Children, Citizenship and Environment

Children growing up today are confronted by four difficult and intersecting challenges: dangerous environmental change, weakening democracies, growing social inequality, and a global economy marked by unprecedented youth unemployment and unsustainable resource extraction. Yet on streets everywhere there is also a strong, youthful energy for change.

This book sets out an inspiring new agenda for citizenship and environmental education which reflects the responsibility and opportunities facing educators, researchers, parents and community groups to support young citizens as they learn to 'make a difference' on the issues that concern them.

Controversial yet ultimately hopeful, political scientist Bronwyn Hayward rethinks assumptions about youth citizenship in neoliberal democracies. Her comparative discussion draws on lessons from New Zealand, a country where young citizens often express a strong sense of personal responsibility for their planet but where many children also face shocking social conditions. Hayward develops a 'SEEDS' model of ecological citizenship education (Social agency, Environmental education, Embedded justice, Decentred deliberation, Self-transcendence). The discussion considers how the SEEDS model can support young citizens' democratic imagination and develop their 'handprint' for social justice.

From eco-worriers and citizen-scientists to streetwise sceptics, *Children, Citizenship and Environment* identifies a variety of forms of citizenship and discusses why many approaches make it more difficult, not easier, for young citizens to effect change. This book will be of interest to a wide audience, in particular teachers of children aged 8–12 and professionals who work in environmental citizenship education, as well as students and researchers with an interest in environmental change, democracy and intergenerational justice.

Introduced by Tim Jackson, author of *Prosperity without Growth*, the book includes forewords by leading European and US academics Andrew Dobson and Roger Hart.

Half the author's royalties will be donated to child poverty projects following the earthquakes in Christchurch, New Zealand.

Follow Bronwyn Hayward's blog at: http://growing-greens.blogspot.co.nz/.

Bronwyn Hayward is a Senior Lecturer in Political Science at the University of Canterbury, New Zealand. She has lectured internationally on environmental politics, public participation and youth citizenship for twenty years. Bronwyn is also a visiting research fellow with both the UK ESRC-funded RESOLVE (Research Group on Lifestyles, Values and Environment) and the Sustainable Lifestyles Research Group at the University of Surrey. She has been a visiting fellow with the Tyndall Centre for Climate Change at the University of East Anglia. In addition to her academic work, Bronwyn is a former Ministerial appointment to the New Zealand Broadcasting Standards Authority with experience in children's television and radio production. She has worked in environmental policy, education and children and youth politics in New Zealand, the UK, the USA and Norway.

'Bronwyn Hayward's magisterial book reminds us that it's not just the biosphere that is threatened through environmental degradation, but our children's imaginations as well, and hence all our future hopes. As we won't achieve sustainable human wellbeing within a flourishing biosphere without citizens who both care about sustainability and are able to act on their concerns, we need to take children seriously as political actors. Bronwyn Hayward argues that, because we cannot live sustainably when social structures and decision-making are unjust, we need to nurture young people as citizens if they are to address the wide-ranging problems we've created: dangerous environmental change, growing social inequality, an unsustainable global economy, and weakening democracies. This wonderful book should be read by all those who think today's childhoods are fine, or who think that children are unfit for democratic involvement, or that we'll get anywhere through individual action – and also by those who already understand the issues, and the importance of children's involvement in their resolution, as they will be re-inspired; in other words, by everyone.' – *William Scott, University of Bath, UK and President, UK National Association for Environmental Education*

'This book is a glorious testament to fortitude, to brilliant scholarship, to the wonderful voices of children's engagement, and to real hope that the future can indeed be secure. Our job is to make it so. Bronwyn Hayward shows how we can do this through the enlightened and patient voices of tomorrow's sustainable citizens.' – *Tim O'Riordan, University of East Anglia, UK*

'Bronwyn Hayward's creative masterpiece describes how we can escape the last 20 years of neo-liberal thinking and its toxic impact on our precious children today and in the future.' – *Susan St John, University of Auckland and NZ Child Poverty Action Group spokesperson*

'A thoughtful and scholarly investigation of how we can create the conditions for children to become confident, participating ecological citizens, capable of collective imagination and action for a better world. There can be no more important task for the future.' – *Jeanette Fitzsimons, Co-Leader of the New Zealand Green Party and Member of Parliament 1995–2009*

'Bronwyn Hayward provides a timely, thoughtful and constructive contribution to an important area of work: understanding how children can develop environmental citizenship. The generation growing up today need to be given the skills and opportunities to engage in shaping their future, rather than be expected to inherit the decisions made by adults now. Hayward makes a strong argument for community collaboration and creative imagination as some of the key ingredients.' – *Lucy Stone, climate change advisor, UNICEF, UK*

'In this inspiring book Bronwyn Hayward explains how children have been left out of the political process or included in only token ways, and the potential cost of this to society. She describes how children can learn to be citizens by engaging in democratic decision-making processes in their local environments. Including children in decision-making benefits the whole of society in unexpected ways. The book is compelling reading for all those interested in the future of democracy and of the environment.' – *Russell Wills, New Zealand Children's Commissioner*

'This book challenges the myths that our kids don't care about what we do as a society and where we are headed. Bronwyn Hayward shows, with alacrity and sensitivity, exactly how the new generation might determine the future. Thought-provoking, controversial and inspiring.' – *David Shearer, Leader of the New Zealand Labour Party*

Children, Citizenship and Environment

Nurturing a democratic imagination in a changing world

Bronwyn Hayward

Routledge
Taylor & Francis Group

LONDON AND NEW YORK

First published 2012
by Routledge
2 Park Square, Milton Park, Abingdon, Oxon OX14 4RN

Simultaneously published in the USA and Canada
by Routledge
711 Third Avenue, New York, NY 10017

Routledge is an imprint of the Taylor & Francis Group, an informa business

British Library Cataloguing in Publication Data
A catalogue record for this book is available from the British Library

Library of Congress Cataloging in Publication Data
Hayward, Bronwyn.
Children, citizenship, and environment: nurturing a democratic imagination
in a changing world/Bronwyn Hayward.
p. cm.
Includes bibliographical references and index.
1. Children and politics. 2. Children and the environment.
3. Citizenship—Study and teaching. 4. Democracy. I. Title.
HQ784.P5H35 2012
305.23—dc23
2012002386

ISBN13: 978-1-84971-436-5 (hbk)
ISBN13: 978-1-84971-437-2 (pbk)
ISBN13: 978-0-203-10683-9 (ebk)

Typeset in Times New Roman
by Book Now Ltd, London

Contents

Illustrations

Figures

Table

Foreword

Andrew Dobson

The issue of 'the future' has been ever-present in green thinking and practice. We are now very used to thinking about the far future and the effect of what we are doing now on people yet to be born. The idea that 'they have done nothing for us' and so we don't need to do anything for them is being slowly eroded, and is at the heart of concerns about the legacy of nuclear waste, for example.

Counter-intuitively, perhaps, thinking about the far future is easier than thinking about the near future: it's 'cleaner' and less cluttered with the messiness of overlapping generations. Thought experiments about the far future can be complex, but that is all they are: experiments, conducted in the clear light of inductive and deductive reason.

In this marvellous book, Bronwyn Hayward urges us to shift our attention from the far horizon to a nearer one, where the 'future generation' in question is the one that will outlive most readers of this book. What is this generation's lived experience of democracy, participation, justice, environmental degradation? What does citizenship mean to them? What are the obstacles to their exercising it? How can we adults support them in their citizenship?

The interviews with children for the book were conducted in New Zealand, but the experiences so vividly conveyed in them are strikingly relevant to any generation, young or old, living through the wave of neoliberalism sweeping through large parts of the world. What emerges from these interviews and Hayward's commentary on them is a challenge to the impoverished, privatized, individualized, and marketised idea of citizenship that neoliberalism would wish to urge upon us.

What we learn from this book is that 'SMART' citizenship is not so smart after all. SMART's faith in self-help, the market, contract, representative democracy, and technology, leaves untouched and unquestioned the systemic underpinnings and relations of power that result in anti-democracy, injustice and environmental degradation.

When we think of environmental citizenship it is probably SMART citizenship we have in mind. This is the citizenship of 'low-hanging fruit' – of individual behaviour change, diligent recycling, home insulation, turning off TV sets instead of leaving them on standby. None of this is wrong, of course, but none of it leads to working on the unsustainable structures within which these practices are embedded, either.

And these structures matter. A sustainable carbon footprint has been calculated at anything between 1 and 1.5 tonnes of CO_2 per person per year. There are dozens of online surveys one can do to work out one's own carbon footprint. The Quaker Green Action online carbon calculator is one example, and it automatically adds 1.8 tonnes of CO_2 at the end of its survey, 'to allow for government activities on your behalf (hospitals, schools, road building, emergency services, the military etc.)'. In other words, no matter how hard you try to change your lifestyle, you will always be over your carbon budget, for structural reasons.

This takes us to 'SEEDS' citizenship, which focuses on collective action to counter the underlying causes of ecological injustice. One of the absolute fascinations of this book is to see where and how SEEDS citizens come to life. These young citizens are forged in the crucible of the everyday experience of relative disadvantage, or what the French call *le vécu*. This is not the politics of government information campaigns, of a well-meaning citizenship curriculum, or of exhortations to buy green, travel less and turn off the television overnight. This is a politics born of lessons learned in mixed community schools, in local protest campaigns, and in connections forged in and through extended families. The vital message here is that children's pro-sustainability values are best supported by not paying too much attention to them (the values that is), but by providing children with opportunities through which they learn how to change the world around them. In this way civic engagement supports, nurtures and develops children's capacity to express empathy.

This book was written in the shadow of the earthquake that devastated Christchurch in February 2011. What better or more terrible laboratory in which to learn the limits of what one can do on one's own, or what happens when democratic life is suspended, even if only temporarily? Bronwyn Hayward and the children in this book have taught me the importance of a democratic imagination, of collective effort, and of structures not surfaces. That's how to get the 'vibe' that 9-year-old Ashley speaks of when 'you feel like you're getting heard and everyone in the world knows – cause you're shouting so loud and you're putting your heart towards something.'

Andrew Dobson
Keele University, UK
March 2012

Foreword

Roger Hart

With a burgeoning literature on the meaning of citizenship in childhood we needed someone to come along and thoroughly address young people's citizenship in relation to the world's environmental problems. This book does just that, with a focus on ecological citizenship. In writing about how to foster and support the growth of a democratic imagination in children, Bronwyn Hayward demonstrates that she has a remarkable democratic imagination. She goes beyond abstract platitudes about planning for the next generation to argue that the next generation is with us now and is ready to play an important role in change – as citizens. For so long environmental education has suffered from the biases of the western middle class environmental movement that began in 1970 with its exclusion of issues of social justice. Finally, the field is beginning to move social justice to the center of the discussions and this book greatly deepens and strengthens this trend.

The focus of most discussions of young people's community and political participation is with teenagers, so it is refreshing that Hayward recognizes that the urge to be involved begins much earlier in life. But while she draws richly from interviews with a large number of children aged 8 to 12 the book also has great relevance for how we should be supporting children in the teenage years. The book adopts the appropriately modest stance of being focused on the young citizens of those countries, like the author's own New Zealand, that are truly neo-liberal democracies. It remains for others to build on this with similar visions of how to promote a democratic imagination and foster the capacities to act upon it in other societies.

With social uprising of youth around the world, it is no longer so easy for social and political commentators to scoff at the idea of young people's participation being an important part of the action on the world's global environmental challenges. Nevertheless, the author does not take a naïve view of the political engagement of children and youth. On the contrary, while she sees the breadth of revolutionary change with youth in recent years as a clear indication of their desire to be involved she also notes the regressive tendency of some democracies to respond with aggressive anti-social behavior legislation to control the assembly of teenagers in public spaces. She presents this as a fundamental backdrop to her argument for the need to enable and sustain youth civic engagement in ways that are deeply authentic yet less susceptible to violent repression by the state. Her depth of analysis leads to a convincing argument that the most promising route to a more sustainable and democratic world is not to avoid politics in environmental education but rather to help build children's capacities to make critical analyses of their own social and environmental situations and provide them with the democratic language and tools to tackle these issues.

The emphasis of this book on the collective agency of children is a most welcome departure from the large psychologically based literature since 1970 on how individual children can help save the planet through their personal actions. Corporations and governments all over the world promote this idea that environmental education and public information leading to individual behavior change is an effective means for addressing the earth's systemic environmental problems. This idea has been given greater strength with the growth of neo-liberalism and the simple-minded notion that free individuals in the marketplace are the key to the world's problems, not governance; that responsible consumption can be taught, just like how not to litter. All of this fits well with the priority in western societies for the promotion of individual autonomy in children's development. This book is designed to help counter this by directing us conceptually and practically towards ways of building the capacity and desire in children for collaborative work, involving critical debate and collective democratic action.

To conceptualize the preparation of children for this new role as committed, engaged activists for social and ecological change, Hayward creatively dovetails together features from a broad range of psychological, social and political theory, thereby providing a much more robust model of the kind of learning required than existing models of environmental learning. There has been much promotion of approaches to environmental education where children are directly engaged in research and encouraged to think critically about environmental issues. But the focus is typically on a specific problem and the end goal is at best to make some local small-scale direct action to improve the environment or to advocate for change through local representative government. The model presented in this book is designed to foster in children a broader and deeper kind of democratic dialogue on social and environmental justice and to build the capacity to flexibly work with others in multiple ways to achieve change.

The author quite rightly recognizes that we cannot entirely rely on local level actions by citizens to achieve the necessary changes. The well worn chant to 'think globally and act locally' has been used effectively by environmental educators and activists for forty years but we may need now to replace it with 'think and act locally and globally'. While Hayward notes that change can come from settings other than schools, she pulls most examples from schools and it is schools that are the most universal setting for children to engage with environmental issues. We already have many examples of networked approaches to environmental education where teachers link their classes of children across regional and even national boundaries to have their children work on joint issues such as monitoring water quality. But under the proposed model networked collaborations would be based on issues that children themselves identify with their different communities as being important rather than on themes that have been proposed from above by well-meaning educators. This is a progressive view of the capacities of children and it will be a challenge for the many educators who are comfortable maintaining their more traditional roles as teachers. The related recommendation that children will need to be prepared for multiple levels of dialogue and possible political action from the local to the national and international levels is an even greater challenge as educators are generally uncomfortable with schools as a place for any kind of real political activity. This is why the arguments of this book need to be heard not only by teachers; they need to be read and debated by people across the spectrum of education, and especially by administrators and policy makers.

Children and youth with a heightened democratic imagination will inevitably come to confront all kinds of powerful groups. One of the greatest challenges for Hayward's model then will be how to convince national educational systems that it is in the interests of the nation and the world to modify their traditional civics models of citizenship based on duty, with the promotion of activist citizenship. But John Dewey's dream of democratic schooling was also radical for its time and while it was never universally adopted, being more the choice of progressive middle class schools, many of his ideas seeped broadly into educational systems. The proposed model moves Dewey's democratic imagination a big notch upwards, closer to the writings of Paulo Freire and Colin Ward. I believe that again a self-selected range of schools will see the value of making themselves vanguards of this deeper kind of commitment to democracy. This time they will not be limited to creating democratic microcosms in the classroom and to simulating difficult societal decisions; the school will instead become a space for children to practice critical citizenship beyond the classroom. By collaborating with citizens of all ages, they will learn the democratic skills of cooperation and collective decision-making and with such democratic solidarity I believe there will be a radical transformation of their democratic imaginations, even when facing the absent, poor or illegitimate decision making of others. We have to believe that, as with Dewey, this more contemporary view of what it means to prepare children to act as citizens will also spread.

Hayward also raises the fear that children's democratic imagination and ecological citizenship could be buried by 'well-meaning environmental campaigns that promote fear, urgency or authoritarianism'. But what she is proposing for children and future generations is not a short-term fix that can be easily suppressed but the creation and social reproduction of a different kind of citizenship where citizens will be prepared to critically engage and flexibly act to counter democratic repression. A more challenging domain of this book for us to debate is the concern expressed by Hayward that much of what we have been seeing lately with youth rebellion in the world is a 'leaderless revolution', and she fears that this kind of non-hierarchical, networked citizenship is vulnerable to co-option, manipulation and disorganisation. As an optimist I personally believe that her model offers a vision of a radical democracy of civil society that would be difficult to repress through coercion or co-option from above, but this is a debate that I hope this book will help foster among environmentalists and educators alike.

Bronwyn Hayward has argued well that we have to create an alternative model of environmental engagement to the 'thin environmentalism' of most current earnest approaches to environmental and citizenship education, with their reliance on the promotion of responsible individual environmental actions and participation in the market, representative democracy and an exaggerated belief in technological fixes to environmental problems. Because we need to find ways of achieving a deeper, more critical engagement of citizens in our transition to a more just and sustainable world I deeply hope that you will read on.

Roger Hart

Director, Children's Environments Research Group
PhD Programs of Environmental Psychology and Geography
The Graduate Center of the City University of New York

Acknowledgements

This book represents a year of 'writing dangerously'. The primary research was conducted in Christchurch, New Zealand, and written up in England on a visiting fellowship with the RESOLVE research group at the University of Surrey. Toward the end of my fellowship, on 4 September 2010, Christchurch was struck by a devastating 7.1 magnitude earthquake. On the day of our return home the following year, Rūaumoko, the god of earthquakes, unleashed his terrible energy in the form of a shallow and therefore more devastating 6.3 magnitude aftershock almost immediately under the city. The impact killed 180 people instantly, injuring more, destroying our central city, and 'munting' or seriously damaging thousands of homes. In the following year, over 8,000 aftershocks of varying intensity have wracked Christchurch, each one renewing our collective grief and exhaustion.

In the scale of a disaster, we are reminded of the limits of our human agency and the grace and power of collective action. It is against this background that I am even more grateful for the support of the following colleagues and friends, none of whom are responsible for errors or omissions but all of whom made this book possible under the circumstances.

First, my sincere thanks to a terrific graduate research team: Jess Buck, Wakaiti Dalton, Holly Donald, Nicholas Kirk, Amanda Thomas, Celia Sheerin, Aramiro Tai Rakena. Thank you too for assistance from Claire Buttiegieg, Sylvia Nissen, Elizabeth Plew and Erina Okeroa. My thanks to Greg Dodds and Paul Le Comte for images and to *The Press*, Christchurch, for allowing the reproduction of news images.

My three-year fellowship with the ESRC RESOLVE Research group on Sustainable Lifestyles, Values and Environment was an intellectually liberating and enriching time of interdisciplinary 're-thinking'. I sincerely thank Tim Jackson (Director) and the whole RESOLVE team from whom I gained so much: Wokje Abrahamse, Alison Armstrong, Tracey Bedford, Catherine Bottrill, Peter Bradley, Kate Burningham, Mona Chitnis, Ian Christie, Alexia Coke, Gemma Cooke, Geoff Cooper, Angela Druckman, David Evans, Shane Fudge, Brigitta Gaterleben, Nicola Green, Michael Peters, Chris Kuklas, Lester Hunt, Scott Milne, Yacob Mulgetta, Niamh Murtagh, Justin Spinney and David Uzzell.

A University of Canterbury College of Arts grant and the New Zealand Electoral Commission Wallace Scholarships for graduate scholars enabled the study, and the University of Canterbury the special study leave.

My sincere thanks also to my co-hosts in the UK at the Tyndall Centre for Climate Change Research at the University of East Anglia, where I conducted my 'adult' research work on climate and governance, especially Neil Adger, Kate Brown, and to Alice Bows, Kevin Anderson and Tim O'Riordan.

In addition I am indebted to the following for specific help and comments related to this book: Benjamin Barber, Gary Birch, Helena Catt, Nicole Dewandre, Andy Dobson, Peter Duncan, John Dryzek, Robyn Eckersley, Rachel and Janine Hayward, Roger Hart, Jane Higgins, Chris Loynes, Karen Nairn, Karen O'Brien, Katherine and John Peet, Kate Rawls, William Scott, Asuncion Lera St Clair, Susan St John, Lucy Stone, Ed Webber Morgan and Pam Williams.

I benefited a great deal from the chance to discuss the themes at conferences and roundtables at Melbourne University, British Political Science Association, The Scottish Forestry Education Institute, Sussex University, Bath University, Keele University, University of East Anglia, Youth 2010, Hornibrook Museum's Youth Panel, University College London, University of Cardiff, University of Oslo, and the United Nations Environment Programme's Global Sustainable Youth Survey Project (with Gunilla Blomquist, Fanny Demassieux and Fabienne Pierre).

The editorial team of Charlotte Russell and Khanam Virjee at Taylor & Francis provided invaluable professional enthusiasm for the project together with care and patience during the earthquakes. My thanks to Gudrun Freese, Alison Kuznets and Jonathan Sinclair-Wilson who began this project and their anonymous Earthscan reviewer.

Finally, my thanks to the principals, teachers and children of Christchurch, who have gone through so much since the earthquakes, and whose daily efforts and democratic imagination will eventually re-create a new sense of community out of our disaster.

For Andrew, Rachel and Ben
With thanks to Jan and John

Introduction

Tim Jackson

Space – not pace. This is the slogan that adorns tourist T-shirts from New Zealand. Pictures of the country often feature craggy snow-capped mountains, crystal clear waters, whales cavorting playfully with sight of gloriously clean white beaches. Such images conjure up a life less ordinary, a life less frantic, a life lived peacefully on remote islands, amid breath-taking scenery. There is some deep truth in that image. But it is not the whole story.

New Zealand, like so many other places, has been marked and occasionally scarred by the 'neoliberal' upheavals in economic and social policy over the past generation. As in many other western nations, a rampant credit-fuelled consumerism has emerged hand in hand with rising inequality and deepening insecurity. The effect on the nation's children has been stark.

In *Children, Citizenship and Environment*, Bronwyn Hayward asks us to take a closer, more critical look at the fine-grained social and economic landscape of her home country, exposing both the strengths and the vulnerability of those growing up in a land, not only of extraordinary beauty, but also of resurgent social, economic and intergenerational inequality.

In bringing the social, economic and environmental injustices which confront New Zealand's youngest citizens into sharper focus, Bronwyn Hayward calls our attention to pressing problems that now confront all economies, both developed and developing. How can we best support people to live flourishing lives? How can we live fairly within the ecological means of a finite planet? How we can create the conditions for a shared and lasting prosperity for ourselves and for future generations?

These questions are particularly pressing when it comes to the lives of younger generations today. One of the biggest challenges is to chart the changing attitudes, values and prospects for the young – those who will feel the impact of the myopic choices made yesterday, and whose ingenuity and resilience will be tested to the full in the harsh conditions of tomorrow. This task was addressed recently, for example, in a global survey for the United Nations Environment Programme in which Bronwyn Hayward and I both participated.

In her role as a visiting researcher in RESOLVE (the ESRC Research group on Lifestyles, Values and the Environment) at the University of Surrey, Bronwyn led both the UK and the New Zealand chapters of the UNEP study and played a vital role in drawing together conclusions from over 8,000 participants in 20 countries across the world. UNEP's report from the study *Visions of Change* reveals a time of profound change affecting the lives of even our very youngest citizens. But it also uncovers remarkable aspirations for real social agency amongst its young participants.

There is no doubt that this is a period of intense change. The years since 2008 have seen the rise of a remarkable global movement of civic activism amongst young people, which mirrored a rise and subsequent decline in public concern about climate change. It was a time in which both the acute and the chronic impacts of the global financial crisis imposed heavy burdens on children globally. Burdens that have been exacerbated by the ensuing, regressive government policy responses. Burdens imposed not only on the nine out of ten children currently living in developing countries, but also on the so called 'shopping generation' of developed economies (young people who grew up during the credit boom of the 1980s and 1990s).

In the case of the very young Christchurch children who are the immediate focus of this study, their lives have been dramatically disrupted not just by growing child poverty and by social inequality, but also by a series of devastating earthquakes after 4th September 2010. This combination of natural disaster and human-made tragedy dramatically underscores the urgent need to create a more just and sustainable future for our children.

In the recent past, governments held out a promise of more flourishing lives for young citizens by relying on models of economic growth that depended on increasing rates of consumption of material resources, growing private debt, and a social logic that seems to defy lasting satisfaction. Relentless advertising pressure reinforces insatiable material consumption as the means fulfil deep, complex human needs. Identity, social participation, status and meaning: we should strive for all of these through a never-ending materialism, if the dogma is to be believed.

Today, however, the instability of global financial markets and the harsh medicine offered in 'austerity' reform packages emphasise the hollowness of the promises we have offered this generation and the ones that will follow. Rising generations in today's society see a future in which they will struggle with significant unemployment, growing social inequality and degrading physical environments. These are the costs of our relentless allegiance to an unsustainable economic model and faulty social logic.

No one should deny that economic growth has delivered us some good things. Improved longevity, better health, education, nutrition, communication, opportunities our grandparents never even dreamed of. These are the rewards to the lucky ones from a century of economic growth. Neither can we deny that improved material conditions are vital for the poorest across the world. Two billion people are still living on less than the price of a Latte Macchiato from the café next door. Growth is desperately needed to lift hundreds of millions of children still living in appalling conditions; to lower infant mortality; to eradicate maternal morbidity; to raise participation levels in basic education.

But in the mature economies, the legacy of economic growth for younger citizens is less clear. Beyond a certain level of affluence, the returns to wellbeing from relentless growth and material consumption are no longer robust. For many children growing up in modern neoliberal 'market societies', the benefits of an economy based on unsustainable extraction of material resources and growing rates of personal debt will be questionable. Growing concerns about children's exposure to stress; declining opportunities for independent free play; erosion of access to quality public space: these are increasingly the prospects for children, particularly those in poor, ethnic minority communities, even in the richest nations.

But injustice and unsustainability are not inevitable. As a passionate advocate for children, Bronwyn Hayward has both anticipated and born witness to the profound change in youth politics. She has personally supported the emergence of youthful anti-consumption movements and protests which question our current economic and political trajectories. Groups such as the UK Uncut movement, the Spanish *Indignados* and the US and UK Occupy protests which followed the remarkable Arab Spring all suggest there is a potent, youthful demand for alternative visions of politics and of more fruitful, less damaging ways to live.

Bronwyn Hayward's study explores a rich and surprising seam of renewed political and social activism, amongst a very young cohort of the population. Her careful listening to youthful voices provides timely insights into a new generation which fiercely protects its own sense of social agency: that is, its ability to both imagine new trajectories and to effect meaningful social change, not just for self-betterment but to make the world a better place.

We dismiss as naive or marginal such youthful pro-environmental aspirations at our peril. In our approaches to environmental education and public policy alike, Dr Hayward argues, we risk underestimating, if not actually subverting, the political energy of youthful outrage at growing social and ecological injustice.

Her arguments resonate with research by others. Taken as a whole, the studies from my own RESOLVE research group reveal the way physical infrastructure and social, economic and political pressures constrain citizens, young and old, in attempts to engage in more sustainable and just forms of living. In our institutional and social structures, in our price signals and performance indicators, in the ease of borrowing and the paucity of saving, in the planned psychological and economic obsolescence of products and pressures, in the efficiency metrics imposed on public servants and fund managers alike, in campaigns of advertising saturation and in the slow erosion of access to quality environments: all these intrusions reduce the opportunities for citizens of all ages and impoverish the lives of our children.

This book suggests that our current attempts to transform the trajectory of our planet rests on a thin, rather ill-defined vision: what Bronwyn Hayward calls 'SMART' environmentalism. It is characterised by mantras of 'self-help' or personal responsibility for individual behaviour change, contractual thinking which underestimates everyday injustice, and a misplaced faith in both 'representative' decision making, and in the power of 'technological transformations', to achieve the dramatic reductions in carbon emissions, energy savings we need for a more sustainable planet.

She is robustly and rightly critical of claims that we can side-step hard political debate and changes to achieve pro-environmental outcomes via market signals and technical fixes. She suggests instead that nothing short of democratic rethinking of the way we invest in and redistribute social goods will achieve more desirable futures for children. 'Nudging' young consumers is not a sufficient, nor desirable way to make the far-reaching and difficult choices which confront our communities.

Nor, she argues, is what she dubs the alternative FEARS model – of repressive governance, riots and violence – the route to secure a sustainable future. These alternatives, she suggests, risk a double injustice, stripping our children of their rights to a democratic future as well as a more sustainable planet. In putting our faith in a relentless pursuit of productivity, we also erode opportunities to treat children with care, and patience, nurturing their democratic virtue and engaging with them in respectful ways as we plan collaboratively for the long-term future.

In contrast, Bronwyn Hayward develops what she terms the SEEDS approach to citizenship and environmental education: one which emphasises Social Agency, Environmental Education (both formal and informal affiliation), Embedded Justice, Decentred Deliberation and Self-Transcendence.

She also introduces a powerful and attractive metaphor – the Social Handprint – with which to argue that significant and lasting pro-environmental transformations will be achieved through the reassertion of democratic, collaborative and active citizenship. In other words, just the kind of action foreshadowed in the emergence of Occupy and other protest networks, as citizens – young with old – begin to cooperate globally to demand changes that can help lead us toward a shared global prosperity.

I am often asked after lectures or in interviews, sometimes by young people themselves, what advice I have for a younger generation. It is always a tough question to answer. So many seem to want to place their faith on the younger generation themselves to solve the problems caused by a previous generation. Not surprisingly, young people themselves resist this pressure. At the same time there is a latent power within the social aspirations of younger people that is at once both exciting and humbling. Question everything, I sometimes answer. Don't wait for people like me to tell you what to do.

Such a response is not a resort to utopianism. In the pages that follow, Bronwyn Hayward offers a refreshing and informed approach to citizenship and environmental education, one which asks us to consider how we can support the young capability of citizens to flourish. The actions of networked citizens are insufficient on their own to make living sustainably an immediate reality. But the seeds of hope documented in this book contribute to visions of change embedded in citizen action.

This thought-provoking re-evaluation of youthful citizenship suggests that our transition to a more sustainable society might be a brighter, more colourful, more promising prospect for our children and our grandchildren than we might otherwise expect it to be. And in this context, nurturing children's democratic imagination and supporting their practical possibilities for citizenship, might be our greatest legacy to a new generation.

Space – not pace. It isn't just a T-shirt slogan. It's a philosophy of change. Giving our children the space – to think, to develop, to act – lies at the heart of the recommendations in this book.

Professor Tim Jackson
University of Surrey, UK

1 Ecology and democracy as if children mattered

For the child ... it is not half so important to *know* as to *feel*. If facts are the seeds that later produce knowledge and wisdom, then the emotions and the impressions of the senses are the fertile soil in which the seeds must grow. The years of early childhood are the time to prepare the soil. Once the emotions have been aroused – a sense of the beautiful, the excitement of the new and the unknown, a feeling of sympathy, pity, admiration or love – then we wish for knowledge about the object of our emotional response. It is more important to pave the way for a child to want to know than to put him on a diet of facts that he is not ready to assimilate.

(Rachel Carson, 1965 (1998), p56)

Young citizens today are growing up in a world that is very different from their parents and grandparents. It's a world in which they are confronted by four difficult and intersecting challenges: dangerous environmental change, growing social inequality, an unsustainable global economy, and weakening democracies as local communities struggle to hold global power to account.[1] Yet today there is also a strong youthful desire for change. As a new generation with vibrant energy explodes onto YouTube and Twitter, through smart phones, Facebook, music and onto streets everywhere, young citizens are finding their political voice. In the diversity of their protests about bank bail-outs, corrupt regimes, income inequality, youth unemployment, education costs, coal mining and climate change, this new generation is calling for action on some of the key issues that underpin the sustainability crisis we face.

As adult citizens we have a responsibility to put things right. We created these problems and we have to address them. Yet the harsh reality is that even with our most concerted efforts, we will not be able to solve these issues within one generation. These challenges will also define the physical and political landscape of our children and grandchildren. We have an obligation to support the capability of young citizens to address the enormous challenges we are bequeathing them. In this book I consider ways we can begin to fulfill that obligation. I focus in particular on the citizenship and environmental concerns of young children aged 8 to 12, a time in young lives when many are learning to reason about moral issues and take an interest in their wider world.[2] It is also an age at which a surprising number of children are now beginning to engage in action for change.[3]

Figure 1.1 Occupy Christchurch protest

Credit: *The Press* Fairfax NZ Ltd.

Perhaps most significantly, at this age children are part of a global cohort which is exposed to increasing levels of child poverty, environmental risk and intergenerational inequity as adult citizens gamble with the future climate, environmental security and well-being of their children and grandchildren.[4]

In a deeply personal reflection, ecologist Rachel Carson urged us to nurture a child's sense of wonder about the natural world. I suggest that we also need to nurture a child's sense of wonder about the democratic world. To appreciate the values of a democracy, children do not need civic lessons about political leaders, voting methods or the politics of corporate board rooms. Some of these facts may matter later. What is more important at first, however, is to nurture a child's sense of wonder about the democratic possibilities of ordinary people acting together in free collaboration to achieve extraordinary change.

Thinking about children as political actors is challenging. Philosopher Hannah Arendt has rightly cautioned us that tyrannical revolutionary movements frequently target children for indoctrination. Children's cognitive skills are still developing, and they can be vulnerable to manipulation or domination.[5] Arendt argued that politics should play no part in children's lives until they are 'educated'.[6] We can take Arendt's concerns to heart while noting that children also need to learn citizenship skills to prepare them for the 'task of renewing the common world'.[7] Moreover, as I argue in the following pages, Arendt overlooked the way children already act as citizens; they are not just citizens in the making, they participate in and belong to our community already.[8] As a result, children need support to develop their capabilities for the political life they have already embarked on.

Rethinking citizenship and environment from a child's perspective

Taking children seriously as political actors in their environment forces us to rethink our adult assumptions about what we mean by the terms 'citizenship' or 'environment'. In policy making we are used to talking about citizenship as a set of legal entitlements conferred on individuals living within nation states or political regions. This approach emphasises adult rights, duties and expectations (for example, voting, paying taxes and support from the state in tough times). Yet this interpretation overlooks the way children also identify with their communities, make demands and contribute to civic life as citizens, in the sense of actors who participate in, identify with and belong to our communities, even in the absence of a full framework of adult legal entitlements and obligations.[9]

In policy making, our discussion about the environment is also often framed in ways that marginalise the experiences of children. The language of environmental sciences and eco-system services is not child-centred, and frequently draws distinctions between the human and the non-human world. Yet, viewed from a child's perspective, the 'environment' and 'ecology' are more fluid concepts. Child development theory reminds us that the child's ecological reality is a complex series of nested interactive systems, in which the child is embedded in a dynamic world of everyday micro-level interactions and indirect but significant macro-level processes, including economic, political, cultural, economic and physical change.[10] At the micro-level, a child's development and daily encounters with family or friends, pets and plants may take place at home, in playgrounds, at school, in the street or in outdoor settings. These complex micro experiences interact with wider events and processes including, for example, conditions of parental employment, media or education policy, and government decisions about urban development or natural hazard mitigation and climate change.[11]

As educators, parents and policy makers, we need to pay closer attention to the complex interactions of the micro- and macro-level changes taking place in a child's environment. There is startlingly little attention paid to ecological issues that currently worry children, let alone the ways that macro-scale, dangerous environmental change will exacerbate these problems.[12] We rarely take the complex ecological reality of a child's world seriously. We invite children to speak at global conventions, and use their art work, songs, and projects to decorate and legitimate policy meetings.[13] We reproduce the question posed by a young child to delegates at the Copenhagen Climate Summit on T-shirts: 'How old will you be in 50 years' time?' But we don't really try to understand the perspectives of a child or the complexity of interactions and relationships that confront them. Children's concerns are not central to our environmental science and policy agendas. Their issues don't often easily fit our conception of what sustainability is all about. Their ecological truths are a little too inconvenient.

As problems go, some of the pressing issues facing children do not seem as terrifying as other 'big' environmental issues.[14] In the global north, children's concerns include climate change and access to green space, but also family strain, school bullying, parental alcoholism, domestic violence, poverty, and whether education is a stimulating experience or a stressful process of constant revision. A recent Cambridge review of education rightly reminds us that many children in developed countries have never had it so good, but the authors also note serious inequalities in children's experience.[15] Children in low-income and minority communities are growing up in challenging environments, while many older students face additional stressors of loneliness and unemployment.[16]

In the global south, children's concerns are also often overlooked or framed in terms of adult (and usually northern) policy agendas. We rarely hear directly from the 9 out of 10 young people aged under 25 who are growing up in developing countries. For these young citizens their problems are myriad. Besides getting ahead in life, getting a critical education and getting connected with friends, they struggle with basic issues of sourcing fresh water, achieving food security, surviving pressures of drug wars, military regimes or famine, all of which add to the insecurity of daily life in a changing climate and degrading environment.[17] Worldwide we have made some significant gains in the lives of infants and babies, but the concerns of the planet's adolescents barely register in the boardrooms of governments or business.[18]

In this discussion I consider the ecology of a neoliberal childhood and issues that matter to children growing up in English-speaking countries. Despite the emergence of new markets, neoliberal democracies continue to be amongst the largest consumers and polluters per capita on the planet. Building from the experience of New Zealand – a country where neoliberalism was arguably rolled out further and faster than any other democracy – I consider how children can be supported and encouraged to think about their citizenship in more sustainable ways. The New Zealand experience presents a stark challenge for those concerned with youth citizenship and environmental education. In an age of consumerism and selfish capitalism, many children interviewed here report a refreshingly 'unbranded' childhood, a wide circle of friends with whom they play outside, and a strong sense of personal responsibility for their environment. As children under the age of 14, many also enjoy belonging to one of the most ethnically-diverse cohorts in the OECD. These are all achievements to be celebrated and are goals of citizenship and environmental education. And yet New Zealand children and young people also experience the highest rate of youth suicide, and some of the higher rates of child poverty, ill health and domestic abuse, in the OECD.[19]

Viewed in this light, I argue that much of our contemporary approach to environmental and citizenship education is missing the point. As adults we show an almost willful disregard for the reality of children's and young people's everyday ecology. As a result, citizenship and environmental education too often fails to meet the needs of a new generation. We teach our children and our students to recycle and reduce waste while ignoring the way domestic violence and poverty are also pressing ecological concerns. While citizenship and environmental education will not be enough to effect significant change for children and future generations, young citizens need democratic language, tools and ways of understanding their situation to re-create a common and more sustainable world.

'It's the politics, stupid'

The complexities of contemporary problems of sustainability have left all citizens, young and old, wondering what we should do. Benjamin Barber reminds us this is essentially a *political* question, one that asks us to consider: 'What shall we do when something has to be done that affects us all, we wish to be reasonable, yet we disagree on means and ends and are without independent grounds for making the choice?'[20] Today, the suggestion that we need a political approach to our complex problems seems almost startling. Over the past thirty years we have grown accustomed to hearing that difficult, challenging problems require more efficient, market-based solutions, more personal responsibility and less government, not more democracy. Nevertheless, I argue that addressing our most difficult ecological and social challenges requires a democratic imagination and a new form of active, ecological citizenship.

I admit it seems an unlikely argument to make. To say we need more democracy in the face of an escalating global crisis sounds like an inadequate response. Everywhere our political leaders and governments appear to be, at best, impotent or inept, and, at worst, calculating and corrupt. Yet all change begins with first steps. To address the complex problems we face, we need to take the first steps to rethink our politics. Rethinking citizenship is part of a vital, wider process of rethinking our democratic practices and institutions, so they can provide better support for our children and future generations who face difficult challenges. Of course we will need to do much more than rethink citizenship and environmental education. However, we cannot achieve sustainable human well-being and the flourishing of a non-human world without citizens who care about sustainability and who are supported and able to act on their concerns.

Faced with our lack of progress to address complex socio-ecological problems, it is understandable that many people might feel increasingly cynical about the potential for a more effective democracy. Given the upward trajectories of carbon dioxide and other greenhouse gas emissions, the accelerating rates of loss of biodiversity, resource extraction, and growing social injustice and power inequalities,[21] many concerned citizens feel worn out and disillusioned by politics and political leaders. In this light, it's also not surprising that a significant minority of young adults we recently surveyed dreamed of living more sustainable lives, but saw the way to achieve this was to retreat to a more self-sufficient lifestyle in a small town or the countryside, preferably generating their own energy and growing their own food.[22]

The temptation to withdraw from our rapidly-degrading and disappointing world in favour of 'do it yourself' independent green living is understandable, but it is not a solution to our collective problems. The desire to opt out of public life, move to the country and erect a solar panel, buy a private education for our children or pay for access to parks does not solve the underlying causes of our collective

Figure 1.2 Protestor at Occupy Vancouver

Credit: Paul Le Comte.

problems, and in many cases the emergence of a green privileged elite or a survivalist mentality will only make growing social and environmental inequality worse.

Some people have become so frustrated with incompetent politicians and communities who are slow to change that they find themselves agreeing with William Ophlus when he suggested we need less open democracy and more green managerialism.[23] Ophlus suggested that growing resource scarcity, social inequality and conflict means we should accept the 'golden age of individualism, liberty and

Figure 1.3 Child making her own Christchurch Occupy sign

Credit: Bronwyn Hayward.

democracy is all but over' and return instead to 'something resembling the pre-modern closed polity'.[24] Yet small, closed communities can also be hotbeds of injustice, and they are unlikely to be effective sites from which to scrutinise global corporate power. Moreover, Ophlus' hopes for a green managerial rule cannot compensate for the loss of citizen freedom to participate in open, account-able democracy. Besides, calls for more authoritarian green decision-making simply miss the point. For all its problems, the ideals of a liberal democracy still matter to many people. The desire for effective political agency, that is, the freedom of will formation (the ability to think independently) and volition (the capability to freely choose to act or not to act), still motivates popular struggles around the world.[25] Internationally, young citizens place a high value on the free-dom of 'agency', so any environmental solution which erodes their agency under-mines a core value which is intrinsic to the vision of sustainable well-being for a new generation.[26] The challenge is to respect and support widely-reported youth-ful aspirations 'to make a difference', enabling young citizens to exercise their agency to recreate a more sustainable common world.[27]

Those who recognise the motivational power of agency sometimes advocate environmental campaigns that appeal to our better natures, encouraging us to adopt pro-environmental behaviours as private individuals. This approach is refreshing, rejecting as it does the widespread assumption that politics must be dominated by self-interest.[28] However, targeting individuals' intrinsic values reflects the growing dominance of a psychological rather than political approach to environmental problem solving. Psychology has taught us much about how individuals think and behave. But the psychological lens inadvertently narrows our vision of citizenship, reducing the potential of political agency to the aggregation of personal value choices, aspirations and psycho-social interactions with the natural world, obscuring the political potential of citizens collaborating and reasoning together to create alternative pathways and forms of public life.

However, the use of psychological techniques to appeal to individual altruism is far preferable to other less democratic options.[29] Social marketing in particular has become a popular method for achieving pro-environmental change. This marketing appeals to social norms, or 'choice architecture' (the context of decision making), to cajole, pressure, 'nudge' or otherwise manipulate people to behave differently.[30] Nudge theory is a form of social marketing which its advocates claim is cost effective.[31] Nudges subtly engineer public behaviour, and are argued to be more effective than embarking on lengthy or uncertain democratic debate to legitimate policy change. The nudge approach is also known as liberal paternalism. The term 'paternalism' underscores the loss of a 'democratic' vision inherent in the approach. Nudging individuals might be an effective way to encourage healthier food choices in the supermarket or school cafeteria, but it is a woefully inadequate method of challenging corporate decision making and advertising campaigns which informed the unsustainable 'choice architecture' of citizens' lives in the first place.[32]

Other solutions to our collective problems similarly attempt to sidestep politics, using a battery of market tools, including fiscal incentives, tax deductions for home insulation and carbon trading.[33] These approaches have many merits, but our intense differences of public opinion about issues like climate change, or the use of nuclear energy, will not be resolved by a tax incentive to purchase a hybrid car. Furthermore, it's unclear that people will continue to act in pro-environmental ways if the financial incentive is removed.[34] This approach focuses our attention on economic solutions, overlooking the way citizens can also engage directly in community action beyond the market to solve collective problems. Market solutions also underestimate how complex individuals are and how our habits, social norms and human interactions can negate the effects of market incentives.[35]

Yet if small scale community approaches, green managerialism, appeals to our altruism or market incentives are not the beautiful solutions to our complex problems that we hoped, the alternative of a 'big fix' political solution appears to be just as unlikely. The buildup to the international climate summit at Copenhagen in 2009 was followed by widespread public disillusionment over lack of international political leadership. Since this event, some people have become so frustrated with the way that supposedly democratic states have failed to act responsibly (for example, condoning use of torture while inflicting climate suffering on future generations with reckless policy decisions), that they advocate giving up on democracy altogether and doing 'whatever it takes' to halt ecological degradation. In their book *Deep Green Resistance*, Aric McBay and colleagues call on citizens to 'fight back'. They argue:

Those who come after, who inherit whatever's left of the world once this culture has been stopped – whether through peak oil, economic collapse, ecological collapse, or the efforts of brave women and men resisting in alliance with the natural world – are going to judge us by the health of the land base, by what we leave behind. They are not going to care whether we were nice people. They are not going to care how you or I lived our lives. They are not going to care how hard we tried. They're not going to care whether we were nonviolent or violent. They are not going to care whether we grieved the murder of the planet. ... They're going to care whether they can breathe the air and drink the water. We can fantasize all we want about some great turning, but if the people (including non-human people) can't breathe, it doesn't matter.[36]

I profoundly disagree. While our present politics are not fit for purpose, our current situation demands more, not less, democracy. It is misguided to imagine that anyone has the ability to determine 'the problem', let alone the right to take any unilateral action they deem correct, to effect transformative change.[37] This approach denies the political reality of the situation we face; our sustainability crisis is a complex, multifaceted series of dynamic problems that we cannot address independently. In this respect, our sustainability crisis is also a deep political crisis. We need new ways of thinking about collaboration. To react in frustration to the collective threats with unilateral action and without careful democratic reflection is a dangerous mistake. We need to retain our ability to remember and to think about what we are doing.[38] It will matter greatly to those who come after, how we lived, and resisted. To surrender our capacity to act as citizens informed by democratic judgment, critical reasoning, compassion, and knowledge of our dependence on each other and the non-human world, is to create a double injustice, stripping our children of their rights to a more democratic future as well as a more sustainable world.

Understanding the citizenship struggles of a new generation

It is common to hear complaints that young citizens are apathetic, or that they will not and cannot act to address long-term environmental and social problems. Moral panic about the young is not new. What is novel about our contemporary debate is not the fear that young citizens are less like their parents, but growing concern they are becoming more like us. Fed a diet of intensive advertising, raised in increasingly inequitable and urbanised lifestyles, legitimate concerns have been expressed that we appear to be teaching children how to become politically passive 'consumer-citizens' who strive for status, novelty and self-fulfillment through competitive, self-centred and increasingly high-energy consumer lifestyles.[39] In his provocatively titled book *Consumed: How markets consume children, infantilize adults and swallow citizens whole*, Benjamin Barber argues that young citizens' potential for engaging in public life is being supplanted by the drive to meet new short-term needs generated by advertising and satiated by products purchased in a commercial market.[40]

Concern about citizen attitudes have been heard before. In 1972, *The Limits to Growth* report argued that, if left unchecked, our current rates of global resource consumption, pollution, industrialisation and population growth would exceed the limits of the planet's physical resources.[41] The authors argued that citizens were unlikely to take effective action because most are concerned only with day-to-day immediate needs. Very few people ever think about issues beyond their own lifetime.[42] With the benefit of hindsight, this seems a startlingly pessimistic conclusion, written as it was in the midst of a period of revolutionary social change and youthful protest about environmental pollution, nuclear disarmament, women's and civil rights – all complex concerns closely affecting the long term sustainability of our world.

There is a risk we will make the same mistake as the *Limits to Growth* team, if we overlook the sustainability implications of contemporary struggles of citizens. The final months of 2010 and the summer of 2011 saw youth-led waves of protests around the world, from the Arab Spring to Spanish '*Indignados*', from Greek uprisings to Wall Street occupations, and Chilean student protests. In their protests against budget cuts, bank bail-outs, economic systems that degrade the earth and its atmosphere while maintaining high youth unemployment, growing social inequality, and lack of access to education or voice in government; these citizens are challenging some of the key elements of our sustainability crisis. The energy of contemporary youth movements reminds us that a combination of youthful populations and frustration has been a key factor in revolutionary change for centuries. The millennial generation is not the first to face tough times.[43] Those born at the start of the twentieth century lived through two world wars and a world depression; their children worried about the threat of nuclear war and oil shocks. However, the challenges facing this generation are qualitatively different. In their struggles with global change, young people are now confronting increasingly intricate webs of financial investment and complex industrial, governmental or military power, problems which have been exacerbated by historical injustices, regional conflicts and colonisation.[44]

Not all youthful action is effective or democratic. If the student protests of 2010 marked the political coming of age of a new generation, the English urban 'riots' of the late summer of 2011 were less effective.[45] Fuelled by a complex cocktail of poverty, rising social inequality and high rates of social immobility, the London unrest that spread to other English cities was sparked by a police incident resulting in the death of a young black man. However, the implications of this death, and the troubling nature of issues facing poor urban communities, was lost from view, as dominant groups reframed the events as 'pure criminality', a 'carnival' of looting and greedy consumption, or (more sympathetically) a fleeting moment of hedonism in a lifetime of alienation.[46] To be effective, citizenship will require more than the unfocused energy of rebellion. As Barber argued, '... a rabble is not an electorate and a mob is not a citizenry. If action is to be political, it must ensue from forethought and deliberation, from free and conscious choice. Anyone can be an actor. Only a citizen can be a political actor.'[47]

Youthful protest and energy for resistance is vital, but by itself it is not enough to bring global power under greater public scrutiny and control, or to transform the trajectories of unsustainable growth and growing social inequity. Young activists are already meeting fierce response from the forces they are seeking to challenge. Many governments attempt to ignore or vilify youth protest. Some democracies seek to protect themselves from their young citizens by routinely deploying anti-social behaviour legislation to control the assembly of teenagers, or using closed-circuit television surveillance or tools like mosquito alarms (a high pitched sound alarm used against vermin now turned on children) to deter youths from gathering in public space.[48] Some states use more aggressive policing practices which routinely infringe human rights, including containing or 'kettling' young protestors for hours without access to toilets and water, let alone lawyers.[49] The most challenging youthful activism is met by covert infiltration (police spying in climate camps), or overt force; armies of police greet student protests with rubber bullets, water cannons and weapons.[50] In this context, the question is no longer '... why don't youth get involved' in politics, but '... which conditions encourage, promote and sustain youth civic engagement', enabling citizens to flourish in a more sustainable and democratic world?[51]

In his classic essay on citizenship, sociologist T. H. Marshall suggested that citizenship can be understood as a reciprocal relationship of rights and duties, between individuals and states. This relationship has evolved through time from initial civil rights (to own private property, for example), to political rights (the right to vote, assembly or free speech) and finally recognition of social rights, such as rights to education, health and secure housing.[52] In reality, however, citizenship rights are rarely progressively granted to new groups as Marshall suggests. More often they have to be wrested from those with power and, once won, these rights must be retained by ongoing struggle.[53]

The United Nations Rights of the Child document was an important international statement of children's citizenship rights. This charter recognises young people belong to their communities and have a right to be heard and treated with respect.[54] In *Kettled Youth* however, David Hancox writes angrily about the situation facing many young people today, who he perceives to be losing their citizens' rights in the face of powerful forces of economic and social retrenchment. While his focus is on the United Kingdom, his arguments apply much more widely. Reflecting on the austerity budget and policy reforms of the Cameron–Clegg administration he argues:

> The worst thing you can say about this government is not that they threaten 'a throwback to the eighties' or a 'return to Thatcherism'. This is less a revival of the 1980s than a revival of the 1880s: a return to pre-suffrage plutocracy – the wealthy propped up by toothless, unaccountable ... parliamentary institutions, nobbled trade unions, and a butchered welfare state, with charities and philanthropists asked to rescue as many of the poor and destitute as they can ... what we are seeing now is the final phase of a Plutocratic Restoration, the re-establishment of Victorian wealth and power inequalities, after the relatively brief social democratic interregnum when we began to build a more equal society.[55]

Strong words, but they highlight the way fixing the climate and addressing related social and environmental problems is only half the battle young citizens face. As financial power is concentrated in fewer hands, and military and corporate decision making grows less accountable, it is increasingly difficult for even the most internet-savvy citizens to participate in meaningful decision making or effectively scrutinise decision making in a global context.

However, not content to burden our young citizens with complex social and economic challenges and barriers to democratic participation, we have also reframed our ideas of citizenship, heaping more and more expectation on youth to take personal responsibility for the problems we have created. As young people attempt to confront complex global issues, they do so in a context of greater emphasis on private action and less, not more, public governance. We foster impossible expectations of individual behaviour change as a method to address global and systemic problems. If we only teach our children that good citizens recycle and vote, are dutiful, obedient, resourceful and resilient, we erode their ability to exercise their agency as freely-chosen collaborative action for a sustainable future.

The shift to citizenship as personal responsibility has been exacerbated by the spread of neoliberal economic theory. While differing from country to country, neoliberalism can be conceived as an economic policy and ideological project that seeks to extend market values into public life. Critics argue that market values of possession and protection of private property have increasingly come to dominate the way citizens think and behave, at the expense of other democratic values such as the civic republican belief of obligation to the state or communitarian inspired values of the common good.[56] Some express concern that children have learned to internalise the lessons of neoliberalism and now equate 'good citizenship' with habits of 'personal responsibility', believing, for example, that 'responsible consumption' is an effective way to address collective problems.[57]

Fostering individual responsibility matters. As the sociologist Zgymunt Bauman reminds us, democracy depends on the courage of individuals to think critically and act morally in the face of pervasive injustice.[58] However, the assumption that private actions are sufficient to re-create a more just, common world or shared prosperity is wishful thinking. Moreover, focusing on individual behaviour change diverts our attention from scrutinising the way power is exercised at a systemic or institutional level. Our sustainability crisis is a political crisis; it involves the whole polity, or community of citizens. We are unable to take effective private or unilateral action to address the complex, interconnected problems we face. But to assert that the way forward is to aggregate individual choices, or effect mass behaviour through social manipulation, morality campaigns or more market solutions, is deeply problematic. These solutions impoverish our democratic imagination. They ignore the potential of citizens acting with political agency to discover new possibilities for collaboration.

Some of these new possibilities for citizen action are illustrated in the non-hierarchical, networked activism of the Occupy movements, the protests of the anti-consumption group UK Uncut, or the Spanish *Indignados* protests. But again, neoliberalism leaves an ambiguous legacy of civic action for this new generation.[59] The current protests draw on ideas of individual autonomy, ecological anarchism and resistance to traditional hierarchy as a 'leaderless revolution'.[60] This approach enables activists to coordinate and respond flexibly to repressive force.[61] But leaderless movements are also vulnerable to manipulation and disorganisation. There is a risk that an emerging vision of non-hierarchical, networked citizenship will be co-opted by established interests before it is more fully articulated.[62] Young citizens need more support if their renewed energy for activism is not to peter out into isolated battles, mindless riots, irrelevant gestures or co-opted ideas.[63]

Environmental and citizenship education: making the connection

It is one thing to recognise we need to strengthen our democracies and support youthful capability for citizenship. It's quite another to achieve this. An undercurrent throughout the book draws on the democratic ideas of a strong, decentred and deliberative democracy, and the human capabilities approach, as ways to encourage new forms of citizenship.[64] I argue we need to bring the threads of environmental and citizenship education together, while placing the concerns of a new generation at the centre of a vision of sustainability. This is easier said than done. Most Anglo-speaking democracies don't really want to think about children or adolescents at all, let alone rethink our ideas about ecology, democracy or citizenship from their point of view. In 2011, opinion poll research commissioned in the United Kingdom by the children's charity Barnardos, revealed that 44 per cent of 2,000 British adults surveyed agreed 'that children in this country are becoming feral'.[65] This research echoes the finding in the same year that Britain ranked bottom amongst European countries with regard to tolerance and appreciation of young adults.[66] In America, poll research in 2011 revealed the biggest generational divide in that country in thirty years, with opinions diverging over a wide range of issues between millennial generations and older citizens.[67]

It is also startling that environmental and citizenship education often continues to evolve in separate silos of thinking. Some individual education programmes have bridged the gap, particularly Danish Forest Schools, English Small Schools, the teaching pedagogy of Vygotski or the US Highland Community Colleges, for example.[68] These education programmes reflect a return to citizenship, asking 'What does it mean to be a citizen in our changing world?'[69] Seen through the lens of both citizenship and environmental education, this is a richly rewarding question, one which recognises that citizenship is not only legally-defined membership of a political community, but also a state of belonging, feeling affiliation and participation in communities that can extend across national borders and acknowledge intrinsic value of the non-human world.[70]

Yet rethinking citizenship in an environmental context is challenging. It has already taken 2,000 years of struggle to extend the novel Greek idea that free men in city-states had the right to govern their own lives to include women or ethnic minorities. We still do not seriously consider the severely mentally disabled or those who live beyond our borders as full citizens.[71] Children, future generations and the non-human world are treated even less seriously as candidates for citizenship. Given the stake children have in the outcomes of environmental decisions, it is concerning they are routinely silenced and sidelined in civic life.

Rather than listen to children, as adults we often simply rehearse expectations of what we think young citizens should care about: recycling and playing outdoors, achieving at school in readiness for participation in a new green economy, reducing carbon emissions, growing edible gardens, exploring new forms of renewable energy, personal resilience, simple living and saving polar bears.[72] Some of these issues really do interest children and are important, but we are so busy setting the sustainability agenda for our children that we have forgotten to stop and hear what they want to have a say about.

Our ambivalent treatment of children includes the roles that children are currently expected to play when learning about the environment or citizenship. On the one hand, children are often cast as passive recipients of information about the natural world, or innocents who need to be rescued from the perils of modernity through unmediated contact with nature. On the other hand, children are viewed as complex actors with the ability to engage with and influence their environment. These conflicting attitudes are illustrated in Jean-Jacques Rousseau's *Emile*, William Wordsworth's reflections on his childhood, and in the writings of early social reformers such as Henry Thomas Seton.[73] There has always been a strong moral narrative in environmental education which suggests nature can heal the effects of modern life.[74] Rousseau suggested that children should be encouraged to freely explore and observe nature. This aspect of his work inspired subsequent child-centered developmental approaches to education including Piaget.[75] Rousseau influenced social reformers such as Seton to provide children with opportunities for informal outdoor play as a counter to the political indoctrination and militarisation of outdoor education in Europe prior to World War Two.[76]

Today, however, there are important contemporary counter-currents in environmental and citizenship education which consider how children can be supported to think critically about their situation and act in ways that are potentially more democratic, liberating and sustainable. In Chapter 4, I review the ground-breaking work of environmental educators, psychologists, political theorists and geographers, including Chawla, Flanagan, Hart, Katz, Orr, Scott, Uzzell and Valentine, for example, who have prompted a rethinking of our understanding of children and their environments.[77] This turn towards citizenship in environmental education is one the discipline of political science has been disappointingly slow to engage with. For that matter, political science has been slow to take a sustained, serious interest in children in many contexts.[78]

Young citizens finally became the focus of renewed and sustained research attention in politics in the 1990s, following concern about a widespread decline in youth voter turnout in established democracies.[79] Debate still rages about whether this decline is a symptom of youth disengagement, or a reflection of new forms of political action (consumer boycotts, volunteering and social media protest).[80] This debate has been usefully informed by reviews of the way citizenship is taught in schools in North America, Britain and Australasia. The 'Crick' report in Britain was particularly influential.[81] That report argued that political literacy and substantive knowledge (about skills, values and processes of democracy) matters, but opportunities to develop self-confidence and moral responsibility are equally important preconditions for citizenship.[82] The report concluded that children learn about democracy 'by doing' democracy, through regular and meaningful opportunities to participate in real life decision making in their school and community.

Despite renewed interest in youth voting and protest, there is little research into how young children experience politics in their everyday world. The received view in political science is that young children's political attitudes or preferences are unstable and likely to change as they grow up, and are therefore of little predictive value in electoral behaviour research.[83] While voter studies continue to dominate political science research, young children's political participation will continue to be neglected.[84] Notable exceptions in this regard which also have implications for environmental education include the recent works of political scientists Joel Westheimer, Judith Torney-Purta *et al.*, Connie Flanagan and Lonnie Sherrod.[85]

Westheimer's report *No child left thinking* is a provocative if pessimistic review of youth citizenship in North America. Westheimer argues that the current citizenship curriculum teaches civic facts in a way that denies children the opportunity to develop their capacity for critical thinking and the chance to practice decision making in real contexts. Westheimer and his colleagues argue that the dominant American models of citizenship as expressed by children emphasises ideas of volunteerism, charity and obedience rather than the values of tolerance, critical thinking and active participation which are necessary for a healthy liberal democracy.[86]

Connie Flanagan and Judith Torney-Purta have also studied the views of children and young people in a series of comparative global surveys.[87] Flanagan's work especially, like that of Hart, and Rathzel and Uzzell, has engaged with liberation psychology to try to understand how young people develop a critical consciousness, discover a collective voice and engage in action to achieve desired goals and aspirations.[88] Flanagan argues the views of young citizens cannot be explained satisfactorily by world surveys of youth opinion which ascribe shifts in post material thinking to economic development and cultural values alone.[89] She calls for a nuanced understanding of how children learn about politics in their everyday lives through small-scale studies that complement the results of large global surveys.

Ecological citizenship

Young citizens' attempts to make a difference on complex issues such as sustainability are both influenced, and frustrated by, our current models of citizenship.[90] Citizenship is often talked of as legal membership in a nation state. Yet this view is problematic for environmentally-aware individuals who wish to act across national borders to address global environmental problems or protest the actions of distant others which impinge on their lives.[91] Andrew Dobson has provided one of the most extensive reconsiderations of citizenship from an ecological perspective.

He developed the concept of ecological citizenship, to describe a form of citizenship that extends across national borders as individuals acknowledge the obligations they owe others as a result of their environmental impacts, and the interdependence and interconnectivity of citizens and the natural world.[92]

For Dobson, citizenship is not a matter of an agreed set of legal rights and duties between a citizen and a state. Ecological citizens have an affiliation and connection with the environment. They recognise their historical obligations and responsibilities for environmental degradation and harm caused to others by their own actions or the actions of institutions that have benefited them. A core principle that drives ecological citizenship is a concern for environmental justice. Ecological citizens aim to minimise environmental harm and take action to address environmental injustice.[93]

For Dobson, ecological citizenship is exercised by individuals rather than companies and corporations, and is couched in the language of liberal autonomy or our freedom to exercise our agency in an international or 'cosmopolitan' world.[94] Yet Dobson's definition leaves open the potential for ecological citizenship to be expressed as collective action, or the free cooperation of autonomous individuals, in ways that echo more communitarian thinking. Others have expanded and developed the innovative idea of ecological citizenship to begin to think about the ecological citizenship of organisations, unions, non-governmental bodies and businesses, and the potential for ecological citizenship to be exercised at all levels of neighbourhood, state and international decision making.[95]

As these new ideas of ecological citizenship emerge, our thinking about sustainability has also taken a liberating turn away from endless definitions of 'sustainable development' towards rethinking sustainability as capabilities for human well-being within a flourishing non-human world.[96] This discussion creates opportunities to reconsider children's citizenship in environmental education. A vision of sustainable communities within a flourishing, non-human world opens up opportunities for conversations about what support citizens will need to achieve political aspirations for pro-environmental change. To create sustainable futures, young citizens will require critical thinking skills, the ability to reason, reflect and communicate clearly; resources to enable mobilisation across place and time, and restraint to live within material limits. To add to this daunting list, citizens who want to make a democratic difference for sustainability will need the virtues of empathy and tolerance, co-operation, moral reasoning, determination and courage.[97]

Yet it's not enough to hope for something better. To achieve a politics that is fit for the future we have to nurture the conditions in which citizenship is formed. In this book I argue that we need to support young citizens as they discover the art, craft and passion of active ecological citizenship. I identify the SEEDS of ecological citizenship: Social agency, Environmental education, Embedded justice, Decentred deliberation, and Self-transcendence. In the discussion that follows, I ask: How realistic are the prospects of a greener, more democratic citizenship? What support will young citizens need to think and act in new, more effective ways as ecological citizens? Building from the paradox of New Zealand's experience,

I will argue that adults also have urgent obligations as ecological citizens to address the injustices we have imposed on children and future generations.

Notes

1 See discussion by Rockstrom *et al.* 2009; Wilkenson and Pickett 2009; UNICEF 2009; UNICEF and Plan International 2011; Hansen 2010; Jackson 2009; Speth 2008.

2 Kail 2010, pp343–434. While definitions of 'childhood' vary significantly amongst communities, here I use the term children to refer to those under 14 years of age.

3 Witness the very young age of some protesters in the student demonstrations in London in December 2010: see Hayward 2010b. See also Our Children's Trust 2011, an organisation suing the US Federal government in conjunction with young plaintiffs, for failing to protect collective resources essential for survival. On youth demographics and protest see Hvistendahl 2011.

4 Hansen 2010; Howker and Malik 2010; Rockstrom *et al.* 2009; Wilkenson and Pickett 2009; Willetts 2010.

5 Bohman 2011.

6 Arendt 1954 (2006), p173.

7 Ibid., p193.

8 Lister 2007.

9 See Lister 2007 for a thoughtful discussion of children as citizens, also Taylor and Smith 2009 and Boulding 1996.

10 Bronfenbrenner's (1979) classic description of children's ecological systems and Kail 2010, pp436–8. For thoughtful reflection on competing definitions of ecology and nature see Smith 2006, pp40–9 and Soper 1995, pp16–20.

11 Bronfenbrenner (1979) defined a child's ecological reality as a complex series of nested dynamic systems including the immediate 'microsystem' of the developing person, the 'mesosytem' of social interactions, the 'exosystem' of communities, and a wider 'macrosystem of social, cultural, economic and environmental systems.

12 Bartlett *et al.* 1999; Bartlett 2008; Hansen, 2010; Tanner and Mitchell 2008; UNICEF and Plan International 2011.

13 See Roger Hart's influential revision of Sherry Arnstien's ladder of public participation highlighting the way children can be co-opted rather than empowered: Hart 1997, pp40–55.

14 Both Murray Bookchin (1990) writing in political theory and Urie Bronfenbrenner's (1979) child development work highlight the social ecology of children's worlds. Bookchin (1990) also discussed his outrage after visiting a New York Museum of Natural History exhibit that confronted children with the assertion that all humans were dangerous species, disregarding the complexity of children's lives, including their different experiences of privilege or oppression.

15 Cambridge Primary Review 2009.

16 See Cambridge Primary Review 2009 and Hayward *et al.* 2011a; Hayward *et al.* 2011b; Layard and Dunn 2009.

17 An image of a small child carrying a bucket of water adorns the cover of the 2007 International Panel on Climate Change (IPCC) report, underscoring the impact on children and the local cultures and communities, interests, development and, in many cases, their very survival (Pachauri and Reisinger 2007; UNICEF 2007). Some children are already experiencing climate hardship on a daily basis (Save the Children 2008; UNICEF 2011c).

18 UNICEF 2011a.
19 CPAG 2011; OECD 2009b, 2011b; Hosking *et al.* 2010; Howden-Chapman *et al.* 2010.
20 Barber 1984 (2003), pp120–1.
21 Hansen 2010; Jackson 2009; Rockstrom *et al.* 2009.
22 Hayward and Jackson 2011; Hayward *et al.* 2011a, 2011b.
23 Ophuls 1977.
24 Ophuls 1977, p145.
25 Barber 1984 (2003), p126.
26 Hayward *et al.* 2011a.
27 Hayward *et al.* 2011b.
28 Orr 2011, p160.
29 Crompton and Kasser 2009.
30 Appeals to altruism in campaigning are advocated by Crompton and Kasser (2009) and Murray (2011), while Thaler and Sunstein (2008) advocate the liberal paternalism of 'nudge theory'.
31 See Thaler and Sunstein 2008, p5; applying nudges to the environment, see pp193–210.
32 See John *et al.* 2011 for a discussion of 'think', a deliberative alternative to nudge.
33 Martinsson and Lundqvist 2010.
34 Rose 2010; Dobson 2003.
35 Incentives to switch to new green technology can have financially unexpected, but increasingly well documented, 'rebound' effects: see Druckman *et al.* 2010.
36 Jensen *et al.* 2011, p13.
37 Freeden 2009.
38 Arendt 1958 (1998).
39 Layard 2005; Layard and Dunn 2009; Mayo and Nairn 2009; Schor 2004.
40 Barber 2007.
41 Meadows *et al.* 1972, p23.
42 Ibid., p18.
43 Willetts 2010; Wolf, J. 2011.
44 Jackson 2009; Leichenko and O'Brien 2008; Young 2007.
45 Hayward 2010a.
46 Bauman 2011; Hayes 2011.
47 Barber 1984 (2003), p126.
48 Green and Hayward forthcoming.
49 Hayward 2010a; Bauman 2011.
50 Bauman 2011.
51 Youniss and Levine 2009, p5.
52 Marshall and Bottomore 1950 (1992); see discussion in Kymlicka 2002, p332.
53 Mouffe 2002.
54 For an extended discussion of the rights of the child see Lister 2007, who notes the UN charter marked an important shift in thinking of children as being, not becoming, citizens.
55 Hancox 2011 (e-book: no page).
56 Dobson 2006; Igoe and Brockington 2007.
57 Baker-Cristales 2009; Doherty 2007; Westheimer and Kahne 2004; Kirk 2008a.
58 For a thoughtful reflection on Bauman's body of writing see Bunting 2003.
59 Blissett 2011.
60 Bookchin 1980.
61 Ibid.
62 Freeland 2011.

63 Young 2006a, 2006b; Hayward 2008a.
64 For deliberative and participatory democracy see Barber 1984 (2003); Young 1990, 2001; Bohman 2007; Dryzek 1990 (1994). For the human development and capabilities approach see Nussbaum 2011; Sen 2009; Hart 1997; Freire 1985. For ecological citizenship, liberal democracy and environmental rights see Dobson 2003; Christoff 1996; Eckersley 1996, 2006.
65 Barnardos 2011.
66 Leach 2011.
67 Pew Research Centre 2011.
68 Ward 1995; Knight 2009; Horton and Freire 1990; Vygotsky 1978.
69 Scott 2011.
70 Heywood 2004, p204.
71 Kymlicka 2001.
72 Duerden 2010.
73 See Jean-Jacques Rousseau's *Emile* (1762 (1966)) and Wordsworth's 'Ode: Intimation of Immortality' from *Recollections of Early Childhood* (1807 (1983)). For a discussion of the life of Ernest Seaton see Witt 2010.
74 McCrea 2005; Loynes forthcoming.
75 Piaget *et al.* 1929; Rousseau 1762 (1966).
76 Loynes forthcoming.
77 Chawla 1999; Flanagan 2008a; Hart 1997; Katz 2004; Orr 2011; Scott 2002, 2011; Uzzell 1999; Valentine 2004; Gough and Scott 2006; Wray-Lake *et al.* 2010.
78 For discussion of political oversight of children from an environmental education perspective see Saylan and Blumstein 2011, and from a political science perspective see Youniss and Levine 2009.
79 Franklin 2004.
80 Brooks 2009; Norris 2002.
81 Qualifications and Curriculum Authority 1998.
82 Ibid., pp35–61; Kahne and Westheimer 2006; Kerr 1999.
83 Krosnick 1991.
84 Cohen 2005; Fiske *et al.* 2010, pp1320–7.
85 Westheimer and Kahne 2004; Torney-Purta 1997, 2002; Torney-Purta *et al.* 1999, 2001; Flanagan and Sherrod 1998.
86 Westheimer 2008; Westheimer and Kahne 2004.
87 Flanagan and Sherrod 1998; Torney-Purta *et al.* 1999, 2001, 2004.
88 Watts and Flanagan 2007.
89 Inglehart and Welzel 2010.
90 Research by Sapiro (2004), along with Flanagan and Sherrod (1998), Dalton and Shin (2006), Inglehart and Welzel (2010), Norris (2011) and Torney-Purta (1997, 2002) has drawn our attention to the way each new generation learns about citizenship.
91 Dobson 2003, pp97–127; Hayward 2008a.
92 Dobson 2003, p8; Melo-Escrihuela 2008; Burgess *et al.* 1998; Christoff 1996; Dobson 2009, 2010b; Dobson and Sáiz 2005; Hayward, T. 2006.
93 See also Young 2011; Pogge 2010.
94 Dobson 2003.
95 Christoff 1996a; Middlemiss, 2010; Wolf *et al.* 2009; Wolf Johanna 2011.
96 Blay-Palmer 2011; Huckle 2010; Leach *et al.* 2010.
97 Barry 1999, pp33–48; Dobson 2003, pp176–89; Fischer 2005; Weale 2009; Finlayson 2010.

2 Neoliberalism and children's everyday citizenship

'Bowling with a sponsor'

He aha te mea nui? What is the greatest thing?
He tangata! It is people!
He tangata! It is people!
He tangata! It is people!

(Traditional Māori proverb)

In this chapter I introduce the children interviewed in the course of this study, to set the scene for a wider discussion of the prospects for nurturing ecological citizenship in neoliberal democracies.[1] As discussed in the introduction, the experience of New Zealand children presents a stark challenge for those concerned with youth citizenship and environmental education. In a small democracy which prides itself on its positive environmental image, New Zealand's youngest citizens face an uncertain future. While New Zealanders report comparatively high life satisfaction, despite low net incomes, young New Zealanders also report some of the highest rates of youth suicide and youth unemployment in the OECD, and high rates of accidents, child abuse, ill health and poverty.[2] This chapter reviews the impacts of neoliberal reform on a New Zealand childhood, and reports on the varied ways children interviewed in this study describe their citizenship. I consider the way growing up in situations of increasing income inequality and declining social support has wide-ranging implications for children's experience of their citizenship and their environment.

Neoliberalism: the New Zealand experiment

Nine year old Ben is leaning on the kitchen table listening as researchers sort through a pile of transcribed notes about children's attitudes to citizenship. 'Why are they talking about bowling alone?' he asks. A quick explanation of political scientist Robert Putnam's book by the same title follows.[3] Putnam argued that democracies are most effective when they are rich in social capital, or networks of trust, mutual support and civic engagement that facilitate cooperation and coordination for mutual benefit.[4] Putnam concluded that 'social capital' is eroding as fewer people take part in activities with others, finding it easier to engage in private leisure experiences. Ben listens patiently but looks incredulous. Finally he replies: 'But everybody knows, if you want to go bowling, you just need a sponsor!'

The belief that sponsorship is the obvious way to foster public participation in civic life is the striking – but perhaps not unexpected – conclusion of a nine-year-old New Zealand child who has grown up observing the way the private sector has increasingly supported his citizenship experiences, from sport to education, as the New Zealand state has been systematically hollowed out and rolled back with the introduction of neoliberal policy.

During the course of Ben's first nine years he has participated in, or observed, countless sponsorship drives and fundraising efforts. Ben walks to school each day in a 'walking school bus' organised by parents. The 'bus' walkers carry fluorescent flags bearing the logos of the sponsors, the city council and a national insurance company. The 'bus' walks past Ben's former kindergarten; a welcome sign on the gate bears the brand of the contractor who built the fence and subsidised playground equipment. Ben's school library was built by donations from an IT company and a publishing firm, matched by a government grant. His school's edible garden was constructed by volunteers using donated garden supplies. His large tree-lined school playground was landscaped following four years of school fundraising. Ben's curriculum enrichment – his school trips, library books and art materials – were subsidised through parent 'donations' elicited by invoice, and by the sale of state school places to fee-paying international students. Ben's local public pool was recently closed. After a storm of protest, a philanthropist offered a million dollars to help build a new pool. Seen through Ben's eyes, is it little wonder he should conclude that a citizen just needs a sponsor?

Over the last thirty years, the introduction of neoliberal economic ideas into political life has transformed citizenship in many democracies, especially the predominantly Anglo-speaking countries of Australasia, Canada, the United States and the United Kingdom, along with South American nations including Chile and Mexico, and Scandinavia's Sweden and Denmark.[5] As discussed in Chapter 1, critics have raised concern that, in the Anglo- American democracies in particular, market values of possession and protection of private property have increasingly come to dominate the way young citizens think and behave. There is concern that values of individualism and competition are encouraged at the expense of alternative values of civic republicanism (a sense of obligation to the state) or communitarianism (an emphasis on the common good).[6] There is also widespread unease that children of the market may have internalised neoliberal lessons to the extent that they now equate 'good citizenship' with habits of private responsibility and 'ethical consumption' in ways that leave the underlying drivers of environmental and social problems unchallenged.[7]

Although the term 'neoliberalism' is regularly used, there are subtle but significant differences in its meaning even amongst the predominantly English-speaking countries.[8] As an umbrella concept, neoliberalism commonly describes a sweeping array of policy changes which have introduced free market values of efficiency, competition and choice into diverse areas of public policy, from trade to education and immigration.[9] In New Zealand, however, the cultural and ideological values associated with the introduction of economic reform have been less socially conservative than the values often associated with accounts of neoliberalism in North America and the United Kingdom.[10] In New Zealand, free market policy reform was introduced by the political left and has been consistently portrayed as a form of progressive 'radical capitalism'[11] in ways that resonated with the cultural mythology of struggling indigenous warriors, pioneers and explorers, striking away from traditional authority and old markets in search of new horizons.[12] This rhetoric ushered in models of 'consumer citizenship' which critics argue have gradually come to usurp other traditional views of citizenship, such as social belonging or tribal affiliation.[13] Research by Nairn and Higgins suggests values of entrepreneurial individualism have now been 'normalised' amongst a generation of New Zealand school leavers who regularly describe their lives as autobiographical projects in which they see themselves as authors of their own destiny, with few agreeing that social, economic and institutional support matters as much as their own determination to succeed.[14]

While many democracies have embarked on neoliberal-inspired reform, New Zealand is remarkable for its speed and scale of change. A Labour government, voted to power in 1984, introduced far-reaching reform in an absence of meaningful constitutional restraints in a small, unicameral democracy.[15] A newly-elected Minister of Finance of the time, Roger Douglas, sought to capitalise on this political opportunity, launching a self-described 'policy blitzkrieg', to address the financial crisis of that period, which included high inflation and unemployment.[16] The Douglas administration aimed to rush through changes before forces of opposition could mobilise effective resistance.[17] The first reforms applied to monetary policy and removed barriers to trade. These reforms were quickly extended to education and environmental planning. After 1991, a conservative National government continued the momentum in the social sphere, cutting benefits paid to single parents to 'encourage' a return to work and 'reduce' welfare 'dependence', while abolishing compulsory union membership to create a 'flexible' labour market.[18]

To illustrate the dramatic effect of these reforms on the landscape of childhood, I focus here on four key policy areas: welfare, demography, education and the environment. Turning first to welfare, New Zealanders like to believe that their country is a great place to raise children, and for many children it is. Our own recent research with the UNEP into the sustainability of the lifestyles of young adults aged 18–35 years revealed a snapshot of high-achieving young New Zealanders who have grown up flourishing.[19] Compared to many international peers, New Zealand's small sample were confident, relaxed and generally optimistic about their future, despite the economic downturn of 2008. This snapshot was supported by wider OECD research, which ranked New Zealand in the same period amongst the top six OECD nations for self-reported life satisfaction, despite comparatively low per-capita net incomes.[20] New Zealanders also report comparatively high levels of social engagement and voter turn-out.[21]

Yet on closer inspection, all is not well for the nation's children. New Zealanders' self-confidence is faltering, with rates of self-reported well-being sliding to 13th place in the OECD.[22] The percentage of children living in poverty in New Zealand doubled between 1985 and 2009, rising to estimates of 26 per cent, with particularly high rates amongst Māori and Pacifica families.[23] New Zealand experienced a rapid rise in income inequality in the 1980s, this rate plateaued in the 1990s, but by 2011 the gap between the richest and poorest New Zealanders had widened more than any other developed country in the OECD.[24] In New Zealand, youth under 25 years (including those not in school or education aged 15 to 18), make up 45 per cent of total unemployed, the highest proportion in the OECD.[25] New Zealand also ranks 28th out of 30 countries of the OECD on a combined range of measures of child health outcomes.[26] Children under 14 years are the group most likely to experience abuse and overcrowding in New Zealand, living in poorly-insulated, damp or cold homes that increase the risk of infectious diseases in a changing climate.[27] Nairn, Higgins and Sligo also note that many children in poor homes live in families experiencing disruptive cycles of short term work contracts.[28] Almost 15 per cent of children live in households of poverty, at half the medium income, compared to only 2 per cent of New Zealand's elderly. In the latter case, the elderly receive universal welfare support payments, but universal support is no longer available to children.[29] As a result New Zealand has the largest gap in material well-being between children and elderly in the OECD.[30]

Perhaps most concerning is the question of whether social and economic reforms have exacerbated New Zealand's shamefully high rates of youth suicide.[31] At its height in 1995, youth suicide reached 28.7 deaths per 100,000 amongst 15–24 year olds.[32] Today, young New Zealand women aged 15–19 years lead the OECD youth suicide rates. Research by Chapman-Howden and Hales highlighted the way closure of larger former state employers, (particularly forestry and railways) in the mid to late 1980s and early 1990s, combined decreasing income support, severely impacted the life experiences of young Māori men, while the New Zealand Mental Health Commission notes social exclusion is a particular problem for young women.[33] While economic growth does not equate to mental well-being, social exclusion is exacerbated under conditions of poverty.[34] A targeted effort has reduced the overall rate, yet youth suicide remains high.[35] While the causes of suicide are complex, a public debate remains to be held in New Zealand over the extent to which an unravelling social contract (or the relationship of rights, support and responsibilities shared between citizens and the state) has made life more difficult for young citizens.[36]

Neoliberalism has also impacted on the demographic profile of children under 14 years.[37] The opening of New Zealand's borders for trade encouraged a more diverse population.[38] In 1987, immigration reforms aimed to encourage settlement of 'entrepreneurial investors' from non-traditional source countries, particularly Asia.[39] In New Zealand's case, children under 14 years accompanied their families to New Zealand for work or travelled to New Zealand for education. This era ended a long-running policy of encouraging 'white' settlement from the United Kingdom, Europe, South Africa, America and Canada, and more restrictive policies for prospective Pacific Island immigrants.[40] Today, young New Zealanders increasingly report multiple ethnicities. The number who identify as Asian-New Zealanders is projected rise from 7 to 15 per cent by 2021.[41] A differential birth rate accounts for the projected increased in the population of indigenous Māori children from 25 to 28 per cent and Pacifica children from 11 to 17 per cent, while number of children who identify as *Pākehā* (or European) is predicted to fall from 79 to 62 per cent over the same period.[42]

Neoliberal-inspired reform has also impacted significantly on the education of New Zealand children. The 'Tomorrow's Schools' legislation of 1987 introduced more parent 'choice' and new locally-elected school boards with power to appoint principals to manage schools as educational chief executives.[43] These semi-autonomous, state funded schools also had greater flexibility to generate revenue by directly marketing fee-paying school places to international students as young as five.[44] While schools followed a national curriculum, they were also encouraged to show diversity in responding to local community needs. These changes have had complex effects. The changes helped create more opportunity for school boards to adopt a flax-roots, indigenous language teaching programme that had grown from kindergarten *Kohanga Reo* (language 'nests') initiatives as *Kura Kaupapa Māori* (full immersion language teaching) programmes at primary and secondary school or 'additive heritage or enrichment models of bilingual education'.[45] Some school boards also used their new autonomy to work more closely with the Enviroschools movement in New Zealand. This voluntary programme is supported by a national association of Enviroschool teachers, and aims to develop whole school, social and ecological well-being teaching and learning programmes. The scheme is currently used by about 20–25 per cent of New Zealand schools, but each school is responsible for funding its additional environmental learning activities.[46]

Neoliberal reform has also had complex impacts on the wider physical environment in which children are growing up. At the height of the reform period, New Zealand as a nation was 'branded' in a '100% Pure' international advertising campaign designed to attract international investment and tourism.[47] However, in reality, New Zealand's environmental track record suggests that the country's green legacy to its youngest citizens has been significantly compromised in pursuit of economic growth.[48] Liberalising New Zealand international trade and removing agricultural subsidies has accelerated a shift in the country's primary production base away from lower carbon sheep production to more intensive dairy farming for export, commercial forestry, mining and mineral exploration.[49] These large-scale land use changes, together with greater private car use, have exacerbated the country's rising greenhouse gas emissions, loss of bio-diversity and high rates of lowland river pollution.[50]

In urban areas, reform of the national planning legislation – the Resource Management Act – was intended to help facilitate sustainable economic development, but critics argue the emphasis in planning legislation shifted away from wider community well-being, especially children's needs for access to green play spaces and warm housing.[51] Estimates suggest that up to one third of children deemed 'at risk' now live in inadequate, poorly-insulated housing.[52] An inadequate house is a key element implicated in New Zealand's high rates of child ill health.[53] Subsequent amendments to planning legislation have failed to effect a significant change in housing priorities for children.[54]

The study method: learning to listen to children

Against this background of sweeping economic reform and an unravelling social contract, we were interested in understanding children's reported experiences of their community, citizenship and environment. The heart of this study draws on detailed qualitative field work conducted over four years (2006–2010) in Christchurch, the largest city of the South Island of New Zealand.[55] The study methods included focus group interviews, community mapping exercises, and field trip or class activity with children aged 8 to 12 years.[56] In this study, 160 children were interviewed in 25 focus groups drawn from nine primary schools from Christchurch and surrounding areas. (One school, a full immersion Māori language programme, was also selected from the rural North Island to reflect the background of the research team).

In selecting the case study schools, we were mindful of Seyla Benhabib's argument that the researcher, positioned as observer, can struggle to see the complexity and fluidity within the inner worlds of a culture.[57] In New Zealand, Bishop and Glynn argue that groups from 'outside' have often dominated research, particularly for indigenous communities.[58] They express concern that the researcher cannot become aware of the meaning of schooling experiences if they 'perpetuate an artificial distance' or 'objectify the subject' by dealing with issues in a way that interests the researcher, but is not a concern of those communities subjected to research. To this end, we worked with our home communities, connecting with the social fabric of the child's world by returning to the primary schools we had recently attended as pupils, or knew well as parents or relatives of current pupils. As a result, the community or tribal events, play areas, school events or neighbourhood references raised in discussion by the children were very familiar to the research team, enabling a deeper discussion about the significance of various events. The interviewers also took part in classroom activities with the children in days leading up to and after the interviews, along with attending field trips, helping children record their own radio shows, or forming a school council and volunteering in the school library and community garden.

The nine schools selected for study included three rural schools: an immersion Māori language school located in a North Island low- income coastal area with 100 per cent Māori enrolment (Kura School); a wealthy rural community on the outskirts of Christchurch city (Tree School); and a small high income rural school in a South Island coastal community with 100 per cent *Pākehā*/European enrolment (Farm-Sea School). Two schools were selected from low- to middle-income urban communities, one of which included a high proportion of refugee and new migrant children from over 40 nationalities (Small World School) and the other a large bilingual Māori-English medium teaching programme (Community-*Kura* School). The remaining four schools were located in locally-comparable high-income

Table 2.1 Profile of the study schools

Socio-economic profile	Decile rating[a]	Location	Name	Roll	Ethnic profile
High income	10	Urban	E-School	500	*Pākehā* 79%, Asian 7%, Māori 2%, other 12%
	10	Urban	GATE School	557	*Pākehā* 80%, Asian 7%, Māori 6%, European 5%, other 2%
	9	Urban	Music School	498	*Pākehā* 64%, Asian 20%, Māori 3%, Pacific 1%, other 12%
	9	Urban	Faith School	323	NZ European/*Pākehā* 62%, Asian 15%, Māori 3%, Pacific 2%, European 4%, other 14%
	9	Rural (Enviroschool)	Tree School	96	NZ European/*Pākehā* 92%, Māori 4%, other 4%
	9	Rural (Enviroschool)	Farm-Sea School	35	NZ European/*Pākehā* 100%
Middle income	6	Urban (Edible garden)	Community-*Kura* School	509	NZ European/*Pākehā* 69%, Māori 18%, Asian 7%, Pacific 0.5%, other 5.5%
	4	Urban (Cultural garden)	Small World School	255	NZ European/*Pākehā* 44%, Asian 23%, Māori 11%, Pacific 6%, other 16%
Low income	1	Rural	Kura School	70	Māori 100%

Source: Bronwyn Hayward.

Note
a   Deciles are ratings constructed by the New Zealand Ministry of Education. 'A decile is a 10% grouping. A school's decile rating indicates the extent to which it draws its students from low socio-economic communities.' Decile 1 schools have the largest proportion of low socio-economic communities, whereas decile 10 schools are the 10% of schools having the highest income communities. 'The indicator is based on Census data for households with school-aged children in each school's catchment area', and includes details about 'adjusted household incomes, household crowding, parental education and dependence on a government benefit for sickness or unemployment' (Ministry of Education 2010).

neighbourhoods typical of the wider population distribution of Christchurch city: an integrated-state funded school with Catholic community support (Faith School); an 'intermediate' school for children aged 11 and 12 years including a gifted and talented programme (GATE School); a specialised extensive IT teaching programme (E-School), and a school with a gifted and talented programme and specialist music teaching (Music School). All schools were state funded. Two rural schools (the Tree School and Farm-Sea School) had active Enviroschools programmes, while the two middle-income schools hosted an edible garden (Community-*Kura* School) and an international community garden (Small World School). The study was a qualitative research project; no attempt was made to gain a representative sample, rather we tried to get as broad a range of school communities and children's views as possible in a city of 376,700 people. The aim was to listen to a range of views of the city's youngest citizens to provoke reflection and a deeper insight.[59]

The children were interviewed in focus groups to help redress the power imbalance often experienced in adult discussions with children.[60] In a focus group, children can be experts, supported by peers, and group reflections can enrich everyone's understanding of the issues.[61] Focus groups were also used to create an opportunity for collective deliberative reflection amongst children about their situation and about the research method, which included construction of a group community map (see Chapter 5).[62] All discussion was taped and transcribed, and all coding was cross-checked on an on-going basis. Analysis was conducted using a constant comparative method that continued during and after data collection.[63] Researchers returned to each group to talk about the resulting themes emerging from the data, and results were presented to children and teachers to test our accuracy of interpreting what the children were reporting, and to re-examine our conclusions and draw on insider knowledge.[64]

The focus groups were conducted in English except for four groups which were conducted in Māori and English in response to the children's conversation. The sample was balanced by gender. Teachers were asked to nominate children to reflect the ethnic diversity of the school's census profile. Within the focus groups, children also collaborated to create 'community star maps', mapping their social capital in response to an opening question, 'What do children from around here do with other people?' Children's cognitive mapping enables children to represent places that are important to them.[65] The primary aim of the 'star maps' was to help facilitate children's discussion of their experience of community interaction with others. The 'maps' were posters, rather than attempts to create accurate spatial drawings.[66] The children were asked to talk about what activities they did with others and to code activities they saw as being similar. Children were then invited to 'weight' the community interactions they enjoyed the most, by placing as many colour coded stars as they liked on their important activities. These star maps are discussed in detail in Chapter 5.

During the course of the study, three small but significant events occurred which were important in the political life of the children we interviewed. The first was the closure of a local outdoor public swimming pool. Amongst the focus groups, nearly all children in eight focus groups had taken part in a series of community protests to retain the pool. Two other protests also occurred which were initiated entirely by children. One was a spontaneous, playground protest over several weeks in a rural school (Tree School) against a ban on climbing tall trees. All children we interviewed at that school had taken part. Teachers, the principal and the children reported students marching and placard-waving outside the staff room. The third protest was fleeting. It took place in the Music School and involved an aborted playground strike during lunchtime, planned by children to protest the age restrictions placed on access to library books and school being 'boring'. Even though it never took place, the planned strike or the debate was reported independently in all four focus groups at the Music School. Simultaneously, workers at a neighbouring supermarket were locked out in a dispute over pay parity with Australian supermarket workers.

Figure 2.1 Children in a protest to retain a local outdoor pool, Christchurch

Credit: Bronwyn Hayward.

Finally, but most significantly, the conclusion of the field work for the study was abruptly framed by a significant 7.1 magnitude earthquake which struck the city of Christchurch on 4 September 2010, and a shallow and therefore more devastating 6.3 magnitude aftershock on 22 February 2011. While field work had ended a month earlier, the on-going grief and exhaustion of over 8,000 earthquake aftershocks of varying intensity which wracked the city in the 12 month period after the initial quake continues to define the lives of the children we report on here in ways that we begin to explore in Chapters 4 and 8.

Introducing New Zealand's children of the market

There were several striking features about children we interviewed. The first was their mobility. This was a sample on the move. Chapter 5 explores the impact of mobile lifestyles on attitudes to citizenship as belonging. Children were invited to introduce themselves by talking about their country of birth and languages spoken at home. A third of the sample was born outside New Zealand and 26 per cent volunteered that they spoke a language other than English at home, with 19 children saying they spoke *Te Reo* (Māori) regularly at home, and the remainder mentioning Korean, Chinese dialects, African, European or Pacific languages.

A second striking feature of conversation with these young citizens was the extent to which choosing their own pseudonym underscored how children are constantly and creatively playing with their identity. The children chose names ranging from political statements ('anti establishmentarianism') to gender swapping (girls as 'Bob', boys 'Daisymae') and favourite food (chocolate). Some children in the bilingual programme at the Community-*Kura* School chose names evocative of North American indigenous communities (Black Eagle) or fictitious characters (Cranberry the 13th). Children in the smallest, full-immersion rural Māori language school (Kura School) chose names of Black American celebrities (Snopp Dogg). No restrictions were placed on the children's choice. Some chose names from books or swapped names in friendship groups, or chose names from fantasy games. A small number of children chose television characters. Their preference for quirky, personal or creative choices adds anecdotal support to Oliver James' observation that material values of branded consumption do not seem to have taken hold in everyday New Zealand life to the extent that is reported in Anglo-American hyper-consumption culture, a suggestion we return to later in discussion.[67]

A third feature of discussion was the way many children talked about citizenship as participation. Previous studies of children's attitudes suggest New Zealand children have a well-developed notion of rights, but correspondingly underdeveloped understanding of the obligations of citizenship.[68] In this sample however, the majority of children expressed a highly-developed sense of personal responsibility for their community and obligations to look after other people and the environment. This conversation was typical of the opening discussion in all focus groups:

INTERVIEWER: What does it mean to be a citizen of this community? [points to community star map where children have written 'Christchurch']

BOB: To be a citizen in Christchurch, you can't litter, and try not to pollute as much as we are right now. You know, try and take public transport instead of taking a rusty old car, and um, be courteous, treat people like they want to be treated, and help disabled people – well, people with problems, like if they're in a wheelchair – to get through the doors.

ACORN: Well, you need to help people, and you should read the newspaper and stuff.

DAISYMAE: Well, just respecting the Canterbury ground [rugby stadium], and Christchurch, and I'm very proud to come from Canterbury, cause the Aero club came from there.

AROHA: Um, look after the environment, and instead of taking public transport you could just bike or walk – that's much healthier and it doesn't pollute.

BOB: That's what I do, I love it!

JASMINE: When you meet people, don't judge them – get to know them a bit more.

(Community-*Kura* School)

As discussion progressed, children spoke about their participation in community life in a wide variety of ways. Some spoke of citizenship as their individual or personal responsibility, to take action in the community. These children I term, 'Self-Helpers' and 'Consumer-Citizens' or 'Green Entrepreneurs'. Others were ambivalent about their ability to participate as citizens, especially 'Eco-Worriers', 'New Arrivals', and 'Streetwise Sceptics'. A third cluster were confident about citizenship as group action ('Team-Tribal Players' and 'Digital Citizens'). These descriptive titles were presented to groups of students in discussion after the research. While these categories are not mutually exclusive (as some children felt they belonged to several), the descriptors were sufficiently evocative that children could recognise themselves and agreed with our interpretation of what they were saying about 'what citizens do' everyday.

Citizenship as personal responsibility for action

Some children were confident that citizens could, and should, take action as individuals to make changes in their community. This group included Self-Helpers, Green Entrepreneurs, Citizen-Scientists and Consumer-Citizens.

Self-help citizens[69]

While all children expressed citizenship as personal responsibility, those I describe as Self-Helpers were children who relished this role and spoke of themselves as expectant and enthusiastic change agents. Self-Helpers believed they could, and should, take personal responsibility for actions, and/or felt that 'good' citizens should additionally engage in fundraising or seek private sponsorship first before looking, for example, to government assistance. These findings resonate with research in the United States.[70] For example, New Zealand Self-Helpers readily volunteered that citizens: 'don't bully', 'don't litter', 'put things in the rubbish', 'respect things and people', 'take care of yourself', 'take care of your family', 'look after your *iwi* [tribe]', 'fundraise', 'eat right', 'help it [your community]' and 'take care of animals'. For the self-help children, good citizenship was equated with a sense of individual responsibility to take action to 'fix' problems. However, in their enthusiasm it was noticeable that that self-help citizens rarely challenged the underlying causes or injustices that might have contributed to a problem. Sir Lancelot-Fakename illustrates this kind of self-help citizenship expectation:

INTERVIEWER:	What do you think it means to be a citizen of these communities?
SIR LANCELOT-FAKENAME:	You should be able to make decisions as well, like help make decisions and like if something could be fixed like when the pool was closed down and they wanted to open it up you could help fundraise for your community so that it could open up again.

(E-School)

Other children also founded a strong sense of identity in taking personal responsibility for the environment, for example, as Bob commented about taking his bike to get to school, 'that's what I do, I love it!' Amongst the children who strongly identified citizenship with personal action were children who specifically framed this individual agency in terms of an ability to participate in the market as consumer-citizens.

Consumer-citizens

When asked what do people do with other people around here, 22 of 160 children reported 'shopping' and spoke enthusiastically about shopping as a form of personal action they strongly identified with. For ten children (all girls), shopping was a pleasurable activity undertaken with family, or friends at weekends, as an event or an outing. (In the same focus groups, other children reported 'hanging out' in commercial spaces including malls and leisure centres, but these children did not equate hanging out with shopping.) While ten children said they liked shopping, most of their friends disagreed:

INTERVIEWER: What have we got listed [on the map] to do with other people?
TINA: I like shopping.
BOB: Nah I hate shopping aye.
BILLY-SONG: Yeah it's boring.
POPCORN: Shopping's boring.
KAJIL: Shops! I like to go to the shops cos I get to buy new things, like new toys.

(Small World School)

Furthermore, only a handful of children spontaneously volunteered any brands in their hour-long conversations. The names of commercial products were only mentioned in association with electronic devices, television characters and music. (One child of 160 drew a picture of a shopping bag and labelled it with a brand name of a girl's fashion label on her community map.) We didn't prompt questions about brands and therefore cannot infer consumer knowledge. However, the absence of brand names in spontaneous conversation (with the notable exception of music and computer games) differs markedly from studies of youth 'hyper consumption' in the United States. For example, Juliet Schor has noted that by 10 years of age, the average American child has memorised 300 to 400 brands, and 92 per cent of child requests for products by children aged 8 to 14 years are brand specific.[71] In the United Kingdom, research by Ed Mayo and Agnes Nairn similarly suggests that at ages 8 to 12 children are similarly brand-savvy, and often promote favoured brands to their peers.[72] In this context the ambivalence of many of these New Zealand children about shopping was striking. Oliver James observed a similar consumer reticence amongst New Zealand adults five years earlier, and speculated that this has resulted from New Zealand's social history of egalitarianism and comparatively low net incomes.[73]

However another 12 children (all drawn from the high-decile GATE School and the Tree School) spoke enthusiastically about citizenship as the responsibility to shop thoughtfully. One of these young citizen-consumers spoke about his family joining the highly popular national second-hand goods trading scheme, Trade Me; 'it's incredible the kind of things that people will buy!' Others agreed that shopping second hand saved 'good money' and 'reduced waste'. Children nominated 'reusing shopping bags' as something 'good' citizens did, and at the Tree School all groups volunteered comments about the importance of buying locally-manufactured goods: 'Stop manufacturing things from China, like plastic things. They just get chucked out after a while, like McDonald's toys, they are plastic and people just end up throwing them out.' Young consumer-citizens in the GATE School also worried about China: 'All these plastic chairs might come from China', and argued that 'everyone should go buy an electric car right now!' or 'Buy stuff in bulk so that there is less waste.'

Green entrepreneurs and citizen-scientists

A particular view of citizenship as a responsibility to take individual action was revealed when children were prompted to discuss climate change.[74] In these groups, many children felt that citizens should be able to invent new processes and technical solutions to encourage clean and green consumption. In these cases, young citizens discussed ways to fix technical problems they associated with climate change, but did not question processes of injustice that may have contributed to the issue, as the extract below illustrates:

KITTY CAT: People today are born with magnificent brains. They have got all sorts of knowledge now that helps them invent new things. There is no point just relying on old stuffs, just invent a new way of getting light and power.
GINGERNUT: People should take the bus more.
SANTA: Electric cars!
KERMIT THE FROG: And the energy efficient light bulbs.

(GATE School)

This type of citizenship I have termed 'green entrepreneurs' or 'young citizen-scientists' to illustrate the way it strongly resonates with ideas of citizenship as ecological modernisation.[75] These children appear to assume that environmental degradation can be and should be addressed by technological innovation, but rarely discussed any underlying questions of environmental justice or fairness that may be raised by the issues they were concerned about.

Ambivalent citizen actors

While many children spoke enthusiastically about citizenship as personal self-help or specific market actions, other children were not confident talking about their ability to participate in the community as citizens, or were hesitant about their capacity to make changes.[76] I describe these children as Eco-Worriers, New Arrivals and Streetwise Sceptics.

Eco-Worriers

In contrast to the optimism and enthusiasm of Self-Helpers, Consumer-Citizens or young Green Entrepreneurs were children I describe as Eco-Worriers, or anxious or concerned citizens with highly developed awareness of environmental issues, but who could volunteer few solutions or actions to address these problems. Amongst the 160 children were 14 who expressed strong anxiety that they or their loved ones may personally experience a variety of threats with little external assistance or relief, most starkly phrased as 'We will die.' These children were often particularly concerned about mitigating problems like climate change but, unlike self-help citizens or entrepreneurs who seemed energised by the opportunity to effect change, some of these children simply seemed overwhelmed by environmental problems. Eco-Worriers may reflect what Jensen and Schnack[77] term 'low action competence' or what Bandura[78] terms 'low external-efficacy' (confidence that if I take action I can effect change). Alternatively, as Woodly suggests, low assessment of efficacy may sometimes simply be realism in the face of large-scale problems.[79] The following excerpt illustrates some of the depth of concern of these children; a sense of personal responsibility, resignation, or uncertainty accompanied the tone of their discussion:

ABBY: I think everyone is responsible [for climate change]. Some say it's the young generation, but it has been going on for quite a while. People think it's just started and they are blaming our generation but really it has been going on for a while so it's from our grandparents down ... If people try really hard we can stop it, well maybe not stop but slow it down.

SAMMY: I agree with Abby about how it's everybody but really umm it's also the people like our mums and dads and stuff and a little bit older than them. They have done it because they had all sorts of things which people would now stop and say 'hey that's not very good for the environment'. It's because nobody really knew that it was happening so they went around as if there were no consequences or anything but now the consequences are really happening.

KITTY CAT: Also when the new sorts of products like the spray cans were invented they didn't know they would have an effect on the environment. They thought: 'Hey this is interesting. Let's make lots and lots of it.' Then they just didn't care about the smoke going out, they just thought it was going to blow away somewhere else.

SAMMY: Basically they have just made a big mess and we have to tidy it up.

(GATE School)

Other Eco-Worriers expressed particular concern about the scale of environmental destruction and the diffuse sources and complexity of the problem, as this continued conversation illustrates:

SAMMY: People from other countries like England and stuff where there is not such a big problem with the ozone layer and that sort of thing, when they come to New Zealand, they don't sort of think of the whole problem of how hot it is getting and they just sit on the beach and get really, really burnt.

KITTY CAT: Also other things which damage the environment are smoking and drugs and drinking. Even though other people don't notice it, they think smoking is cool, lets smoke, but it can actually cause deformations of children. It's just not helping.

(GATE School)

These anxieties have been echoed in a study by Constance Flanagan which suggests some children growing up in modern democracies are reporting increased rates of anxiety in response to constant change, and a heightened sense of uncertainty.[80] This anxiety is starkly illustrated by Poppy:

INTERVIEWER: Well, what sort of effects do you think that climate change will have on you in the future? We have talked about some sort of extreme examples like New Zealand flooding …

POPPY: We will die. How are we supposed to die? It's not like we can just die? That's no fair. God? [Can] God create something to protect us?

(Tree School)

Discussion will consider the implications of eco-worrier anxiety in greater detail in Chapter 3. Other children who had recently arrived in New Zealand were also unsure about equating citizenship with participation

New Arrivals

While the majority of children interviewed in this study reported citizenship as active participation (as individuals or groups), at least one child in every urban focus group was less confident. These children were new migrants or in the country as fee paying primary school students with few community supports beyond their school and church. When asked if they knew others who could effect change, a few of these children could think of few people, and all expressed some anxiety that they belonged to only a small number of community groups compared to their peers. In the extract reported below, Crystal had come to New Zealand from China one and a half years earlier. All the other children in this discussion had been born outside New Zealand, but Crystal lived alone with her mother to attend a New Zealand school as a fee paying student:

INTERVIEWER:	Do you know people that have made changes in these communities?
LEONARDO DA VINCI:	Yeah I know the mayor I've met him … because my friend's friends with him.
INTERVIEWER:	Cool, not everyone knows the mayor …
PUFF:	My mum's a lawyer and she's made heaps of changes.
GINGA:	My dad's a teacher and sometimes a principal and he changes the school around like how it runs …
CRYSTAL:	[softly] My mum changes the house around, like moving stuff.

(Community-*Kura* School)

Crystal's quiet comment sits in a wider context of an hour-long conversation in which she struggled to think of ways she could make a difference to her wider New Zealand community. Given her friends were enthusiastic self-help citizens, her reserve and hesitancy was noticeable in group discussion. Her sense of social isolation may have been heightened by her experience as a fee paying student. In conversation with parents of fee paying students after interviews, being a fee paying student appeared to complicate citizenship. Fee paying students have no legal rights of citizenship, but some parents felt they contributed to the community through fee payments, yet 'too much' was 'kept' by the school. Two principals commented it was hard to integrate fee paying families into the school because there was less 'commitment to get involved' and some 'tension between families here to settle and children staying with mum for education only'.

Streetwise Sceptics

Amongst the children who were ambivalent about participating as citizens were a third group of young Streetwise Sceptics. In 17 focus groups, children had taken part in, or observed, a local protest. In all 25 focus groups, children also reported that their parents or family friends volunteered at school (on the board or parent teacher association). However, not all children agreed they could participate effectively as citizens through protest or volunteering. Students at the Tree School who had protested to be allowed to continue to climb the trees were particularly sceptical about citizenship as active participation in community life:

EVE:	… Everyone wants to climb the trees at our school.
INTERVIEWER:	Yeah I heard about that.
EVE:	We wrote a letter and the principal wrote back saying because we just wrote it on a pad of paper she wanted us to type it all up and that. And we just thought it was real stupid because we wrote it.
JASON:	Last year people protested.
EVE:	And they didn't come and tell us [to], we just did it and then there was no talk about it after we stopped.

JANE:	Yeah.
JAMIE:	No one said anything.
INTERVIEWER:	So you protested and nothing happened afterwards?
EVE:	They never brought it up again and they try their hardest not to bring it up.

(Tree School)

These children at the Tree School also commented with similar scepticism about local politics, describing the parent teacher association as 'our mums who help out at the school' and who were 'on our side', while members of the school board were described as people who had children who 'left our school ages ago but they just stay'. These children also reported that decision-making in local clubs (the pony club and tennis club) was dominated by 'people who just stay and stay'. In discussion later, teachers agreed that children were sceptical and felt it was exacerbated by wider community tension between new families commuting into town for work and old established rural farming families.

Some children at an urban school who took part in a neighbourhood protest to retain a local community pool were similarly sceptical about equating citizenship with active participation:

ROBERTA:	We've written petitions and done protest marches but the council won't listen to us, well it's going to cost too much to fix it so there's no point.
LEONARDO:	Yeah, like 300,000 bucks.
PUFF:	Because there's a crack in the ground underneath the pool and they'd have to lift everything up and then fix it and that would cost thousands of dollars.
INTERVIEWER:	So when you said that you didn't think that the council listened … to children like you?
ROBERTA:	They probably did listen but they didn't …
JUSTIN:	Care.

(Community-*Kura* School)

In later discussion in Chapter 4 we will return to consider whether a sense of healthy civic scepticism is a barrier to participation, or encourages critical thinking and greater action. Overall, however, Streetwise Sceptics stood in marked contrast to children who defined citizenship in terms of collective action and belonging.

Citizenship as collective action

Approximately one third of the entire sample of children felt that citizens could effect change as members of a group, a tribe, a church, or in collaboration with others. The social contract may be unravelling at the macro scale, but these children saw themselves as citizens who played active roles as members of community groups or tribes or through digital action.

Team-Tribal Players

Team-Tribal Players were young citizens who strongly identified as members of a team or tribe, multiple ethnic communities or church groups. These children belonged to an extensive array of formal and informal sports clubs, afterschool activities and church or community groups. 'You must never forget your mother tongue', 'I'm gonna make church rich, man. Make church full of stickers so it's got more than the other ones', 'I belong to my tribe, I belong to our *marae* [sacred communal meeting place]', 'I am very proud to come from Canterbury because the Aero club came from there'. Many of these young citizens had also taken part in the pool protest, but unlike Streetwise Sceptics, they felt positive about equating citizenship with collective action. These children often also reported detailed positive observations of parents, grandparents and older community members taking part in school board, local council, tribal or national decision making (see Chapter 4). These young team and tribal players expressed enjoyment and confidence in collective action as way to achieve change. Taking part in local protests and observing tribal politics often had a profound effect on some young citizens as this discussion illustrates:

DAISEYMAE: You could write a bit, you could protest – cause there's nothing stopping people at our age from going out protesting, and keep on writing letters to the government. Cause it's not illegal or anything, and you shouldn't be embarrassed to do that if you really want something.

INTERVIEWER: Have you done anything like that?

DAISEYMAE: No, I haven't – but I could if I wanted.

AROHA: You could protest, or you could make a group of people who want to do something like for the Pool. And you could make a petition for something too.

(Community-*Kura* School)

Similarly, some children in bilingual programmes observing the interaction of tribal and national politics could report remarkably detailed political insights, as this discussion amongst 8- and 9-year-olds reveals:

CRANBERRY THE 13TH: In the *iwi* [tribe], the top *iwi* person is probably my *taua* [grandmother or elderly female relative], my *taua*'s on the [tribal board], and she's one of the big people who's going to have that meeting at [place], you know what it is? They're doing something and they do it every year, a real special thing, I just forgot the name.

INTERVIEWER: A *hui* [meeting]?

CRANBERRY THE 13TH: *Hui-ā-tau* [annual general meeting]. Yeah, she's one of the big people.

STAR FLYER: I've got [a relative] that's in parliament and he was arguing with …
[group then discusses in detail a current parliamentary debate]

(Community-*Kura* School)

One feature of the team player and tribal citizens was that the community events they recounted were also activities that involved other generations (parents, teachers, and older siblings). The effect of intergenerational support in creating a politically-engaged community is a theme I examine in Chapter 4.

Digital Citizens

Given the mobility of these children, some reported that 'good citizens' maintained connections with friends and family in other countries, kept up their other language and did this by using electronic media. Several children, all boys, were enthusiastic about children participating with other people through computer games. Boys and girls in every focus group mentioned that citizens participated with others via the internet. At the time of the study, internet usage was uneven, with less penetration in rural and Pacifica New Zealand homes.[81] Children at the highest income schools most often reported using email and home phones to contact friends overseas, but few reported mobile phone use. 'I have lots of friends too and most of them are in England and I email them and I phone them sometimes but it costs too much.' During the study period only 27 per cent of 6–13-year-old children owned their own mobile phones, due to the comparatively high cost of phones:[82]

BLOB HEAD: [Things I do with other people around here] going on the internet which I don't get much chance to do unless I go to the library.
INTERVIEWER: So what do you do on the internet? And do you guys go on the internet as well?
                          [general chorus of 'yes'; someone sad you're not allowed on the internet at school]
BLOB HEAD: At Christchurch City libraries. That's where I do the internet and stuff. I look for Harry Potter sites and Tamagochi sites, and sometimes my sister, I do a job for her and I go on Barbie sites and print off colouring-in pictures.

(E-School)

However, following up the interviews in 2011 revealed a very different picture of electronic communication use. Teachers and students commented that they now used email and social media frequently, although high costs still made internet access uneven. All schools reported that after the earthquakes, mobile phones were now widely used as an essential tool for keeping in contact with home and school, given on-going aftershocks.

Summary: citizenship as sponsored participation

Will Kymlicka has described our communities as the 'seedbeds' of citizenship.[83] Children learn the values and virtues that are expected of citizens in their communities. What kind of citizenship flourishes in New Zealand children's everyday communities? The introduction of neoliberalism has dramatically changed the education, health and physical environments of young citizens at a macro level, eroding confidence in a shared social contract and increasing suffering and disruption for some families. Critics have expressed concern that children now equate citizenship with individual responsibility and that market values of selfish capitalism tend to crowd out other communitarian values. However, a closer look at the micro level of children's everyday experience suggests a more nuanced experience. New Zealand children are surprisingly unbranded and many experience social capital as voluntary action. The New Zealand social contract may be unravelling for young citizens, and the gap between rich and poor increasing, but many still see themselves as active participants recreating communities through their own individual efforts or as members of extended family, tribes and community groups.[84] There were significant exceptions to these positive citizenship experiences. Some fee paying overseas children and new migrants reported belonging to fewer clubs, while other children were sceptical their actions to effect change would make a difference. Some felt anxious and unsure or excluded. Discussion now turns to consider the implications of these diverse everyday citizenship experiences for nurturing new forms of ecological citizenship.

Notes

1 Graduate research projects associated with this study include: Jessica Buck 2009; Wakaiti Dalton 2008; Holly Donald 2009; Nick Kirk 2008b; Celia Sheerin 2007; see also Hayward *et al.* 2006.
2 Hayward, Donald and Okeroa 2011a; CPAG 2011; OECD 2009b, 2011b.
3 Putnam 2000.
4 Putnam 1995, p67.
5 Ong 2004; O'Brien *et al.* 2009.
6 Dobson 2006; Igoe and Brockington 2007.
7 Baker-Cristales 2009; Doherty 2007; Westheimer and Kahne 2004; Kirk 2008a; Thompson 2007. The current emphasis on personal responsibility was reinforced, but did not begin, with neoliberalism: see Curtis 2002; Bookchin's (1990) critique of the introspection of the 'psychotherapy industry'; Rose 1999; Foucault *et al.* 1991.
8 Harvey 2007.
9 Dalziel 2002; Kelsey 1996.
10 Duggan 2003; Giddens 1998, p7; Larner and Craig 2005.
11 Duggan 2003; see also a discussion on Bourdieu's radical capitalism in Leyva 2009.
12 King 2003, p509; Mulgan 1972; Walker 2004.
13 Larner 2000.
14 Nairn and Higgins 2007, p266.
15 Palmer 1979.
16 For a discussion of the older children affected by policies of this period and a comparison with their UK counterparts, see Nairn *et al.* forthcoming.
17 Douglas 1993.
18 Dalziel 2002; Boston *et al.* 1999; Kelsey 1996.
19 Hayward *et al.* 2011a.
20 OECD 2009a.

21 Hayward 2006; Vowles 2009.
22 OECD 2011a.
23 Where poverty is defined as living within 60 per cent of the median disposable income. CPAG 2011, pp18–19; Children's Social Health Monitor 2009. Grimmond (2011) draws on the OECD report, *Doing Better For Children* (OECD 2009b), arguing it 'indicates that child poverty rates in New Zealand are about midway between those of the UK and the US (using the poverty measure of 50 per cent of median household income). In New Zealand 15 per cent of children were deemed to live in poor households in 2005, compared with 10 per cent in the UK and 20 per cent in the US', p4. New Zealand is notable for a very low number of elderly in poverty, fewer than 2 per cent.
24 Johnston 2011; OECD 2001b.
25 Boven *et al.* 2011; OECD 2011a.
26 Gluckman and Hayne 2011.
27 Grimmond 2011; McMichael *et al.* 2003; Gluckman and Hayne 2011.
28 Nairn *et al.* forthcoming
29 Collins 2010.
30 Ibid.
31 OECD 2009a.
32 Ferguson *et al.* 2005.
33 Howden-Chapman *et al.* 2005; New Zealand Mental Health Commission 2011.
34 Wilkinson and Pickett 2009, pp66–70, 175.
35 Ibid.; OECD 2009a.
36 Stylianou 2011; Howden-Chapman *et al.* 2005; Hayward and O'Brien 2010. See also Johnston 2011 for a discussion of the comments by the OECD secretary at the unveiling of the *Divided We Stand* income report on the social contract in many countries.
37 Flanagan 2008.
38 Ong 2004; Putnam 2007.
39 Bedford 2002; Spoonley 2006.
40 For discussion of the way New Zealand attempted to maintain a white immigration policy through assisted migration and entry permits, see Phillips 2009.
41 Statistics New Zealand 2004, p12.
42 Ibid.; Bellamy 2008.
43 Codd 2005; Woodfield and Gunby 2003.
44 Lewis 2005; Butcher and McGrath 2004; Ong 2004, pp137–8. This move to sell school places has also contributed to the rapid diversification of New Zealand children's demographic profile.
45 May *et al.* 2004.
46 The Enviroschools Foundation 2011.
47 True and Gao 2010.
48 New Zealand Ministry for the Environment 2007.
49 MacLeod and Moller 2006; Barnett and Pauling 2005; Statistics New Zealand 2011.
50 New Zealand Ministry for the Environment 2011.
51 Stevenson 2007; see also Blaiklock *et al.* 2002; CPAG 2011; Children's Social Health Monitor 2009.
52 CRESA 2010.
53 CRESA 2010; Children's Social Health Monitor 2009.
54 Ibid.

55 The study included subsets of research interviews published by Kirk (2008b) and Dalton (2008); see also Kirk 2008a, 2008b; Donald 2009; Sheerin 2007; Buck 2009; Dalton 2008; and research assistance from Amanda Thomas and Ara Tai Rakena.

56 Kail 2010, pp362–93.

57 Benhabib 2006.

58 Bishop and Glynn 1999.

59 Clark and Moss 2001 discuss a mosaic approach to collaborative research, using a range of techniques with young children to reflect on the meaning of experiences from different perspectives. With older children, focus group discussion prompted reflection on class activities and 'maps'.

60 Punch 2002. See Appendix for discussion question prompts for this study, and see Kirk 2008a, 2008b.

61 Heath *et al.* 2009, pp89–92.

62 Bagnolia and Clark 2010 also note the way children and young people's focus groups help students to feel confident and make critical comments about the research method.

63 Strauss 1990; Westheimer and Kahne 2004.

64 Westheimer and Kahne 2004.

65 Halseth and Doddridge 2000.

66 Freeman 2010.

67 James 2007, p104.

68 Smith 2005; Taylor and Smith 2009.

69 I am indebted to Westhiemer and Kahne 2004 for the term 'self helper', a term they used for personally-responsible citizens they observed in US-based child citizen research.

70 Westheimer and Kahne 2004.

71 Schor 2004, p25.

72 Mayo and Nairn 2009, pp185–7.

73 James 2007.

74 For an extended discussion of some of these groups, see Kirk 2008b.

75 Weale 1992; Hajer 1995; Mol and Spaargaren 2009.

76 Here, in thinking about children's experience of citizenship at a broad level, I am indebted to Ruth Lister's (2007) thoughtful discussion of citizenship and children.

77 Jensen and Schnack 1997; see also Reid and Scott 2006; Bishop and Scott 1998.

78 Bandura 2007.

79 Woodly 2006.

80 Flanagan 2008.

81 Access to the internet in 2006 among Māori was 46.7 per cent and 37.7 per cent among Pacific peoples. These levels were well below those of Europeans (70 per cent) and Asians (77 per cent) in the same year (New Zealand Ministry of Social Development 2010, p113).

82 Colmar Brunton 2008.

83 Kymlicka 2002, pp302–19.

84 New Zealand Ministry of Social Development 2010 reports overall high rates of social capital in New Zealand (pp110–23). See discussion in Chapter 4.

3   Growing greener citizens

SMART, FEARS or SEEDS experiences?

Na ono kahona iti rawa, ko ngā Ooka teitei rawa; Tall oaks from little acorns grow.
(Wiremu Ruwhitu, personal communication 2007)

Discussion in Chapter 2 identified a variety of ways children experience citizenship everyday as participation and belonging in communities. Some participate as enthusiastic individual Self-Helpers, Consumer-Citizens, and Green Entrepreneurs. Others experience citizenship through belonging to groups, tribes and teams, churches or ethnic communities. However, some children are diffident and uncertain about their citizenship, including those described as Eco-Worriers, Streetwise Sceptics or New Arrivals.

What are the implications of children's everyday citizenship experiences for sustainability? What are the prospects for children to learn new forms of ecological citizenship? To begin to understand the environmental implications of children's citizenship experiences, I offer a typology of environmental citizenship education, which I describe here as the SMART experiences of *thin environmental citizenship*, the FEARS of *non-citizenship*, and the SEEDS experiences of *strong ecological citizenship*.[1] Each of the three forms of citizenship education are summarised here with a handprint diagram. The idea that we leave a legacy or handprint of our citizenship is expanded further in Chapter 8.

While each individual child's formal and informal citizenship learning will cut across these broad categories, I offer this typology as a tool for highlighting the environmental implications of young citizen's attitudes and expectations about their political agency, environmental experiences, observations of the way decisions are made, their experiences of justice and their opportunities to exercise political imagination.[2] In comparing these three broad forms of environmental citizenship education, I argue that SEEDS experiences provide the strongest support for children learning to exercise their capability for democratic citizenship for a just, sustainable, common future.

The SMART citizenship education for thin environmentalism

Citizenship education takes place formally and informally throughout life. Children learn about citizenship by observing and exercising citizenship in their

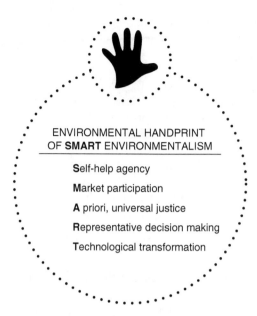

Figure 3.1 Environmental handprint of SMART environmentalism

Source: Bronwyn Hayward.

families, school and wider community. Many children interviewed in Chapter 2 had learned to feel confident about their citizenship as personal responsibility. These Self-Helpers, Green Entrepreneurs and young Citizen-Scientists were citizens who reported that citizens can and should take individual action to effect positive environmental change. While a strong sense of youthful efficacy is valuable and important in a democracy, I argue that too great an expectation of citizenship as individual responsibility for change can be a recipe for ineffective action and anxiety, particularly in a context of diffuse global decision-making power. Yet many children's expectations of personally responsible citizenship are reinforced by 'SMART' environmental citizenship education and lessons of: Self-help agency, Market participation, A priori justice, Representative decision making and Technological transformation. I argue the net effect of SMART citizen education is a thin environmentalism in which citizens learn that desired environment outcomes are achieved through individual efforts in the market, guided by universal rules or contractual agreements, representative decision making, and a political imagination informed by technological problem solving. These SMART education experiences help young citizens address some of the symptoms of our sustainability crisis, but they leave the drivers of ecological and social injustice unchallenged.

Self-help agency

Growing up under neoliberalism, many children are socialised to see themselves as individual authors of their own destiny, relishing the opportunity to take personal responsibility for their lives.[3] SMART citizenship education reinforces this confidence in self-help agency, encouraging children to take personal responsibility as citizens to address environmental problems. The following example illustrates the way children express this personal responsibility:

THE NUT: We can make changes to the environment by using less pollution.
ROBIN: Everyone can make a change in their own way, it depends what change it is. Like the government and Prime Minister, they can make changes in rules and everything, and other people can make changes in climate change.
TAILS: And us, we can make changes in ourselves.
ROBIN: Yeah.
SANDWICHES: I think everybody can make changes, but I don't think they actually do – we have to make them happen, like we can't go up to the Prime Minister and *ask*, we have to make them ourselves.

(Music School)

Some children at the Faith School also framed citizenship as individual autonomy:

INTERVIEWER: Who or what do you think should be responsible for doing something about our changing climate?
MILLY CYRUS: God, as well as us because of free choice, the option that humans have to do bad things.

(Faith School)

Feelings of personal responsibility are laudable, but are they an adequate preparation for the scale and complexity of the problems that will confront young citizens in the future? On the one hand, a strong sense of self-help initiative can foster creative problem solving. On the other hand, children growing up in an environment of a minimal state in which they are encouraged to look to themselves first to solve collective problems can find life stressful, and may adopt anxiety reducing behaviours that are unhelpful for the child's own wider development.[4] Feeling too much pressure can cause children – like adults – to deny the seriousness of the problems, withdraw, take risks or blame themselves for personal failure (see Chapter 4).[5]

Market participation

Through the SMART experiences of thin environmental citizenship, children are also continually encouraged to equate good citizenship with active participation in the market as green entrepreneurs, inventors and thoughtful shoppers. Only a few children, 10 in the 25 focus groups (all girls) identified shopping *per se* as an experience they enjoyed at this age. New Zealand children are exposed to high rates of advertising about sugary and fatty foods, and many struggle with child obesity, yet the children in this study can hardly be described as rampant consumers.[6] Consumer products play a more significant role in the lives of older New Zealand children, but the findings of this study are in keeping with other research that suggests that at ages 8–12 years New Zealanders tend to limit brand discussion to music, digital media and computer games.[7] When children expressed pleasure in shopping for toys and 'new stuff', others in their focus groups normally responded in a derogatory way.

If few of these children could be described as hyper-consumers,[8] many were keen to learn to participate in the market in other ways, as entrepreneurs, responsible consumers or inventors of new products. Some children (12 of the 160) strongly identified themselves as ethical or green consumers: 'Everyone is buying more X-boxes and stuff, and they are wasting energy and stuff when they could be playing outside and enjoying all the fresh air!' The children in the two gifted and talented education programmes (GATE School and Music School) in particular discussed many possibilities for developing new energy-efficient technologies or new green products, and trading second-hand goods. Here, children discuss their family experiences of Trade Me, a successful national online second-hand trading scheme which involves the whole population:[9]

ABBY: … my dad was fixing some stuff in our house and he bought a big bag of wood, and he only used about a quarter of it and he put it on Trade Me and it sold for good money. Because he could have thrown it out, or kept it and never used it but now someone else is going to get to use it.

(GATE School)

Children at the rural Tree School also advocated buying locally-made New Zealand products as something 'good' citizens should do. Children's desire to participate responsibly in the market can be underestimated and misrepresented. A 2011 opinion poll of 24,000 British children aged 11–16 years reported that 'owning a house and earning a lot of money were top aspirations of the young people surveyed'.[10] Yet on closer inspection, children were not offered an option in the survey to simply say they wanted to be secure or comfortable.[11]

However, some children are very concerned consumers and want to use the market to achieve positive environmental outcomes or promote local industry; very few children we interviewed discussed the market as a site of social or environmental justice. Children may be routinely encouraged to buy environmentally-friendly products, but is this approach helping students learn the skills they need to make value judgments about fairness of the impacts of a market economy?[12] It seems unlikely. Market thinking frequently narrows citizenship identity. In reality, young citizens who want to exercise green choices through the market frequently find their options are constrained by costs, products and distribution processes beyond their control.[13]

In general, learning to exercise citizenship through the market has an ambivalent potential. As Kymlicka argues, markets are seen to promote a variety of important virtues including self-reliance, but, on the other, in an era of 'unprecedented greed and economic irresponsibility' evidenced in the savings and bond scandals, bank loans and increasing social inequality in developed economies, markets 'fail to teach social responsibility, public reasonableness or dialogue',[14] let alone other useful citizenship values such as civic solidarity.[15] Psychologist Albert Bandura illustrated the underlying limitations of consumer-citizenship when he argued:

> As long as consumers' daily needs are met, they have little incentive to examine the humaneness of the working conditions, the level of pollution by the production processes, and the costs exacted on the environment to produce, ship, and market the profusion of goods and dispose the wastes. Under these modernised conditions, lifestyle practices are disconnected in time and place from the very ecological systems that provide the basis for them.[16]

Mayo and Nairn[17] also capture the ambivalence of citizenship in the market when they argue that young consumers' loyalties are not nailed to a board marked 'citizen of a nation state', but are a form of 'Post-It' citizenship:

> … adhering to different communities, causes and concerns over time that, with different degrees of ease, can be picked up or put down. They are aware of issues of power, such as those around gender and race, even if they express them in new ways. They are less likely to set consumer action apart from citizenship. This is a generation that has internalized branding as if it was their first language, and they can use consumerism or indeed anti-consumerism as a form of self-expression and protest.[18]

However, Mayo and Nairn express concern that youthful enthusiasm for ethical consumption may be self-defeating in the long run, and that the potential 'insulation from nature' for young shoppers may 'hamper' the ability of young citizens to embrace a more sustainable future.[19]

A priori principles of justice

Through SMART citizenship education, children learn to equate just decision making with abstract or a priori rules and contractual agreements. Many children we interviewed referred to fair decision making and to classroom rules and school behaviour contracts as the basis for just decision making. These everyday constitutional agreements and rules were not simply parroted by children as reviewed wisdom (see the discussion about justice in Chapter 6), in some cases children had internalised the rules in ways that made sense to them: 'In school sometimes when you do something bad the teachers tell you think about what you have done and to earn it back you have to pick up rubbish around the school.' Andrew Dobson cautions us about the limits of universal rules and contracts or reciprocal agreements as the basis for fair and just environmental change. Dobson argues much public discussion about environmental citizenship assumes that citizens should take action to improve the environment in anticipation that others will act in a similar fashion. As Ollie at the GATE school put it: 'Everybody is just sort of doing their bit, and that is really good because the more people that do their bit that means the less and less waste we have and everybody's actions count and that sort of thing.' Dobson argues this reasoning is often summed up as 'I will if you will'.[20] However, he cautions that this assumption provides a thin grounding for pro-environmental behaviour, because it implies citizens are not obliged to act if others don't. For example, children at the Tree School argued that New Zealand was a small country, which should not have to do as much to mitigate climate change because other countries weren't 'doing the right thing'. Others suggested New Zealand should not make changes because: 'I don't think New Zealand is making as much of a problem as other countries. Places like New York have huge factories that make more pollution than we make in New Zealand.'

Critics of contractual and universal approaches to justice education also argue that it is not enough to agree to a set of given rules, citizens need to learn to develop skills to challenge everyday injustice when it is encountered (see Chapter 6). In the focus groups, however, it was noticeable that few children at the high income schools who advocated market solutions for environmental issues raised questions of justice or fairness. One child expressed anxiety about China, framing her concern as: 'I don't really agree with people that work there because they hardly get paid and they work like every day.' Another child, again Ollie in the GATE School, argued 'I think industrial pollution, all the big oil, gas – that sort of thing – big companies like on the edge of town, they are sort of out to make money and not really thinking about the future and the greenhouse effect.' However these two comments were some of the very few examples of children questioning the justice of a market economy. Viewed in this light, SMART environmental citizenship education offers inadequate opportunity for young citizens to learn to reason about everyday justice.

Representative decision making

In SMART environmental citizenship education, children observe or experience decision making as representative model decision making and voting. Many children were enthusiastic about voting. The majority of New Zealand children we interviewed spontaneously volunteered voting as 'the best' method of making decisions for a community. 'Voting' was spontaneously mentioned in focus group discussion twice as often 'shopping' by children when asked to discuss what people do with other people 'around here'. While voting turnout is declining in New Zealand, and lower amongst younger age groups, turnout remains comparatively high at 75 to 80 per cent.[21] Through watching their own parents vote or through taking part in school council elections, many children reported voting was an efficacious or useful method of decision making, with comments such as 'we can't vote in the elections because we are too young, but we can decide the people we want on the school council, so I guess it's kind of even'.

In the thin environmental model of SMART citizenship education, however, children are routinely encouraged to participate passively as voters or citizen consumers rather than active decision makers. Children learn to select leaders through school council elections or they observe that teachers or the principal 'chose the school council and ask us what we think'. In these experiences of everyday school decision making, many children we interviewed reported feeling they were consulted but the final decisions were usually made by smaller groups of representatives. Under SMART, democratic individual votes or choices are counted up. In this process, children are encouraged to think of democratic decision making as aggregating individual preferences. This approach differs from models of democratic decision making where children learn to engage in public conversation with others in ways that might create new collective visions or to change a point of view and values (see Chapter 7). In the summary under SMART experiences of environmental citizenship, children learn to contribute to public decisions in passive roles as voters or ethical consumers rather than citizen activists.

Technological imagining

Finally, through the SMART experiences of citizenship, young citizens are encouraged to imagine technical solutions to our sustainability crisis. As has already been noted in the gifted and talented classes in particular, several of the children readily identified themselves as young entrepreneurs, arguing that technological innovation is the best way to reduce environmental problems: 'people are born with magnificent brains'. There is a fine line between creative innovative problem solving and what Tim O'Riordan has described as a 'technocentric' mode of policy making that 'is almost arrogant in its assumption that man is supremely able to understand and control events to suit his purposes'.[22] While technological innovation is important and valuable, technocratic solutions address symptoms, but not the drivers of the underlying injustice that has caused the problems. The following conversation delightfully illustrates young citizens' enthusiasm for creative problem solving of a technocratic bent, although it is salutary to consider that in desperation some adult citizens are clutching at not too dissimilar possibilities:

TOM: We could shoot rubbish into space.
BOBBY: We could fire it into the sun …
RED: To burn it up!
BOBBY: Yeah … it will send off gases and things.
RED: We could get a container, and get all the gases into a container and then chuck it into space!
BOBBY: Wind turbines and water things will help also. Energy and things that will contribute to climate change …

(GATE School)

In overview, the SMART citizenship education for thin environmental citizenship is promising but ultimately disappointing. In the SMART experiences of citizenship, children learn to internalise a strong sense of personal responsibility as Self helpers, and experience opportunities to make changes through Market participation. They are encouraged to understand justice as a priori rules and reciprocal agreements. Participation is relatively passive as children learn to value Representative decision

Figure 3.2 Authoritarian handprint of FEARS of non-citizenship

Source: Bronwyn Hayward.

making and Technological imagining is encouraged. In SMART citizenship education, children are rarely confronted by questions of social or environmental justice. Moreover, children are often encouraged to assume heroic possibilities for individual action to effect environmental change using their 'magnificent brains'. While a technological imagination is important, technical solutions will not be enough to effect change on the scale required to avoid dangerous environmental change.[23] Young citizens also need wider ways to understand the sustainability challenge we face and more support to exercise their capability for sustainable citizenship.

The FEARS of non-citizens

Growing up today, not all children are learning to think of themselves as citizens or to value democracy. Some children struggle to experience citizenship as any form of democratic participation or belonging. The experience of domestic violence, poverty, increasing securitisation and threat of environmental risk and disaster can inhibit children's capacity for citizenship. While there is growing recognition that children have significant potential to exercise agency in the face of very difficult circumstances, we cannot ignore the way suffering undermines many children's capability to act as citizens, testing their physical, emotional and social resilience and well-being.[24] I summarise these children's experiences as the FEARS of non-citizenship. These experiences include: Frustrated agency, Environmental exclusion, Authoritarian decision making, Retributive justice and Silenced democratic imagination.

Frustrated agency

Frustrated agency can be observed where children's opportunity for both inde-pendent thinking (will formation) and action (volition) is undermined or inhibited by a range of coercive, physical, economic, social or cultural barriers and prac-tices. Children forced into slavery for military, labour or prostitution purposes, for example, cannot be described as exercising freedom of agency. In *The Wealth of Nations*, Adam Smith expressed his concern about children who labour at a young age. Smith argued that their experience is 'both so constant and so severe that it leaves them little time for leisure and less inclination to apply to, or even think of anything else'.[25] In contemporary times, Pogge has been fiercely critical of con-sumer societies which are complicit in reproducing modern slavery by ignoring the inhumane conditions endured by many labourers who produce the goods for consumer societies.[26]

Martha Nussbaum's work on human development has highlighted ten central capabilities she argues any decent political order must secure for its citizens to flourish and be able to exercise their agency effectively. These include: the ability to live life of a normal length; to be able to have good health, including adequate nourishment and shelter; to be able to use the senses of imagination and thought; to have bodily integrity, free from domestic violence or assault; to be able to form emotional attachments, including with the non-human world; to be able to express affiliation and identity; to exercise practical reasoning, including planning; to be able to play; and to exercise sufficient control over one's political and material environment.[27]

Nussbaum's work reminds us that children's capacity for citizenship can be frustrated by the absence of any combination of these factors, from lack of educa-tion and poor nutrition, or high levels of physical risk in their environment, which are well beyond a child's capacity to manage, and where a child is not offered appropriate mentor support or skilled peer encouragement to help them learn to meet the challenges they face.[28] Children in developing countries, for example, will face a difficult challenge to exert the full potential of their agency in the face of storms or severe droughts associated with climate change, particularly if they are also struggling with social inequalities.[29] In 2011, an international report esti-mated that up to 80 per cent of deaths in the 2004 Asian Tsunami were female.[30] This stark statistic underscores the way adolescent girls often struggle to exercise their agency in situations of domestic violence and inequitable access to educa-tion, or where their work and living conditions place them at disproportionate risk of natural hazards and undermine their ability to adapt appropriately.

Furthermore, in a rapidly mobilising world, some children are excluded from citizenship as a result of social isolation and the loss of confidence that results from relocation. Social isolation is likely to compound these children's vulnera-bility to other environmental risks. For example, we could anticipate that when faced with additional environmental risk, like the natural disaster of the earth-quakes which followed this study, children like Crystal, living with one parent and knowing only few people in her community, might face greater difficulty exercising her agency in the absence of community support than her more highly-networked peers with access to wider immediate social support to assist them to cope with the disaster.

Children's agency is also frustrated by inequalities which undermine a child's health and access to education. In New Zealand, high rates of child poverty and life in cold, poorly insulated homes has created a legacy of ill health that is amongst the worst in the OECD.[31] While no children in this study complained about their housing inhibiting their ability to participate as citizens, in 7 of the 25 focus groups, children volunteered concerns about domestic violence, parental alcoholism or school bullying, as the following extracts from children's focus group discussions illustrate. In the first conversation, Black Eagle, a girl, comments on her frustration about not being heard:

INTERVIEWER: In your family, you said your dad's in charge. Does he listen to you?
BLACK EAGLE: Not really, because when he's drunk he doesn't.

(Community-*Kura* School)

Other similar serious causes of frustrated agency were noted by children who casually commented on smacking at home:

KAJIL: Um, some people, lots of people, people that are smart enough to care about the world, do this – protest! That's the foremost best way to get what you want in a community.
BEN TENISON: So you could protest against your mum? [giggles]
BOB: If I did she'd just give me a smack, aye. [more giggles]
BRITNEY: But what about the anti-smacking law?
BOB: She doesn't care about that.

(Small World School)

Bob's casual comments were greeted by sympathetic giggles, suggesting this was an experience at least acknowledged by others. Children also spontaneously mentioned adult alcohol abuse, bullying, domestic violence or alcohol as factors inhibiting their participation in community life. For example, the following extracts are from another conversation amongst children at the Community-*Kura* school:

ROBERTA: I haven't had a personal experience but sometimes with kids at school if they've been bullied they don't feel safe here. They hang around with the teachers and just try and hide.
PUFF: Sometimes I feel unsafe at other people's houses, like my dad goes around to his softball mate's houses and I don't know them and they're like 'do you want a drink' or something and I'm like 'no thanks' because I don't like know what they do to their drinks and all that. So I feel kind of unsafe going around to parents' houses that you don't know them.

TROY: Sometimes I feel unsafe at my friend's place because their dad owns heaps of guns, and there's always these shotguns and stuff lying around the place.

INTERVIEWER: If you guys wanted to change a decision or something, how would you go about making a change, be heard?

ROBERTA: Write some petitions, but it probably wouldn't help, and making protest marches and, well we wouldn't make it but we'd put up posters and stuff. And we'd write persuasive letters.

(Community-Kura School)

These comments are of concern, suggesting children's citizenship is inhibited by everyday injustice. In 2011, a report by the New Zealand Chief Scientist, Peter Gluckman, commented that alcoholism, domestic violence and bullying are significant issues for New Zealand children who report some of the highest rates of these problems in the OECD.[32] The comments also illustrate a glaring gap between citizenship education strategies that encourage children to effect change in their wider physical environment by 'putting up posters and writing persuasive letters', and the grim reality for some children of domestic violence and alcohol abuse inhibiting their flourishing in their home environment.[33]

Environmental exclusion

FEARS experiences, which undermine the citizenship of children, also include environmental exclusion. Crompton and Kasser, like other environmental psychologists, argue that early and extensive exposure to the natural world matters, because it enables children to develop place attachment and empathy with non-human nature and fosters well-being in communities.[34] The experience of environmental exclusion reported by children was both physical and social, and the causes were complex. Some children we interviewed expressed concern that they feel excluded when play space is lost or constrained, as this discussion amongst pupils of the Tree School (which also banned climbing trees) reveals. The children in this school face urban development and roll growth which is impacting on sports fields ('paddocks') used for school ball games like Touch (rugby):

SEZ: At the moment the touch people that are out there playing soccer like there are three games happening on one field.

HAMFISH: It is real squeezed … because all the balls they all go onto the different fields so there is like rugby, then touch, then cheese slice or something and then soccer.

LEWIN: In the morning tea and lunch the little kids play soccer, and the older ones play touch and they playing on the same field running into each other.

(Tree School)

In the following example, another form of exclusion is explained by Puff, who vividly describes her concern that a lack money can exacerbate environmental exclusion in its broadest sense:

INTERVIEWER: What issues matter to you?
PUFF: Money.
INTERVIEWER: Money is an issue that matters to you?
PUFF: Well if we lose more money we won't be able to have homes, like we won't be able to afford them, they'll become dearer and there will be hobbies that we won't be able to do in our life and there will be clubs that will close down because they haven't got enough money. And schools will start to get smaller. And the malls will become more expensive, I don't know if that's a word? And suburbs will just become smaller.

(Community-*Kura* School)

This description of social-environmental exclusion is revealing from a 9-year-old. Here, Puff simply articulates her concern that children's access and enjoyment of public life as citizens can be diminished by lack of financial support. A number of international studies would support her concern. In poor urban neighbourhoods in the United States, for example, studies show that lack of access to public services compounds children's disadvantage, which in turn 'may hinder children in the development of academic and other abilities'.[35] In her brief précis of the implications of financial exclusion, Puff captures the problems facing an estimated 1 in 4 poor children in New Zealand who live on 60 per cent or less of the median income.[36]

Authoritarian decision making

In addition to frustrated agency and experiences of environmental exclusion, children's citizenship can also be thwarted from flourishing by authoritarian decision making. In the New Zealand study, Streetwise Sceptics were children particularly concerned by what they perceived to be adults not listening to them. Streetwise Sceptics were especially frustrated, remaining unconvinced that anything would result from their actions. At the Tree School, for example, children felt frustrated by the decision to ban climbing tall trees, and they felt being asked to type up a letter to the Principal was 'stupid' because they'd already written their demands on 'paper' and mounted protests. The Tree School children also observed decisions being made in ways that were not democratic in clubs in their wider community beyond school:

INTERVIEWER: How do decisions get made in your communities? Who makes these decisions?
JILLO :   The organiser of events [horse riding]

SAM:	The headmaster, the principal.
PIPPI:	The manager.
SAM:	They have normally been to that club for ages. And so they have just slowly got higher and higher. And at school there is a board and that. But the principal has the final decision.

(Tree School)

Where decision making is authoritarian, young citizens do not gain an opportunity to see how decisions can be formed through inclusive dialogue or passionate, respectful argument. Children in the Tree School went on to discuss the way they felt local decision making in their school, parent associations and wider council was dominated by the 'higher ups', or people on decision-making boards who had 'just stayed and stayed' or who dominated community positions by virtue of being there a long time. However, the same children who complained about community decisions made by 'higher ups' also reported that decisions about use of the play-ground and games should be made by older children who'd 'been there' longer.

Retributive justice

FEARS experiences of non-citizenship are compounded by attitudes to justice, which tend to be retributive or expressed as blame. Both approaches are less con-ducive to developing sustainable, fair and equitable community outcomes.[37] Retributive justice at its most basic level is the vengeful spirit of an eye for an eye. Iris Young describes this as a backward looking liability model of justice in which 'the harm for which we seek to assign responsibility' is usually conceived as a discrete event that already has taken place: 'We look back to punish the culprit', to blame some (and thereby absolve others) or to compensate victims in an 'effort at restitution'.[38] Rather than looking to understand shared responsibility for systemic injustice or ways to take collective action to transform the processes that produced the injustice, the use of blame attempts to provide a shortcut or a quick fix to solve the immediate problem. In the Tree School, children debated what should be done about climate change. Some wanted to 'blame it' on bigger countries and, when challenged by the interviewer, one child responded in the following way:

INTERVIEWER:	So you can't just blame one country or one group of people [for climate change]?
M:	Yeah … you probably could if you biked everywhere and didn't use electronics or anything.
SEZ:	Like there will be like run out of CO_2, because the trees make CO_2.
HAMFISH:	I reckon what they should do is make a law, a law that says if you don't recycle and do all this stuff here you will get jail time and if you are really bad you might get the death penalty!

Just as children need support to learn about environmental processes (in this case, for example, the role of trees in the carbon cycle), children need support to learn moral reasoning: learning to think beyond blame and absolute rules of good and bad, to understanding reasons for problems, or to express ethics of care (see Chapter 6).[39] Without support, and under conditions of fear, people may feel less inclined to listen and understand the perspectives of others. Blaming someone or something is the easy expression of fear. For example, when asked about climate change, a child at the Tree School joked: 'I blame the Chinese.' In subsequent discussion, and with some challenge, the child reflected, 'I guess you can't pin it all on them.' However, a tone of fear was expressed by several students in this rural community about immigration from China (see Chapter 6). In the context of different discussions, anxiety about jobs being taken by people paid less in China, Chinese food products being poisoned, and an urban myth about the local Chinese takeaway shop serving rat were all raised.

This low level of racism and anxiety is troubling, and reflects the fears of immigration to New Zealand which increased after 1987. Media widely reported public tension during this period, including concerns by parents as predominantly European/*Pākehā* communities like the Tree School began to include more families from Asia. A parent interviewed in a national newspaper has described this period as a time '... of confusion, of bewilderment, for a little while of absolute fear [about immigration] thinking, "I don't understand this [arrival of new immigrants]".'[40] However, in the case of the Tree School, the school roll has remained almost entirely European/*Pākehā*.

Silenced imagination

Finally, as a result of children's everyday FEARS experiences, their imagination for citizenship may be silenced. Bonnie Honig argues that under conditions of disaster or emergency, our political imagination can become reduced to experiences of 'mere' survival, rather than an imaginative creative experience of 'more' life.[41] Children whose daily experiences are consumed by a struggle for mere life need to direct much of their energy to survival. In this process, young citizens are drained and exhausted, and it is very hard for them to think imaginatively about democracy. No children in the New Zealand study reported this exhaustion at the time, but two children at high-income schools reported feeling 'stressed'. However, since the Christchurch earthquake, many have experienced exhausting and difficult times. Reported rates of domestic abuse have climbed dramatically, up by 47 per cent in the months after the quakes of 4 September 2010 and 22 February 2011.[42] Principals and teachers interviewed at the end of the study period commented that many families were under strain, but also that they felt there was a stronger feeling of community within the schools. One principal reported arranging activities like fundraising for the communities affected by Japanese disasters as ways to encourage children to 'look and think outward' after hardship.

Children's imagination for democratic citizenship can also be silenced or hampered by well-meaning environmental campaigns that promote fear, urgency or authoritarianism. Some Eco-Worriers struggle with anxiety and lack of social support, which exacerbates their sense of vulnerability and loss of agency.

UNICEF reports, for example, that some Pacific children living in atoll communities appear to have absorbed environmental campaign messages about sea level rise and feel heightened fear about their immediate future, without a corresponding sense of any wider practical support for their efforts to adapt to these threats.[43]

Other well-meaning environmental campaigns also inadvertently promote unhelpful messages to children. For example, the 2010 advertising campaign of a United Kingdom-based climate change charity called 10:10 graphically illustrates the way children's opportunities to take an imaginative and democratic role in environmental debates can be narrowed by public campaigns of fear and securitisation. In an effort to reduce carbon emissions, 10:10 produced a video clip called *No Pressure*.[44] The video depicted a teacher encouraging children to cut their carbon emissions by taking small actions, for example encouraging their parents to insulate their house or buy energy-saving light bulbs. The teacher asked for a show of hands about who thought they could undertake the behaviour changes discussed. A forest of hands went up. Only two students were unsure or unconvinced, their arms firmly crossed, eyes cast down. 'Fine', says the teacher, 'no pressure, your choice'. In the video, as the children stand to leave, the teacher turns and presses a button on her desk, detonating explosives which kill the two dissenting children, leaving a bloody mess over the other shocked and cowering students.

There was significant public outrage at this advertising campaign, and it was quickly pulled from public circulation in mainstream media.[45] On reflection, however, it is disturbing that a pro-environmental campaign should use fear and satire when faced with citizen dissent or apathy. This mixed message reinforces unhelpful assumptions that young citizens will not act unless forced to do so. Campaigns based on green authoritarianism and fear are unhelpful in environmental citizenship education.

Strong ecology and the SEEDS of citizenship

Some children, however, have opportunities to learn about citizenship in ways which I argue offer more promising foundations for a new kind of sustainable democracy. I summarise these experiences as the SEEDS of strong ecologism. These experiences include: Social agency, Environmental education, Embedded justice, Decentred deliberation and Self-transcendence. I briefly introduce these experiences here and expand on the these themes in discussion in the chapters that follow.

Social agency

How do children learn about citizenship as social agency or the ability to affect choice and act in collaboration with others? Iris Young speaks of social agency as a citizen's 'collective ability' to make use of the resources of established groups to which they belong, and to act in concert with others.[46] A sense of social agency was eloquently illustrated by 10 year old 'Cranberry the 13th' from the Community-*Kura* School who said: 'I am nothing without my tribe.' Some children clearly felt their citizenship is most effective when exercised in collaboration with others. Children had the opportunity to experience citizenship through classroom-coordinated letter

Figure 3.3 The social handprint and the SEEDS of ecological citizenship

Source: Bronwyn Hayward.

writing campaigns or when enjoying a shared activity ('we all learn together'), or by taking part in community protests and activities to create a community garden. Children at the Small World School were disarmingly confident about collective agency, given over 40 nations represented at the school:

POPCORN: Communities work together, most of us are really good at cooperat-
           ing and we're all really good at something else –
MARY: Teamwork!
POPCORN: Yip, *and* we play tag!

(Small World School)

Social agency is a key element of ecological citizenship. The actions of citizens in their private lives (for example in keeping home energy use to a minimum) are vitally important. However, to be effective in the face of large-scale threats and challenges, citizens need to learn to collaborate with others.[47] Many children in the two bilingual schools (the Community-*Kura* School and the *Kura* School) readily equated their citizenship as collective action. This was particularly evident when children were coding activities they did with others. Children in the bilingual groups used verbs for collective action in English and Māori, for example, putting political parties and children's clubs like Guides under the title 'they all *hui* [meet] together'. A comparison of the comments of children in the large urban bilingual school and the small full immersion rural school and suggests children at both schools were 'very unambiguous in the way that they coded their communities, ... emphasising the way in which their *whānau* [extended family], *kura* [school] and wider neighbouring communities were seen as "one close group" which *hui* [meet and gather] together'.[48]

Environmental education

The SEEDS experiences of children's citizenship also include experiences of formal and informal environmental education. Many researchers, notably Louise Chawla and Harry Heft, have argued that informal opportunities for children to identify with outdoor space is very important for well-being.[49] Informal environmental affiliation was vividly illustrated by Māori children in this study, who often identified with a mountain or waterway as part of their tribal identity in *mihi* [greeting]. Non Māori rural children similarly listed local outdoor places as being important for their sense of citizenship and community identity. For example, two boys from the Farm-Sea School identified with 'eeling in the creek' so much that they had a lengthy conversation over what to call it (a sport? an activity?). In the end, they decided eeling was so important to their everyday lives that they associated it with their town's name:

FRED: Eeling's not a sport ... that's outdoor activities.
RON: It could be in [name of town] as well?
FRED: Yeah! Do it in eeling equals [name of town]!

(Farm-Sea School)

Other children in Ron and Fred's Farm-Sea School similarly reported informal environmental education, enthusiastically describing 'going on big walks' or making 'big huts'. Many have argued that informal opportunities to enjoy nature are a vital foundation for pro-environmental citizenship. It is also hard to envisage how children without any opportunity to enjoy the natural world could prioritise environmental values. Yet informal exposure to the environment is not sufficient: children also need some substantive environmental education. For example, some children in rural communities reported significant confusion over sources of greenhouse gas pollution, or felt they knew very little about climate change despite strongly identifying with outdoor physical locations as spaces for their collaborative play.

INTERVIEWER: What forms of pollution do you think are causing these [climate] changes?
JENNY: Pollution and smoke and things like that. I don't think it's true about the animals causing it, because animals were made to go on the Earth and they wouldn't cause any trouble.
PANSY: Yeah? The poos, the farting, the farts! [laughs]

(Tree School)

Children also benefitted from opportunities to learn skills to help them reason about justice.

Embedded justice

In addition to Social agency and Environmental education, the third of the SEEDS experiences which characterise strong ecological citizenship is a sense of Embedded justice. In Chapter 6, I argue that ecological justice is best understood as everyday practical reasoning about procedural and distributional fairness, and our responsibilities to put right any harm we have caused through our actions or the actions of others that have benefitted us.[50] Ecological citizens also have a wider moral obligation to address injustice, to enable others to live as well as they are able. These are demanding ideas of justice, and all citizens, young and old, need support to develop their ability to reason about what is fair and unfair in our local places.[51] Child psychologists, arguing after Vygotsky, suggest a child's ability to reason about justice is accelerated when children have the opportunity to debate moral issues with more experienced adults or peers (see Chapter 6).[52] For example, in the New Zealand study, one Māori child at the bilingual Community-*Kura* School argued that New Zealand's founding document, the Treaty of Waitang[53] (a treaty signed between the British Crown and Māori chiefs) should be used as a model to help people think about ways they could collaborate as citizens, or make changes in their community: 'You could make a treaty, like the Treaty of Waitangi, to agree on something.'

In the Small World School, children were debating who should have access to school resources. Several children said that other children (specifically Korean–New Zealand children) were going 'crazy' doing a paper game they called '*dgakgi*' which others felt was 'not fair' because it was taking resources (paper) away from the school which did not have many resources: 'It's really taking away the paper of the school. It's getting hard cos the teachers have to buy paper all the time and it's really taking of the money they need for the junior school safety matting.'

We also observed children engaged in practical reasoning in the Small World School where children spoke of their frustration with their playground equipment, and that the government was being 'mean' or 'unfair' not giving more resources to their school. In the smallest and poorest Kura School, children discussed the fairness of fishing quotas imposed to protect local fish stock. In the rural Farm-Sea School, they debated the fairness of fishing restrictions over floundering, and the need to protect a rare local dolphin species threatened by floundering nets. In the Tree School, children raised concern about the way the decision was made by the principal and teachers to ban them from climbing tall trees. In each of these detailed discussions about distributional or procedural justice, children drew on real world observations to enrich discussion about what was fair or just (see Chapter 6).

Decentred deliberation

The SEEDS of ecological citizenship education also include the opportunity to engage in discussion with children across community boundaries to enrich understanding and enable wider public opinion to begin to consolidate.[54] Strong ecological citizenship is strengthened through these experiences of decentred community deliberation. Decentred deliberation aims to both open decision making to wider scrutiny and to link local sites for discussion with debates in other communities as citizens learn ways to challenge illegitimate expressions of global power (see Chapter 7). Some children were also acutely aware of the need to 'decentre' their debate not only spatially but intergenerationally, to enable their concerns to be heard. Some children argued that adults often dominated decision making. For example at the Farm-Sea School, children considered mass advertising in the local newspaper to encourage adults and the wider community to listen to them:

INTERVIEWER: Do people who make decisions listen to children?
MILEY: Well we've got a community paper with notices, if you want to put something in, you could put it in the newspaper.
MICKSTER08:   Yeah say like in big huge letters "DO NOT POLLUTE THE PLANET".

(Farm-Sea School)

These children recognised the importance of getting more people to hear their concerns. Others also felt public discussion was important. Eighteen of the 160 students volunteered that they'd had an opportunity to take part in a school council, but other students complained that the number of people that could be involved in that way was limited. Children did give other examples of opportunities to have their say which they also valued, including school surveys, family or class meetings, and making decisions in groups on school camps.

Self-transcendence

Finally, some children had opportunities to exercise their political imagination for citizenship as self-transcendence. In these situations, children reported thinking beyond their own immediate concerns to emphasise the needs of others, and of the non-human world.[55] Some children in the bilingual schools spoke of identifying with their tribal land and communities: 'I belong to my *marae* [sacred meeting place]'. One of the most mundane but significant experiences that appears to have supported many children's ability to transcend their own self-interests in the New Zealand study were opportunities to take part in sports teams. Over half the sample spoke positively or very positively about their membership in sports clubs: 'I love it'. Children also reporting observing parents, teachers and grandparents engaged in voluntary and collective action over time for their school or the wider community, including fundraising, working for the parent-teacher association and school board, or taking part in tribal events. Observing these intergenerational voluntary experiences appears to have helped some children think about how change happens over time, and to take the needs and rights of others seriously. This was movingly expressed by one child from the Community-*Kura* School. When asked if she knew who made decisions or was in charge in her community she said:

BLACK EAGLE: Well, in my family it's my *koro* (granddad) cos he wakes up at six o'clock in the morning and does *karakia* (prayers).

(Community-*Kura* School)

This quite simple suggestion that early morning prayer was a way to make positive change resonates with another simple thoughtful comment of Lewin, a child at the rural Tree School. Lewin described his frustration that the local council had wanted to cut down a grove of trees near his home. He spoke with pride about helping his mother stop the council by finding the council phone number in the telephone book. He then summed up why the trees could not be cut down by saying simply 'some of those trees are *over 160 years old*' (speaker's emphasis). In Lewin's comment on the age of the trees, he suggests a scale of time that transcends human life.

Summary: SEEDS of citizenship

In overview, young citizen's understanding of their everyday citizenship is reinforced by their formal and informal citizenship education. These interactions have implications for the attitudes young citizens express about decision making and the actions they may or may not consider taking. Within children's everyday interactions in family, home and school they learn new ways to think about citizenship agency, their environment, how decisions should be made, what is just or fair, and empathy for other ways of living. Amongst the three dominant forms of environmental citizenship education I identified in this chapter, I argue that the SEEDS experiences are most likely to help children learn to exercise their capacity for citizenship in more sustainable ways. But the SEEDS of Social agency, Environmental education, Embedded justice, Decentred deliberation and Self-transcendence need tending if we want a just and sustainable democracy to flourish. In the following chapters, I consider ways we can actively promote experiences of strong ecological citizenship.

Notes

1 Barber 1984 (2003); Dobson 2003; Bohman 2007; Dryzek 1990 (1994); Eckersley 1996; O'Riordan 1976; Young 2006a, 2006b, 2011.
2 Milbraith 1984, p21; O'Riordan 1976, pp2–5; Martinsson and Lundqvist 2010.
3 Higgins and Nairn 2006; Westheimer 2008.
4 Hamilton 2010, pp118–23; see also Clark 2011 who argues that ironically, in a 'risk society', the public are sometimes less familiar with some things that should frighten them.
5 Hamilton 2010; Kail 2010, pp343–8.
6 Oommen and Anderson 2008; Hammond *et al.* 1999; James 2007.
7 Zanker and Lealand 2009.
8 Kasser *et al.* 2010; Schor 2004.
9 Keale 2009.
10 BBC 2011.
11 By comparison, in the same year, qualitative research conducted with colleagues at Resolve for the United Nations Environment Programme of a sample of the British shopping generation (young adults aged 18–30 years) invited respondents to describe their economic aspirations in their own words. Given the opportunity to say anything they liked, many young people commented they wanted to be 'comfortable not rich'. See Hayward *et al.* 2011b.

12 Cambridge Primary Review 2009.
13 Seyfang 2005.
14 Kymlicka 2002, p304.
15 Sandel 2009. In addition, Inglehart and Welzel argue that post material values are self expression values that emphasise tolerance of diversity, and rising demand for participation in decision-making in economic and political life. They suggest these values produce a culture of tolerance in which people place a high value on individual freedom and self-expression, and have confident, activist orientation (Inglehart and Welzel 2005, p56).
16 Bandura 2007, pp14.
17 Mayo and Nairn 2009.
18 Ibid., pp284–5.
19 Ibid., p285.
20 Dobson 2003, 2005; see also Sustainable Development Commission 2006.
21 Elsewhere I review New Zealand's high voter turnout (Hayward 2006). In focus groups, voting was mentioned 100 times in discussion compared to 'shopping' (51 times across 25 focus groups) as something people did with other people.
22 O'Riordan 1976, p1.
23 Jackson 2009, pp71–86. On the limits of technological thinking, see Speth 2008, pp200–4.
24 Mitchell *et al.* 2009.
25 Smith 1776 (2008), p432.
26 Pogge 2002.
27 Nussbaum 2011, pp33–4. Nussbaum also begins to think creatively about these capabilities in relation to non-human nature and future generations: see pp157–66.
28 Plan International 2011; Mitchell *et al.* 2009.
29 Hansen 2009; UNICEF 2007; Plan International 2011.
30 Plan International 2011.
31 Children's Social Health Monitor 2011; CPAG 2011.
32 Gluckman and Hayne 2011.
33 This problem of unsafe domestic environments is also shared by children in the global South: see Plan International 2011.
34 Crompton and Kasser 2009; see also Chawla 1999; Louv 2005; Orr 1994; Hart 1997; Uzzell 1999. By contrast, for a discussion on social exclusion as a cause of youth suicide, see New Zealand Mental Health Foundation 2011.
35 Hart and Kirshner 2009.
36 Grimmond 2011.
37 Dobson 2003; Young 2011.
38 Young 2011, pp180–1.
39 Crain 2005, pp158–69.
40 *Sunday Star Times* 2008.
41 Honig 2009, pp1–4.
42 Lynch 2011.
43 UNICEF 2011b.
44 McVeigh 2010.
45 Ibid.
46 Young 2011, pp146–51.
47 Christoff 1996; Dobson 2003; Wolf *et al.* 2009.
48 Dalton 2008.
49 Chawla and Heft 2002.

50 Dobson 2003; Young 2011.
51 Barratt-Hacking *et al.* 2007, Chapter 7.
52 Daniels *et al.* 2007, p138.
53 Hayward and Wheen 2004.
54 Young 2006b, 2011; Bohman 2007.
55 Freeden 2009.

4   Social agency

Learning how to make a difference with others

In the last few decades we have learnt a lot of new words: 'ecology', 'ecosystem', 'biosphere', 'symbiosis', 'Gaia', 'sustainable development' and the rest. These are words that are framed to express a cooperative rather than a competitive relation with other life forms ... Moreover, this cooperative approach clashes strikingly with the competitive individualism that has lately been so prominent in our social and political life.

(Mary Midgely, 2004, p174)

In her important discussion of how ideas about wilderness and nature change over time, Mary Midgely reminds us that the ways we think and talk about ourselves and our environment can commit us to certain pathways of action, not all of which are helpful or desirable. She argues we have framed much of our political thinking as myths about individualism. Today, however, in communities from Tunisia and Wall Street, to the earthquake-shattered pavements of Christchurch, young citizens are beginning to question political life as an expression of individualism, and to rediscover the citizenship power of social agency.

In Chapter 2, I defined agency as a citizen's capacity for developing independent thought (will formation) and the capability for freely choosing to act on those ideas (volition).[1] In this chapter I review the importance of agency and identify barriers that citizens of all ages face as they learn to exercise agency. I argue young citizens also need opportunities to learn about practical social action and critical resistance. In conclusion, I consider ways that children can learn to exercise social agency as ecological citizens in their family, school and community.

Why agency matters

Over the past century there has been widespread acceptance that, in a democracy, individuals should be free to determine the conditions of their lives.[2] Environmental philosopher Freya Matthews has gone so far as to argue that when liberal democracies are 'stripped bare' of all their economic, institutional and procedural differences, they are 'a system of governance dedicated to individual freedom and "self-rule" or autonomy'.[3]

Research from many disciplinary perspectives has examined how individuals exercise agency to effect desired change. Psychologists draw attention to the way we express our agency through actions of habit, imagination and judgment; economists have examined the role of agency in the market; political science considers agency as an expression of power; child development theory explores how opportunities to exercise agency improves our understanding and well-being; geographers are reconsidering agency as a source of creative resilience in the face of disasters; while sociologists have drawn our attention to the potential and limits of our agency in the context of the social world.[4]

Given this rich vein of interdisciplinary interest in understanding agency, it is surprising we still know so little about how children express agency in everyday life as young citizens. We have very conflicted attitudes to children's agency. On the one hand, as dependents, children are often assumed to exercise limited agency, yet as recent research in community disasters and development has shown, even very young children can make a significant difference to the world around them.[5] We are startled whenever a young child performs a selfless or heroic act, and the wide reporting of the event only serves to underscore more prevalent media narratives that focus on children exercising agency in defiance of authority, or as victims or as bullies.[6] There is less thoughtful public reflection about the conditions under which children learn to exercise their agency democratically, and in ways that promote justice and sustainability.

Understanding youth political agency, its possibilities and its limits, helps us understand how young citizens learn to shape their environment by making choices, developing new plans and acting on alternative options. Hannah Arendt coined the term 'natality' to celebrate the imaginative, unexpected, disruptive and creative power of citizen action.[7] Arendt painted a vivid image of the potential power of an individual to act in unexpected and innovative ways. Likening it to a birth, she argued that citizens acting with agency can take a political community in new directions that challenge dominant thinking. To act with natality is literally to create something new, to form ideas and take action in ways that can be creative, playful, ingenious and transformative.[8]

Over the past thirty years, however, many citizens – young and old – have been encouraged to direct their agency toward the market as entrepreneurs and citizen-consumers.[9] Agency in this context is narrowly reconceived as freedom to make consumer choices, rather than, for example, freedom for creative, public engagement for a common purpose. If we wish to broaden children's imagination about the possibilities and opportunities for agency beyond thin environmental visions of technocratic entrepreneurs and green consumers operating in the market, we need to think seriously about the conditions in which children grow up, form their ideas, and learn to exercise their will.

In this context, returning to Arendt's writing on agency is both refreshing and problematic. On the one hand, her ideas of agency are refreshing because they suggest our futures are not inevitable, and that the actions, hopes and decisions of ordinary people can make a positive difference. When citizens participate in determining community choices, they strengthen our democracies. Community

Figure 4.1 Christchurch children digging liquefaction after the 22 February 2011 aftershocks

Credit: *The Press* Fairfax NZ Ltd.

engagement can improve our knowledge about complex problems, enhance public accountability and legitimise decisions.[10] When citizens actively participate in democratic life, they can affirm their innate right to shape their destiny, and develop a 'non-servile', deeply democratic character.[11]

On the other hand, Arendt's optimism is not a celebration of unfettered individual agency, the latter is highly problematic. In reality, we are never entirely free to determine our life conditions. Our lives are complexly influenced by the structures and institutions and demands and needs of our society, or families, schools, cultural practices, legal frameworks, economies and the material world (including limited resources and hazards encountered on a dynamic planet).[12] In turn, our actions affect these institutions and structures.[13] Moreover, green critics argue that rights to exercise our freedom should be tempered by the recognition of our dependence and obligations to others, including the non-human world.[14] Our agency freedom from this perspective is better conceived as an interdependent autonomy: my freedom cannot be achieved without yours and, in turn, all human freedom depends upon the limited and finite resources of our planet.

In light of both our interdependency and a desire for autonomy, we could reconsider agency from the perspective of Amartya Sen's description of 'sustainable freedom'. Sen argues that to sustain the freedoms we value, we need to broaden the classic concepts of sustainable development, '… to encompass the preservation and when possible expansion, of the freedoms and capabilities of people today without compromising the capability of future generations' to have similar – or more – freedom.[15] Sen is optimistic that when we have the freedom and support to reason about what we value and how we might achieve this, we can think far beyond our immediate needs and interests. Others go even further, arguing that rethinking agency in sustainable ways might require us to acknowledge our obligations not only to each other but to our ancestors, future generations and non-human nature.[16]

These ideas enrich our understanding of what it means to exercise our freedom for agency in a finite planet. After three decades of neoliberalism, we almost started to believe that agency was simply exercising individual choice; my freedom to buy things here and now in a market. Suddenly, a new generation is rediscovering the power of social action and collective will formation, redefining the ideas of agency beyond making choices, to consider life's purpose and meaning. Can autonomy, will-formation and volition be rethought as social freedom to collaborate to make a difference, in a generation that also values individual autonomy?

There is certainly no lack of interest in rethinking agency amongst a new generation of citizens. The importance of agency was underscored for me during research conducted alongside colleagues at Resolve, for the United Nations Environment Programme. A number of the young adults we surveyed placed great value on their autonomy when questioned about their attitudes to sustainability and their ability to 'make a difference'. For example, when asked what their worst ways of living would be, the majority of respondents from the United Kingdom and New Zealand mentioned loss of agency freedom, articulated as 'living without a life purpose' or 'being kept from achieving my potential', being 'unable to control the conditions of my life' or unable to 'live according to my values'.[17] This was often expressed graphically. For example, when asked what their worst way of living would be, a young UK woman aged 23 replied 'I think the worst way of living would be in a situation where I am passionate about making changes but not in the position to', while a New Zealand student said he feared being a 'factory worker in mainland China'.[18] Another student said they would hate 'being caged or kept from achieving my potential'.[19]

The common thread woven through many of the comments was the importance of agency, not only choice or freedom, but the desire to use freedom in purposeful ways. A common refrain across many countries in the survey was that young adults 'wanted to make a difference'.[20] Reflecting on the importance many young citizens place on agency casts a new light on behaviour studies, suggesting young citizens growing up in neoliberal states may need fewer lessons in how to change their behaviour, and more support to confront the barriers that limit or constrain their ability to exercise their agency in imaginative ways as ecological citizens.[21]

Barriers to agency

Expressing our agency as independent thought and reflective action in the face of threats or complex problems is not easy. Children, like all citizens, face several barriers when learning to exercise agency to address difficult problems like climate change. In the first instance, as Clive Hamilton notes, humanity has evolved psychological dispositions which equip us with skills to address immediate short-term threats, but makes thinking about future threats more difficult.[22] Our common coping strategies in response to unpleasant, dangerous or overwhelming situations include denial, distraction, blaming others or enforced optimism, all of which reinforce a natural tendency to think in the short term and avoid addressing difficult, long-term issues.[23] Even if young citizens overcome these psychological barriers and anxieties, they face political 'neutralisation' as the current turn to responsible citizenship. A curriculum that focuses attention on agency as personal responsibility deflects attention from exercising our collective agency to address systemic injustice (see Chapter 6). Expressing our agency as responsible participation in a market, or as green entrepreneurs and conscientious shoppers, is a poor substitute for the democratic freedom and capability to envisage new forms of collective cooperation to achieve a common purpose.

Young citizens concerned about environmental and social change also face barriers to exercising their agency as citizens in an atmosphere of growing securitisation, urgency or fear. As leaders urge people to act quickly (while government and businesses appear to do little) or conjure up memories of wartime combat against a common enemy, they erode opportunities for citizens to engage in reflective, thoughtful action. Sherilyn McGregor argues that vulnerable voices of women and children are silenced and further marginalised in a process of securitising the environmental debate, as policy debate becomes mired in technological complexity and fear.[24] Children's charities, notably UNICEF and Save the Children, also argue the language of environmental security shifts priorities away from understanding issues facing children and supporting their priorities for action, toward protecting 'assets' for economic growth and 'essential services'.[25]

In political science, Easton and Dennis' classic essay on children and politics suggests children's agency (measured as a sense of efficacy or confidence in their own ability to effect change) is also constrained by family income. They argued a child's efficacy correlates with their parent's socioeconomic status.[26] A subsequent study by Almond and Verba confirmed this view, noting also that children from wealthier socio-economic backgrounds tended to have more opportunities to practice agency at home and school.[27] Traditional approaches to citizenship education and research in North America have often discouraged citizens from exercising agency. The experience of World War Two and the rise of youth fascist political movements in Europe prompted a flurry of studies in the 1950s and 1960s by political scientists who aimed to understand how young people thought about citizenship, to prevent political socialisation as youth indoctrination. During this period, the focus of research was very much on understanding how society 'transmits' political orientations, knowledge, attitudes, behaviours and values to the child as a one way process to ensure political stability rather than encourage critical thinking.[28]

In the late 1980s, the growth of political psychology offered a promising new focus on the ways young citizens might exercise political agency. However, the results of that research were underwhelming. There was some valuable reflection on tensions between a young citizen's sense of internal efficacy (their belief in their capability to understand politics and their right to have a say on issues that concern them) and their external efficacy (their belief that if they do take action, political institutions will be responsive to citizen involvement), concepts due to Albert Bandura.[29] Yet the research of the period was coloured by institutional racism of predominantly white male researchers who concluded that young minority communities simply lack information and training to participate effectively in politics.[30] Alternative explanations for low levels of self-political efficacy, such as observations that political institutions might actually be resistant to the needs of young minorities, were not widely debated. The 'problems of youth citizenship' were treated as problems of 'citizen information deficit' and youth civic disengagement was to be fixed by more citizenship education.[31]

Contemporary research by Chawla and Cushing takes a different view. These authors suggest a child's agency is nurtured when surrounded by peers and adults who also feel confident and politically efficacious.[32] Yet not everyone has the same opportunities to acquire confidence in their right to have a say, and not everyone grows up in politically-confident efficacious communities. How can we encourage efficacy in communities where children do not regularly encounter confident political mentors? Interviews with young people who report low efficacy suggests we have been too quick to assume low efficacy equates to an information deficit. Devra Woodly's study regarding Black American citizenship argues that a low sense of external efficacy[33] should not be interpreted as an indication of insufficient political knowledge, or lack of hope, but rather a realistic self-assessment of the unlikely possibilities for these individuals' ability to affect change.[34]

Work by the social theorist Bourdieu has also challenged romantic notions of citizens being able to act with unfettered agency. His work has revitalised interest in the factors that influence children's understanding of their agency beyond their family and socio-economic status. Bourdieu examined the social world and children's experiences of social, economic and cultural power.[35] His observations that children adopt 'self-limiting habits' as a result of community and cultural influences, inspired new thinking about what ignites people to change their habits. It has sparked much research into social practice.[36] In the United Kingdom, the Sustainable Lifestyles Research Group have examined the way individual citizens try to live more sustainably; they argue individual lives are both constrained and enabled by their social world. Sometimes, it requires a major lifestyle change (such as the birth of a new baby, going to a new school or retiring) to create a moment for critical reflection, yet, even then, without surrounding conditions which are supportive of change, individuals often fail or are simply unable to act in new, more pro-environmental ways, despite their best intentions.[37]

Social agency for a new generation

Despite formidable barriers to exercising agency, there are also important counter currents and opportunities for young citizens to rethink the power of their agency. These trends point to other ways of thinking about agency beyond individual action. A number of theorists and writers have highlighted the role citizens can play in enhancing collective responsibility for justice and pro-environmental decision-making. In the first instance, Roger Hart's ground-breaking study of children's participation in environmental planning took a firmly child-centred view of planning and public policy processes.[38] Hart criticised the passive role children are often expected to play in urban planning. He noted that many efforts to 'engage' children in decision making reinforce this passive vision of children's agency, and amount to little more than window dressing to legitimate policy or planning recommendations already prepared by adults. Hart developed Sherry Arnstein's ladder of effective citizen participation and Paulo Freire's ideas about education as liberation.[39] He argued that children and young people's democratic capacity to effect change is nurtured when they have the opportunity to play an active role in all stages of local environmental decision making.[40]

Youthful agency can be powerfully effective. As I write, my home city of Christchurch is still being wracked by a series of devastating earthquakes and aftershocks, with one over 5 magnitude earthquake every 10 days on average, for the period February to June 2011. In the scale of this emergency, everyone – young and old – is reminded of the limits of personal efficacy. In the aftermath of the earthquakes, the city's young citizens have learned about their capacity for collective action and put this thinking into action with powerful effect. While there were some remarkable and moving examples of individual heroism and selflessness, one student in particular captured national imagination. Wanting to make a meaningful difference in the face of the emergency, second year university student Sam Johnson organised a Facebook campaign which eventually communicated with over 24,000 people. This campaign coordinated an on-the-ground volunteer student 'army' of over 10,000 to clean up the city.[41] The effort of university and local high school students inspired many other communities, albeit not in such spectacular numbers, to come together and build on existing networks, such as a baking army, a farming army, a 'Gap filler' creative theatre scheme, and a Greening the Rubble community gardening scheme. In the latter cases, groups of young artists and environmental activists and professionals worked to provoke creative thinking and some low-level resistance to centralised government plans to rebuild the city using a newly-created central administrative agency (see Chapter 8). These groups, by staged films and created temporary exhibitions, sought to reclaim public space by literally planting seeds in the rubble.[42] Other communities – again, young and old – developed time bank schemes and built on ideas of transition town networking to help local communities draw on pre-existing networks and build new bonds to recover through collective agency.[43] While the 'student army' limited participation to those over 13 years, Principals reported many children in the primary schools we interviewed knew about the initiatives and regarded the secondary school and university students as 'heroes'.

In the scale of an emergency, people recognised the need for social agency. Despite these demonstrations of spontaneous community collaboration by young citizens, the New Zealand government's response was less inclusive and democratic. In the wake of the disaster, the constitution was suspended for weeks, and the powers of Christchurch's struggling local elected council suspended and

Figure 4.2 Christchurch student volunteer army clean up liquefaction in the city following earthquake aftershocks

Credit: Eve Welch.

replaced for five years with a central authority accountable to central government. Given that the children we interviewed in every focus group spontaneously mentioned the role of their respective local council, the effect of the loss of this form of grass roots democracy on youthful agency remains to be seen. This decision, and the ongoing cordon of the central city for building demolition, was a small but salutary reminder of the point made in *Emergency Politics* by Bonnie Honig. Honig argues a traditional interpretation of the resources of democracy – as rights, rule of law and faith in progress – is ill-suited to supporting citizens to take back power and continuously 'found' and recreate democratic visions in daily life.[44]

Agency as resistance

Observation of both the spontaneous, collaborative student responses to the Christchurch earthquake, and the authoritarian and centralised response of the New Zealand government in the period after the earthquake, forcefully underscored Honig's point that citizenship agency is not simply action to address common problems; it is also action which recreates democracy and democratic values of popular sovereignty.[45] A critical form citizenship agency involves resisting and challenging illegitimate power. Agency is complexly expressed as creative problem solving, civil disobedience and dissent. Given that many of the most significant environmental impacts today, such as tar sand mining, fracking, large scale logging and growing food insecurity, are tacitly endorsed by government policy, it is disturbing that both citizenship and environmental education are becoming increasingly depoliticised. A great deal of attention and funding has focused on teaching children to recycle, grow their own food and reduce their carbon footprint, but startlingly little emphasis is given to providing children with opportunities to learn to resist the illegitimate exercise of state power. James Bohman reminds us that, in a globalised world, the ability to extract yourself from the plans of others is a very important form of exercising agency.[46] As the actions of state governments and distant others (corporations, investment companies and consumers) affects the local weather and food security of the growing number of children in developing countries, learning strategies to extract your community from the plans of others will become a more and more challenging issue for those who want to exercise agency meaningfully.

The importance of thinking about agency as resistance was highlighted by John Barry who argues that '... states, economies and cultures show little sign of independently becoming more sustainable without citizen action'. Comparing classroom civics lessons with the experience of environmental protest, Barry concludes, '... critical or resistance citizenship is more important to cultivate and support'. Barry notes however, that '[i]t is highly unlikely, though, that state-based citizenship modules in education, workplace, or corporate notions of environmental citizenship ... will cultivate and encourage this activist and duty-based notion of citizenship'.[47] Children's agency is cultivated differently in different contexts and power relationships, and, as a result, children may need support to learn when to exercise their agency in tactical ways, as short protests for example, or when to adopt more long-term strategies.[48] In this light, Barry asks provocatively,

> [w]ill nonviolent direct action tactics, the ethical and political dimensions of civil disobedience, and other dimensions and potentials for citizen activism be taught in (environmental) citizenship classes? Will the educative capacity of political struggle itself be conveyed? Will students of such citizenship classes be exposed to ethical arguments highlighting such forms of citizen action as positive for democracy? Will such forms of resistance citizenship be seen as caring for and defending democracy?[49]

Learning to resist illegitimate power, like learning to resist peer pressure, is an important skill. Even when resistance fails, the experience of thinking and acting with independent thought is often liberating. Emirbayer and Mische argue that the presence of sceptics in the community may be an indicator of future political transformation, as these are people whose political capacity to imagine an alternative future has already been enlarged.[50] Sceptics may have hit a structural 'barrier' which they do not yet know how to surmount, however they argue this feeling sows seeds for new thinking. Seen in this light, the Streetwise Sceptics identified in this study may be as important in creating political change as tribal and team players who are confident they can make a difference. Ronald Inglehart and

Christian Welzel argue that 'elite challenging activities' are an important indicator for a liberty-orientated critical public,[51] while Cohen and Arato go further and describe civil disobedience as the motor of social change.[52]

However, before we are tempted to romanticise agency as resistance, it is important to also recognise how difficult it can be for young adults to practice agency as resistance, particularly in an environment of growing securitisation and surveillance (see Chapter 5), or in an education system which emphasises increasing testing and skills-based learning for short-term economic growth and which enacts penalties on non-conformists. Cunningham and Lavalette, for example, document the harsh way discipline was imposed on children engaged in civil disobedience during a wave of school strikes over the Iraq war.[53] Furthermore, children can exercise their agency to reproduce repression as well as democratisation. Paulo Freire suggests education can be a liberation process through dialogue, which exposes dehumanising and unjust practices.[54] Yet, Jeffrey has also documented the way some children use their agency to oppress others and reproduce new forms of hierarchy and control.[55] Given these conflicting experiences, what are the prospects of nurturing ecological citizenship as social agency and critical resistance in families, schools and communities in neoliberal democracies?

Ecological citizenship as social agency in family, school and community

For Barry at least, effective citizenship requires new skills and virtues, including the ability to act collaboratively with others, and to resist illegitimate power with courage.[56] What are the prospects for learning about collaborative and courageous social agency in neoliberal democracies? Peter Levine argues all efforts to support young people's voice in politics often contains an embedded seed of hope for a more positive future.[57] But Levine acknowledges we cannot rely solely on seeds of hope which are not spread uniformly. The kind of agency that children need to exercise as ecological citizens will require more than energetic, hopeful self-determination. Given the complexity of the problems confronting this generation, effective ecological citizens will need to learn to exercise agency as social action and critical resistance in family, school and wider community settings.

Families and social agency

Since the 1950s, significant studies, including Talcott Parson's general theory of action, have identified the role that family and peers, as well as school and personal traits, have as key influences shaping individual agency. Nussbaum argues that children's opportunities in life are shaped even before birth, and that feeling nurtured and loved from an early age makes an enormous difference on a child's confidence to participate in public life.[58] One of the most important primary conditions that nurture an expansive sense of agency, which is required for ecological citizenship, is the ability to express empathy for others. This ability to feel empathy is nurtured in strong attachments in childhood. As Nussbaum reminds us, it is the sense of being worthy and capable of love, and the ability to feel empathy, which is an important precondition for political agency that is more open, inclusive and compassionate. We can see examples of this seed of expansive agency fostered in the tribal and extended family setting of many children we interviewed in the Community-*Kura* School.

The role of *whānau* [family] and tribal membership in nurturing strong attachments, empathy and agency came into stark relief in conversation with several boys who knew the interviewer well and are young leaders amongst their peers. In describing how much their family and tribe mattered, several children came close to tears. Part of an intense and moving conversation is reported here with permission of the children and their school community:

INTERVIEWER: How about I use this word, what does it mean to be a citizen or your *iwi*? Or what does it mean to be a citizen of your *whānau*? What does that mean?

PARK MASTER: A lot.

EVIL HAWKE: Special.

CRANBERRY THE 13TH: I reckon my family's cool and stuff and they're the best family in the world and stuff, and I like them. ... Well there some things I don't do 'cause my *iwi* doesn't like me doing it and I don't like doing it ...

GHOST: I feel real happy that *whānau* [family] makes me feel special.

EVIL HAWKE: Well really good because you get to see what you haven't seen before, like in your family.

CRANBERRY THE 13TH: If wasn't for my family, back me up and support me and stuff then I reckon there'd be like no meaning to my life and stuff 'cause I don't wanna live without a family.

(Community-*Kura* School)

Many groups of children shared a similar intensity of feeling when talking about their home and family; this was evident in the number of stars children placed on their family and home when allocating stars on their community maps. In the context of wider tribal and friendship networks, these children are already expressing agency that is mutual support and, as 'Evil Hawke' indicates, extended families can help children expand their knowledge 'to see what you haven't seen before' and to express citizenship identity in collaborative ways around food sharing.

David Uzzell and Patrick Devine-Wright *et al.* have examined how children learn to exercise their agency for pro-environmental change in their homes and families.[59] Their respective research suggests children and parents have to be willing and able to communicate with each other, and the environment has to be regarded as an appropriate topic for discussion, conditions which both conclude are rarely met. This work echoes the results of Wood, which suggests family backgrounds can undermine agency if parents themselves feel they are unlikely to effect change, or felt pressured to give up valued freedoms.[60]

Schools and social agency

Beyond the family, environmental educators have highlighted the role that schools also play in fostering collaborative learning and action while respecting the autonomy of the individual.[61] For example, rather than teaching that emphasises environmental 'facts' and desired 'behaviours', William Scott and colleagues have argued that effective learning begins with an understanding of what the learner needs and wants to learn, rather than what the outcomes of education should be, as dictated by adults.[62] Scott highlights the potential for greater synergy between citizenship and environmental education.[63] He advocates providing children with opportunities to engage in action learning, that is, the chance to take part in – and critically reflect on – real decision making within their school and their wider community.[64] He argues environmental education is most effective when it provides children with opportunities to think critically about the world around them and to reflect on how their views and experiences shape their environment.[65]

Recent research by Rickinson, Lundholm and Hopwood takes up this emphasis on understanding the complex decisions that young citizens wrestle with whenever they take action in everyday life.[66] They argue pupils need support to debate the values embedded in environmental choices, but caution that students can be 'switched off' by too much moralising. In New Zealand, Wood has similarly highlighted the need for teachers to pay careful attention to the role peer groups and classroom expectations play in encouraging children's interest in political debates and their belief and confidence in their ability to effect change.[67]

Striking an effective balance between providing substantive environmental content and nurturing a critical appreciation of the processes of political, social and economic decision making is a concern of environmental psychologists David Uzzell and Nora Rathzel.[68] These writers are particularly critical of teaching that focuses on sustainable development. They argue the classic concept of sustainable development (as development that meets the needs of today without compromising the needs of future generations) is a policy construction that was designed to assist negotiations amongst those concerned with promoting economic growth and those worried about degradation. The concept may have helped environmental policy negotiation, but is an inadequate focus for teaching children to think critically or act in new ways to advance sustainability because, as a policy concept, sustainable development was designed to conceal, not reveal, deep value conflicts in communities.[69] Rathzel and Uzzell argue schools can play a more useful role in nurturing children's capacity for critical thinking and action by providing opportunities to practice debating real issues that involve deep dissent. Drawing on ideas of psychological liberation, such as Boal's theatre of the oppressed and Vygotsky's theory of education, they argue children need more opportunity to develop conflict-generated problem solving skills. These authors describe this approach as 'transformative' sustainability education, in which children learn how to challenge powerful groups and individuals.[70]

Not all schools offer similar support for children to learn the virtues of social agency. In the New Zealand study we heard from children at the Faith School who struggled with the issues of agency:

INTERVIEWER: Who do you think is responsible for taking action on climate change?

JIMMY: God [is responsible for floods] ... it's God's tears because he is angry ... God controls everything. It's a cycle, I read a book about it and it was on *Suzie's World* [a television science programme].

(Faith School)

Other children like Jimmy were very worried about climate change and felt they had to look to God: 'How are we supposed to die? It's not like we can just die. That's no fair. God, create something to protect us.' Here Poppy echoes Jimmy's suggestion that God controls everything. In contrast, a few city blocks away, other children at the Small World School reported school councils as empowering experiences even in a changing climate:

POPCORN: Yes. I am a house captain and I think that we can make changes in the community, because we're kids too so we listen to kids.

BRITNEY: I think, um, that, um, the house captains, I mean pupil council can change things.

TINA: That's house captains.

BRITNEY: No, pupil council too can um, will change things and they like organise things. I think pupil council can change things and the school.

(Small World School)

These markedly different views of agency raise the question of what difference can a school make in teaching agency? The Crick review of the citizenship curriculum suggests the impact can be quite significant. The Crick Report explicitly draws out this relationship between the structural organisation of schools and citizenship education. That report suggests: '[t]he ethos, organization, structures and daily practices of schools have considerable impact on the effectiveness of citizenship education'.[71] In the light of this assertion, it is interesting that in the New Zealand case study some children appeared to gain a great deal of confidence in their ability to exercise their agency as a result of their school-based activities. Many children, for example, commented with pride on performing in *kapa haka* groups [cultural performance] or in choirs. School camping trips were also often cited as valuable opportunities to 'learn to do things with others' (see Chapter 5). Many children were acutely aware of the attitudes of their classroom teacher, reporting if they voted or if they listened to the children. In addition, sports and cultural clubs, and the coaches of these clubs, were frequently cited as important supports for children learning to do things with others; sport in particular was listed by nearly all children at this age.[72]

Supporting children to learn to collaborate as citizens matters. Elizabeth Beaumont reminds us that learning political confidence and skills to act with others can be a disruptive force in public life.[73] She examined four situations in which students in the United States learned about political agency by taking part in various community and political activities. She argued that students learn politics by doing politics. However these lessons tend to advantage those who come from homes that encouraged political debate, and those who are already advantaged in education: they had a wide range of similar opportunities increasing their confidence. Her work is underscored in our field observations of children in a gifted and talented programme at the Music School. The children we interviewed commented with disarming and frank confidence on their abilities:

TAILS SINGING: I love singing.
SIMON BUDDY: She's really good at it, she sang in front of the whole school.
ROBIN: In my house we garden as a family.
THE NUT: Sometimes we play board games.
ROBIN: Oh, yeah, speeches. I'm really good at those.

(Music School)

The relaxed confidence of these children and their belief about their agency can be compared to some of the new migrant children in other classes, who were so shy about making comments, that they whispered their thoughts to the interviewers. Other children felt that there were more appropriate ways of expressing political agency, such as 'backing up my *iwi* [tribe]' or taking part in religious activities 'we do prayers'. The cultural nuance of nurturing agency was brought home to me at the end of one interview in the Small World School. One child, Bob, who was from Samoa, said: 'I think it's stupid we can't have a vote over whether we do speech competitions or not because I hate them.' There is significant expectation in many communities in New Zealand and the Pacific about leaders as orators; the English term 'speech competition' does not adequately capture the intense, exciting, community experiences of the speech and *kappa haka* [cultural dance] events children like Bob are referring to. While many children rise to the occasion, not all children choose to express their sense of agency in speech making.

By contrast to children in tribal communities, where there is a great deal of emphasis on speaking, and speechmaking, children at the Tree School complained they were not being listened to in their protest about their right to climb trees. They clearly felt their agency was frustrated. Yet teachers at the Tree School also commented with concern about a 'culture of low-level playground bullying' which they were attempting to address. In conversation with these students, many complained that 'higher ups' dominated decision making in the clubs and activities in their community, yet these same children also argued that older children should make most playground rules (like who could sit on which seats) because 'they had been there the longest'. In this light, the critical question is how can agency be nurtured in ways that foster young citizens democratic and sustainable values?

In the New Zealand study I was also struck by the value of schools as safe spaces for children to practice citizenship as critical resistance. In the course of the research, a confrontation broke out one morning between protestors protesting the closure of the local pool and a demolition contractor driving a large truck. As the situation threatened to escalate out of control, so children began screaming and crying. Two researchers and I happened to be near the protest and parents and children asked us to take children to the school 'where it was safe'. In this situation, schools are embedded in local communities supporting children as they cope with difficult change in their wider world.

Communities and social agency

Children's confidence in social agency appears to be reinforced at times where communities work with schools, and can provide significant support for children as they learn about social agency. In the study, two middle-income schools (the Small World School and the Community-*Kura* School) actively built close working relationships with parents, grandparents and other relatives, who would often spend spontaneous time in classrooms as helpers. Social spaces were created for parents and relations to have a cup of tea, and day classes were offered in parenting skills, family *kapa haka* or cultural performances, or to help parents learn about what was being taught at school. These intergenerational learning interactions were reported by children, and the pride children took in learning an indigenous language and performing in front of family and communities appears to have reinforced both social agency and opportunities for intergenerational learning and conversation.[74] In turn, intergenerational learning can help sustain children's agency over time. Mary is 8 years old and attends the Small World School; here she makes a direct link between the value of learning to give speeches and cultural performances and her enhanced sense of agency in other situations:

INTERVIEWER: Do you feel people that make decisions in your community listen to you?
MARY: When you're afraid, you can maybe stand up and speak, and say your own words, like to a bully ... like for speech. If you're scared you don't have to be scared at school, cos it's not like those big [speech and cultural] competitions, it's just like a normal practice, small one for children.

Many children in the bilingual programme, at the Community-*Kura* school also reported observing grandparents and relations taking active roles in the community. Elsewhere, Sacha McMeeking, as a representative of the South Island's *Ngāi Tahu* tribe, has spoken of the value and strength she and other young leaders draw from reflecting on a political struggle over seven generations by the *Ngāi Tahu* tribe to settle their claim for loss of cultural *taonga* or treasures including land.[75] Historian Ranganui Walker speaks of this strength of resistance as '*Ka whawhai tonu mātou* – Struggle without end'.[76]

Intergenerational support is a powerful boost to children's confidence in their ability to effect change, enhancing children's capabilities to exercise citizenship.[77] Inglehart and Welzel argue that people are also supported in their community to exercise agency in non-material ways, when freed from the immediate demands of survival.[78] When people are disempowered, tired, or simply scared, it can be very difficult to exercise agency by speaking out. Often, as the earthquake experience in Christchurch revealed, nurturing agency in these situations requires helping a person simply to survive. But as Sen has pointed out, survival is not all that people are capable of, and should not be the sufficient condition for fostering agency.[79] In my own observation of children and adults, feeling a sense of agency is a key part of recovery after a disaster for young citizens. Children, like adults, value the ability to be able to effect changes in their world in ways that are meaningful to them.

However, the New Zealand study also reveals how agency can be eroded in subtle ways, particularly through children's experiences of poverty or income inequality. In the two poorest school communities, all children in the focus group agreed that a lack of money limited collective agency (negatively affecting the conditions school grounds or their town, and constraining their opportunities to learn new things that were available to other schools – see Chapters 5 and 6). At age 8 to 10 years, these children are observing the way New Zealand has experienced rapid growth in income inequality in the OCED since 1984. The small comments were told with some wry humour and collective solidarity, yet they are poignant reminders that agency depends on economic resources.

Humour in the face of frustrated agency was also evident when children discussed who 'gets the belt' from mum or dad if they are 'cheeky' or 'speak out'. These latter comments are disturbing and should give pause for thought to those who rush to argue that children lack agency, are apolitical, pre-political or consumer orientated. These efforts to address inequality in local environments should not rest on the agency of young, personally-responsible citizens.

Rethinking the 'power of one': a leaderless revolution?

The experience of global economic recession, high youth unemployment, dramatic cuts to public services, the bail-out of failing banks, and growing concerns about lack of accountability in decision making, has sparked worldwide protest. As protest spreads with the aid of rapid social communication, young protestors have begun to connect in a 'leaderless revolution' to challenge financial power and growing social inequality. Such leaderless revolutions have ambivalent potential. At once a powerful restatement of new forms of community organisation that do not rely on hierarchy,[80] they are also strikingly vulnerable to manipulation and reframing to capture emerging concerns of a new generation before the new concerns of discontent are articulated.[81]

In many ways, the Occupy protests in particular resonated with the neoliberal rhetoric in which citizens are encouraged to govern themselves with a minimal state.[82] This self-governing autonomy is a powerful motor for change, but it can be co-opted to deliver yet more of the same, individualism rather than encourage greater civic collaboration across deep differences. At the opening of this chapter, Mary Midgely urged us to challenge the dominant myth of competitive individualism. This is a difficult task. As Rose reminds us, individualism is complexly embedded in contemporary ideas of citizenship. Liberal 'strategies of government' have made effective use of a variety of 'devices' of governance, from schooling to the domesticated family, '… to create individuals who do not need to be governed by others, but will govern themselves, master themselves, care for themselves'.[83] The challenge for a new generation of ecological citizens is to turn this strong sense of individual autonomy toward a collaborative democratic purpose and a more sustainable future.

Notes

1   Barber 1984 (2003), pp126–7.
2   Dewey 1916 (1966).
3   Mathews 1996.
4   Bourdieu 1998; Brofenbrenner 1979; Brown and Westaway 2011; Emirbayer and Mische 1998; Giddens 1998; Hart 2008; Norris 2011; Weale 2002.
5   Katz 2004; Tanner and Mitchell 2008.
6   Aqtash *et al.* 2004.
7   Arendt 1958 (1998).
8   Ibid.
9   Seyfang 2005.
10 Fischer 2003.
11 Pateman 1970 (1990); Barber 1984 (2003).
12 Clark 2011; Shove 2010.
13 Giddens 1986, p5; Jackson 2009, pp87–102.
14 Smith 2006, p56.
15 Sen 2009, p251–2.
16 Clark 2011, p50–4.
17 Hayward *et al.* 2011a; Hayward *et al.* 2011b.
18 Ibid.
19 Hayward *et al.* 2011b.
20 Ibid.
21 See for example Shove 2010; Whitmarsh *et al.* 2011.
22 Hamilton 2010.
23 Ibid., pp210–33.
24 McGregor 2006.
25 Save the Children 2008; UNICEF and Plan International 2011.
26 Easton and Dennis 1967.
27 Almond and Verba 1963 (1989), pp369–70; Pateman 1970 (1990), p49.
28 Easton and Dennis 1967; Greenberg 1970 (2009); Verba *et al.* 1995. See also Flanagan 2008b.
29 Bandura 1997; Fiske *et al.* 2010.
30 Woodly 2006.
31 Greenberg 1970 (2009).
32 Chawla and Cushing 2007.
33 Bandura 1997.
34 Woodly 2006.

35 Bourdieu 1998.
36 Swartz 2002, pp61–9.
37 Burningham *et al.* forthcoming.
38 Hart 1997.
39 Arnstein 1969; Freire 1970, 1975.
40 Hart 1992, 1997.
41 Johnson 2012.
42 Brett 2011; Hayward forthcoming.
43 Buttigieg 2010; Brett 2011; MacLeod and Moller 2006.
44 Honig 2009.
45 Honig 2009.
46 Bohman 2004.
47 Barry 2005, p34.
48 Honawa cited in Moncrieffe 2009.
49 Ibid.
50 Emirbayer and Mische 1998, p1009.
51 Inglehart and Welzel 2005, p191.
52 Cohen and Arato 1994, p567.
53 Cunningham and Lavalette 2004.
54 Freire 1985, pp84–5; Horton and Freire 1990, p47.
55 Jeffrey 2011.
56 Barry 2005.
57 Levine 2011.
58 Nussbaum 2011, p34.
59 Uzzell 1999; Devine-Wright *et al.* 2004.
60 Wood, J. 2011.
61 Orr 1994; Reid and Scott 2006; Sobel 1996.
62 Reid and Scott 2006.
63 Scott 2011.
64 Bishop and Scott 1998.
65 Scott and Gough 2005; see also Scott 2011.
66 Rickinson *et al.* 2010.
67 Wood, J. 2011.
68 Uzzell 2010; Rathzel and Uzzell 2009.
69 Rathzel and Uzzell 2009.
70 Boal's (2000) theatre of the oppressed and Vygotsky's (1987) theory of education as conflict-generated problem solving are discussed in Rathzel and Uzzell 2009.
71 Qualifications and Curriculum Authority 1998, s9.1.
72 See also Bengry-Howell *et al.* 2010.
73 Beaumont 2010, 2011.
74 Hart 1997.
75 McMeeking 2011.
76 Walker 2004.
77 Nussbaum 2011.
78 Inglehart and Welzel 2005, p33.
79 Sen 2009.
80 Blissett 2011.
81 Curtis 2011.
82 Dean 1999; Kirk 2008a; Lukes 2005; Nairn and Higgins 2007; Rose 1996.
83 Rose 1996, p45; see also Kirk 2008a.

5 Environmental education
Growing up on Google Earth

> When we walk, we naturally go to the fields and woods; what would become of us, if we only walked in a garden or a mall?
>
> (Henry Thoreau 1851 (2007), pp12–13)

What kind of environmental education will young ecological citizens need? The children in the New Zealand study are amongst a global cohort born during the launch of the world's largest internet search engine, Google, in 1998. Their world is characterised by growing contradictions. On the one hand, for many of these children their horizons are constantly expanding, facilitated by internet communication, new social media and international travel.[1] Yet, at the same time, many children in English-speaking democracies are losing independent, unsupervised access to valued local places.[2] For many children, their physical and temporal freedoms to roam or to 'waste' time are under threat in highly-urbanised, digital, monitored and commercialised spaces.[3] These children are variously described as a gated, chauffeured, 'bubble-wrapped' or hot-housed generation.[4] Media alarm is sounded about children growing up without access to wild or risky play, at risk of a 'nature deficit disorder', deprived of access to the outdoors or effectively living as 'pampered prisoners' under the anxious surveillance of 'helicopter parents' who hover in the background, ever fearful of traffic or strangers and anxious to ensure their children's leisure time is used productively to develop skills they will need to 'succeed' in a competitive, global marketplace.[5]

However, there is a real danger that in our moral panic, adult attention is drawn away from the more mundane ways that children growing up in cities are suffering in everyday environments of 'sterile surveillance', domestic violence, multiple deprivation and risk.[6] In this context, I argue the biggest problem that many children face is not a 'nature deficit' but an adult attention disorder. Loss of independent access to natural environments is a serious issue, but I suggest children in developed countries are at greater risk of adult policy neglect, as public attention is directed away from the socio-ecological realities that trouble children – including growing social inequality, family strain and lack of access to education or employment – all of which may be exacerbated by dangerous environmental change, particularly for minority communities. In developed economies, policy attention is increasingly focused away from children and toward concerns of an aging baby-boom cohort who dominate the ballot box.[7]

The problems children face in their home environments are exacerbated by changes in their wider physical environment, including a changing climate.[8] These changes increase the likelihood that the most vulnerable children will suffer from a 'double exposure' to economic and environmental problems.[9] Socio-ecological suffering is not experienced uniformly. Its impacts are disproportionally felt by the poorest children, girls, and children of indigenous and ethnic minorities[10] who experience higher overall exposure to environmental risks of polluted and degraded local neighbourhoods.[11] A report by the international aid agency Plan estimates, for example, that 80 per cent of all deaths in the 2004 Asian Tsunami were women and girls.[12] Re-thinking ecology from a child's perspective also means recognising that children's valued home environments are increasingly subject to domestic strain and economic uncertainty, as well as pollution and climate change.[13] Lessons in recycling are irrelevant if these wider pressures are eroding children's conditions of life and their opportunities to flourish. Viewed in this light, an effective environmental education needs to support young citizens as they learn to ask political questions about how power is exercised in their community, by whom, and with what effect. A relevant environmental education will also provide children with opportunities to learn about the complex situations they face, practice skills to resist or challenge illegitimate decision making, and begin to learn strategies to bring about desired change.

Mobile worlds: understanding children's environmental experiences

In a ground-breaking study of the processes of economic development and global change as experienced through the eyes of children growing up in a Sudanese village and a suburb of New York City, Cindy Katz observed children on the cusp of a time–space expansion, as communities began to imagine vastly-expanded horizons for study, work and trade.[14] A decade later and a hemisphere away, we see the effects of a dramatic time–space expansion on New Zealand children's lives. Children in every focus group we spoke with (except the two smallest rural schools) casually reported complex migration stories. These children belong to a cohort of those under 14 years who have experienced a remarkable demographic transition, as New Zealand immigration policies have been relaxed to facilitate trade and international investment.[15] Many children had moved to New Zealand with their families for work or education. In the latter case, children were normally living with a guardian or parent, while the other parent worked offshore. Some had moved for refuge. A typical example of the mobility of these young lives is reflected in this a focus group conversation amongst children in the E-School:

Figure 5.1 Children's informal outdoor play develops environmental affinity (Lake Pukaki, New Zealand)

Credit: Bronwyn Hayward.

GOTHIC BUBBLE SKULLS:	Hi, I'm Gothic Bubble Skulls and I'm 11. And I've come here from Singapore and I've been basically all the way around the world. And I've lived in many places and I go to [school] and I live in [area]. And I live with my mum, and my dad lives with his girlfriend in Singapore. And yeah, that's about it. I came here at the start of last year.
INTERVIEWER:	Ok, cool. And what language do you speak at home?
GOTHIC BUBBLE SKULLS:	I speak English and I used to speak fluently Chinese.
TONY HAWK:	Hi, I'm 10 years old. I live with my mum and dad and little brother. And I go to this school, and my teacher's Susie. I was born here and I've lived my whole life here.
SEMAJ:	My name is Semaj and I was born in Seoul in Korea.
CHLOE:	My name is Chloe and I was born in England and I came to New Zealand when I was 4, and I started school at [school]. I'm 11 years old and at home I speak English. Sometime this year I went to South Africa on holiday. And I've got a twin brother and a little sister who's 9 and a mum and a dad.

(E-School)

Making sense of life in a highly mobile world was a motif running throughout many conversations as young citizens re-created a sense of community and belonging. Some found support through their cultural identity: 'you must never forget your mother tongue'. Others found solidarity with the experience of other new migrant classmates as the following conversation captures. Here Jordan and Ben have both arrived in New Zealand about three years earlier. Jordan came from China with his mother and grandparents who run a small corner store, or dairy, while his father works in China, and Ben came from India. All the children in this discussion had lived in New Zealand for less than four years:

BEN: I belong to India, and you belong to China.
JORDAN: Can I write, 'I belong to a dairy?'
HEATHER: Yeah, 'cause his mum and dad like work in a dairy.
JORDAN: No, my dad's in China.
BEN: His dad went back to China.
JORDAN: My dad has never been here.
BEN: Oh, I belong to my mum and dad! I belong to my family!
JORDAN: I belong to Asia.
BEN: Oh yeah! [writes Asia too]

(Community-*Kura* School)

Ben's epiphany that, like Jordan, he can identify as 'Asian' too is sometimes described negatively as an 'othering' identity experience, when dominant cultures define a minority. But here, Ben, as an immigrant from India, drew strength from connecting in a moment of shared solidarity with his friend Jordan from China. There were many such instances of children trying to find places of belonging or shared reference points in a mobile world. For Jordan it was his family-owned corner store, and a popular destination for children to bike to and buy sweets.

In another group at the same school, European/*Pākehā* children discussed the place of commercial shopping malls:

INTERVIEWER: Can anyone belong to that community? [points to children's community-star headed 'places to hang out' and 'malls']
NEARLY ALL: Yip.
GINGA: They'd have to move there.
PUFF: No, because there's malls everywhere.
GINGA: Yeah but if you're in places in Australia, you can't be a part of that community because you're not even living there.
PUFF: They have malls there too, you know?
ROBERTA: They could just stay there for a day and they would adapt to that community. They could stay there and it doesn't matter who you are, you could go into it.
TROY: Anybody should be allowed in a mall as long as they're not going to steal anything or kill anybody.

ROBERTA:	Why would you kill somebody in a mall?
TROY:	Murderers normally do it.
GINGA:	No they don't!
LEONARDO DA VINCI:	Not in the middle of the mall they don't.
GINGA:	They do it in the street at night.

(Community-*Kura* School)

In their reflections on mobility and threats to personal safety, the familiarity of a mall is described as facilitating a sense of belonging and reassurance. Here these children are adding nuance to Marc Augé's description of the 'non-places' of supermodernity as spaces (like hotel rooms or airports) which look exactly the same the world over, and where there is little to no personal culture embedded in the environment.[16] Augé suggests the rise of these non-places can be understood as the consequence of increasing global trade, and pressure to homogenise needs and consumption patterns to expand consumer markets. However, this conversation also suggests that, for some children, the sameness of these non-places makes them appealing sites of reassurance given wider changes they are less able to control. Their comments reflect what Constance Flanagan describes as the 'private anxieties and public hopes' of a generation of children whose lives have been made more precarious by the uncertainties of growing up in a world of highly mobile capital.[17] The ubiquitous sameness of malls creates a space of respite where children know what is expected of them and how to 'adapt' to fit in.[18] Yet even the children who said they regularly hung out at malls could hardly be described as hyper-consumers in ways comparable to research in North America and the United Kingdom.[19] As noted in Chapter 3, brand names were only volunteered in discussion about the internet, electronic devices and music, and in one case a girls clothing range.[20]

However, for most children, it was not the shopping mall but their local school which was their most important public space and source of identity in a changing world, as this conversation illustrates:

SAMMY:	[pointing to a big map with all the countries children come from] There's heaps and heaps of different country people in our school.
ABBY:	Like me!
KITTY CAT:	And that makes us really cool because we are a cool school.
SAMMY:	Going to this school is really exciting because half the class or more than half the class is from a different country but at my old school there was about one or two people from a different country. Everybody else was from New Zealand.

(Small World School)

The large green playgrounds of local schools also emerged as spaces where children enjoyed hanging out with friends after hours. School playgrounds were surprisingly important public spaces for nearly all children. Michael Sandel has argued that in large, highly diverse democracies, access to public space matters because it provides an opportunity for citizens to encounter others and develop a sense of solidarity and mutual responsibility.[21] Sandel argues that equitable access to public space is vital for democracy. Schools, parks, playgrounds, community centres, swimming pools and recreation centres (and we may add public libraries and museums) matter as the sites for creating a 'public realm' where citizens from 'different walks of life' encounter one another.[22] Sandel fears that these public spaces are being hollowed out by the 'secession' of the 'privileged' who are leaving these public facilities to those who can't afford anything else. Sandel argues this process is eroding the institutions that 'once gathered people together and served as informal schools of civic virtue'.[23] He suggests the driving force in this process is growing income inequality that undermines the '… solidarity that citizenship requires as rich and poor lead increasingly separate lives'.[24]

Sandel makes an important point, yet children's access to public space is not only under threat because the well-heeled are withdrawing from these places; children are also actively excluded from urban space. This process is worst for children from low-income communities and communities with large ethnic minorities.[25] Children in all English-speaking countries are experiencing exclusion as loss of access to outdoor public space,[26] and many children are also finding it harder to get around or get away independently.[27] In the space of just a single generation, the unsupervised physical roaming distance for many children has contracted dramatically.[28] Social norms are also used to exclude and constrain children's access to and use of public space. 'Chauffeuring', or escorting children to school and clubs, is the bane of many families, even though many children report they would enjoy being able to get around independently.[29] The reasons for children's exclusion from public space include 'safety conscious' risk adverse parenting norms and 'auto centric' urban design.[30] Research by Gill Valentine suggests the privatisation of public space (the creation of malls and retail centres policed with surveillance) is redefining many urban areas as adult zones and relegating children to private indoor home spaces.[31]

Cindy Katz goes further. She traces North American children's loss of access to public space to the urban policies and practices of the 1980s, which increasingly 'demonised' powerless people though a 'diabolical assortment' of social and economic practices.[32] She describes this as a process of 'revanchism', or the material and social practices of 'meanness and revenge', that include policing 'gang youth' rather than providing parks, and funding prisons rather than schools.[33] Katz's discussion of revanchism, written in 2004, could equally be applied to the near apoplectic reaction of British politicians and media in the wake of the English urban disorders of August 2011. The overwhelmingly youthful riots were described as the 'sheer criminality' of 'feral youth'.[34] The English use of the word 'feral' to refer to children and young people is a particularly unpleasant term that has crept into common conversation in the United Kingdom.[35] It is also disturbing that some governments and private retailers now use a high-pitched alarm originally designed to deter pests to disperse groups of young people and prevent them from gathering in public spaces.[36] These high-pitched sirens, known by trademarks names including 'Mosquito', hurt children's ears, but cannot be as easily heard by those over twenty-five. Despite complaints from the European Commission that these devices infringe children's human rights, the alarm is now widely used in Britain and in some retail spaces in New Zealand, including supermarket doorways and bus shelters.[37] Sadly, these alarms are just one of the insidious weapons in a burgeoning tool kit of control and surveillance techniques that are used to regulate and monitor children in their physical and digital environment.[38]

Against the background of children's struggle to gain or maintain access to public space, this study was interested in understanding New Zealand children's experience of belonging to communities as citizens. We asked children: 'What sort of things do children do with other people around here?' The question and a subsequent group exercise to construct a community map was originally conceived as an ice breaker to open a conversation about citizenship. However, the community mapping exercise itself revealed some significant differences in children's interactions and use of public space which are reported here.

Children's segregated public space: commercial, outdoor and social places

At the age of 8 to 12 years, all children in this study emphasised their home environments as their most important places where they enjoyed interacting with others: 'playing with friends', having 'sleep overs' or 'birthday parties', 'baking', 'gardening', enjoying 'family celebrations', 'doing jobs', 'sharing food' and 'playing computer games'. Their descriptions of home based interactions reflected a casual 'drop-in' lifestyle, with many children reporting friends 'coming over' or 'coming around'[39] to play after school, especially at the weekends.[40] Nearly all the children also listed sport, including outdoor sports (netball, rugby, soccer, pony clubs, touch rugby and tennis) as community activities they enjoyed doing with other people. Surveys indicate children's participation in sport peaks for children in New Zealand at ages 8 to 12, with 67 per cent of children in national benchmark studies reporting interest in taking part in new activities.[41] From 13 years that participation declines. The important role that sport plays for many New Zealand children under 13 was underscored by the comment of one boy who, when told his group would be 'mapping' activities that children did with other people, replied: 'But won't like the whole page be sport?!' Other activities children reported enjoying included clubs (Brownies, Scouts and Pony Club) and place-based activities like biking to the local dairy (corner store). Public libraries were mentioned by children in 10 of the 25 groups as spaces they used with other people, particularly to access the internet.

Despite growing up as part of a wider international Google generation, these New Zealand children had uneven access to and experience of the internet and electronic communication. Children from rural and Pacific communities are least likely to have internet access at home.[42] At the time of the study, the internet was a digital place where children in 24 of the 25 groups reported doing things with other people. The children at the smallest rural school did not mention the internet. Internet penetration has been uneven in New Zealand. However, all focus groups reported enjoying playing computer games with other people (especially boys): 'At Christchurch City libraries that's where I do the internet and stuff. I look for Harry Potter sites and Tamagochi sites or, sometimes … I do a job for [my sister] and I go on Barbie sites and print off colouring-in pictures.' Some children also mentioned *What Now*, an interactive, state-funded television programme, as something they 'did with other people'.

Beyond these shared activities, the children constructed three strikingly different types of community map. The differences were surprising for the research team, given that seven of the nine schools were within a 20 kilometre radius of each other and some were separated only by a few city blocks. In the first instance, children from the schools drawn from high-income communities were distinctive for the high proportion of map space children devoted to escorted, structured, commercial or digital activities. Most children in these high-decile school communities reported a very structured leisure time filled with orchestra, ballet, sport, maths tuition, brownies, dancing and piano. While the children enjoyed these activities, some complained there was little time for informal play and interaction with friends except at home at the weekends (sleepovers), or when cycling or walking to the local shop or school. It was also striking that, in constructing their community maps and in their focus groups, none of the children from the high-income schools described the physical characteristics of the locations where they undertook activities with others. These schools were located in pleasant 'leafy' suburbs, but the quality of the environment was not commented upon. The only time physical places were mentioned with pleasure ('the beach', 'Le Bons Bay' and camping) was in connection with holidays or special weekend activities. Physical space was also discussed when talking about commercial spaces (malls, movie theatres and leisure centres) as important sites for meeting friends and shopping. (Shopping was listed only by girls.)

Some children discussed 'digital' spaces in detail; boys were especially keen to describe things they enjoyed about computer games. No girls mentioned computer games, but they did discuss using email to talk to friends. At the time of this research (2006–2010), it was surprising no one from the high-income schools mentioned Facebook, social media or even mobile phones. The fact so few children mentioned digital communication technology at the time of the study may reflect the comparatively high cost of this technology in New Zealand. Children used digital media, but it was not a dominant element in their public interactions. However, when I visited schools at the end of the study in 2011, the situation was very different. All schools mentioned that mobile phones were important in helping children and teachers manage in the earthquakes and aftershocks, and many children had access to Facebook.

A second distinctive type of community map were maps constructed by children living in rural communities; their community maps were distinguished by 'big' or expansive outdoor play. Unlike Louv's observations of rural children in North America (who he argues are increasingly playing inside), these rural New Zealand children still played extensively in the outdoors.[43] Children in rural schools reported a vast array of informal outdoor activities and a wide independent

Figure 5.2 Detail of E-School children's community star map: 'Digital places'

Credit: Bronwyn Hayward.

roaming range. Compared to their urban peers, these rural children took part in fewer formal clubs but many participated in more sport. Rural children were the only groups to comment on the physical location in which their sport took place (carefully distinguishing, for example, between water sports or beach activities, and places where they went fishing, eeling, horse riding or competed in dog trials etc.). These children also commented in detail on the physical sites of their informal social interactions, distinguishing between activities with others at home, *ngāi mahi I te kainga* [things we do near home], or places where they undertook collaborative tasks with friends such as 'making big huts', making 'tracks going down to the creeks and into the bushes', 'eeling by myself and fishing with the *whānau* [family]', 'jumping off the wharf', going on 'big walks together', helping dad on the farm, and looking after 'our horses and dogs'.

A third distinctive community map was developed by children in the low- to middle-income urban schools (the Small World School and the Community-*Kura* Schools). The community maps made by these children were comparatively thick and dense networks of social interaction. These children listed a huge range of formal and informal clubs and activities. These children spoke about interacting regularly with parents, siblings, cousins, friends, the parents of friends, grandparents, and older and younger associates they knew well in a neighbourhood that defined their primary ecological world. The New Zealand family is changing,

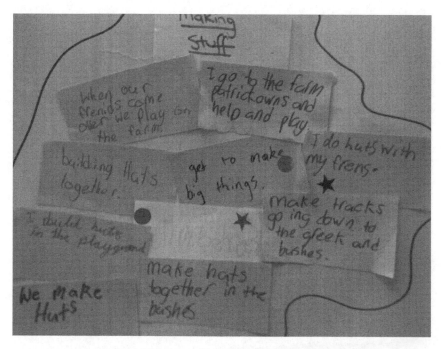

Figure 5.3 Detail of Farm-Sea School children's community star map: 'Making stuff'
Credit: Bronwyn Hayward.

with higher rates of single parent, female-headed households, especially for Māori.[44] However, extended family, tribal and community networks of friends also matter for many children. For example, one child commenting on his *whānau* or extended family experience simply said: 'It's really good because you get to see what you haven't seen before.' This thick network of family and friends differs significantly from David Willet's portrait of the 'dominant' Anglo-American family structure, which he characterises as distinctively nuclear, 'tall and thin' as grandparents live to older ages with fewer grandchildren, in a family often geographically separated by significant distances.[45]

There was one important exception in the dense community maps of low- to middle-income urban schools. For some new migrant children, their family was portrayed as a thin, fragile thread stretched between New Zealand, where they currently live with their mother, and another country, often in Asia, where their father works: 'My dad's never been here', 'I live with my mum and my dad lives with his girlfriend in Singapore'. While some new migrant children spoke confidently of a citizenship which crossed national borders facilitated by travel and electronic communication: 'I'm Asian!', 'I found it really easy to make new friends here'; others were less confident. A discussion with a Principal about this prompted the observation that children who attended his school as fee paying students with one parent were most likely to feel isolated:

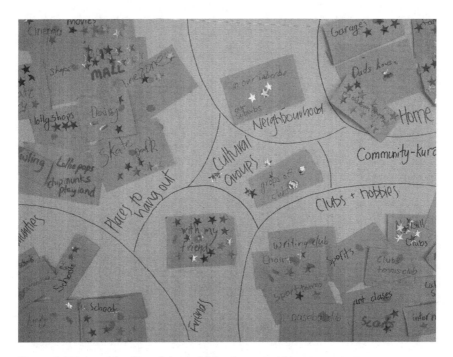

Figure 5.4 Community-*Kura* School children's community star map

Credit: Bronwyn Hayward.

> Mum often walks the child to school and as a little family, well, they don't
> seem to have quite that same, commitment – they are just here to learn
> English so we have to work quite hard to connect them [both mum and
> child] into the community, you know, shared meals, sports and the garden.
> Having a few dads coaching sport helps as often the child will have no dad
> living here.

Overall, however, the children at low- to middle-income schools also recorded
the widest range of unsupervised urban roaming spaces and 'hang out' places
(school playgrounds, malls, dairies, leisure centres, parks, the local pool and
libraries) where they met friends, or took part in activities with adults and siblings. This finding supports independent research undertaken by Claire Freeman
which noted that children in lower-income communities in another New Zealand
city, Dunedin, had the widest independent urban play range.[46]

In overview, the community mapping exercise suggests these young citizens
of Christchurch use public places in differing ways and, as a result, have fewer
opportunities to encounter each other than we might expect. Many children
attending schools in high-income communities had very structured afterschool
experiences with significant access to digital media and fewer opportunities

for informal street play. The physical environments they mentioned included shopping malls, home based play, biking to school and the local dairy. In contrast, none of the children from the smallest (and poorest) rural school mentioned the internet, but all rural children valued a range of informal play activities undertaken with a few other friends in 'big' or 'wide' outdoor spaces. Children in the middle-income bilingual Community-*Kura* School and the Small World School reported roaming more widely in urban play and the thickest webs of social interaction.

Pressures on children's public places

Many of the varied public places and the activities which mattered to children were also the subject of a variety of pressures. In the first instance, the high-decile children reported enjoying their structured clubs and activities, but at least one child within each of these focus groups mentioned that time pressure and having to go in transport by car prevented them from playing informally with their friends or 'mucking around'. Three children went further and described this problem as feeling 'stressed'. They said that they liked their home environment because they were able to 'just relax'. The idea of needing to relax was not mentioned by any other children.

The rural children attending the Tree School were very concerned about urban development, and being banned from climbing tall trees (see Chapter 6). These children were wrestling with the conflicts of development; on the one hand they did not want to lose their quiet, roaming lifestyle, but they also wanted more children to play with:

LEWIN: Everyone at the school sort of lives around here like, Diddy, you used to live down the road, and Ben ...

SEZ: Lots of people live around here.

HAMISH: Our teacher lives down there ... N is moving down our road. W lives on [that] road. G lives down there. Heaps of people.

LEWIN: I think that our country should stop letting other people in ... because the [main road] which is down there, is quite a busy road and they are thinking of making that into a highway.

SEZ: Yeah it's a country ...

HAMISH: Yeah it's a country ... it's a flat ground country, other than the hills and that. And its normally like real quiet. Me and my brother go on road rides together at 6 o'clock and it's really quiet. If they make a highway me and my brother won't be allowed out because there will be so many trucks coming down there.

EMILY: People won't be able to bike to school and stuff. I just live down that road... if that's a highway people will come this way.
        [group begin talking over the top of each other, about where they live, and the problem of roads]

LEWIN: And then school will be real loud ...

HAMISH: The school will be overloaded if they make that highway. And I think it's a risk that our community is going to get too big … I just think they're making schools too big and they're making the communities too big. And it's quite nice knowing everyone but that can get annoying just having such little people to know and that …

EMILY: You have to be friends with everyone else.

(Tree School)

These children were wrestling with their concern about the pressure of urban expansion and migration on their public space. The comment 'I think the country should stop letting people in' was typical of concerns expressed by all the children from the Tree School who expressed anxiety about immigration from China.[47] In reality, however, this community school roll remained entirely European/*Pākehā*. The children at the Tree School also discussed the way they felt adult awareness of risk limited their outdoor play:

INTERVIEWER: So do you guys reckon that as students you should have more of a say in those sorts of matters [like climbing trees]?

HAMFISH: I think you should just get permission to climb trees and if you fall off then it's your fault.

SEZ: Yeah you should like get permission from your parents or something. And if you get permission from your parents then it's not the principal's fault so they don't have to worry.

INTERVIEWER: [clarifying] If you fall off a tree then it might be considered their fault?

HAMFISH: I guess being a principal is probably harder than it sounds.

(Tree School)

When she remarks that being a principal is probably harder than it sounds, Hamfish has a point. I presented this case study of tree climbing to a group of teachers in England. I indicated some of the trees these children enjoyed climbing were extremely tall and asked them how they would handle the question of risk or respond to a children's protest about wanting to continue climbing trees. There was a silence. Then one teacher said politely: 'for a start children don't climb trees at my school so this is just something that would never arise'. In New Zealand, children are two times more likely to die in accidents than they are in the United Kingdom, presenting a real dilemma for teachers who value wild, outdoor informal play experiences but also wish to keep children safe.[48]

Children at the lower-income Small World school were also concerned about the physical deterioration of their public spaces. They were particularly frustrated there was not enough money to enable improvements to be made in their school playground. These children from this low-income urban school were very aware that the quality of their play environment was significantly lower than other neighbourhoods. They complained about vandalism, graffiti and having fewer quality play resources than other schools: 'There is actually one thing that we don't have that other schools do have … two [basketball] hoops! We only have one! Yeah someone broke off the other one' (see Chapter 6).[49] Similarly, many children at the Community-*Kura* School reported participating in protests to keep their highly-valued local pool open. Nearly all children were infuriated that this space was being closed by the local council.

Of most concern was that children at the Tree School and the Community-*Kura* School also reported they felt their freedom to enjoy public space was curbed by instances of school bullying, fear of domestic violence and adult alcoholism. In this extract, children at the Tree School describe an annual university student binge drinking event euphemistically known as a 'garden party':

GOODY GOODY GUM DROPS: [I'd like to have a say about] Garden parties [university student drinking events], I think they should go because whenever the Garden Party's on I have to stay home because there are drunk people all over. We can't go anywhere because there are like drunk people and bottles and stuff. So I think they should higher [raise] the age [for drinking] and don't get too drunk or anything. Because if you do that you're going to do something really silly and you're going to have to go do community services or something.

BUBBLE O' BILL: Police should keep a closer eye on parties, because a lot of people that we know have been, people get hurt and killed at them.

(Tree School)

Bubble O' Bill and Goody Goody Gum Drops raise an important issue for rural communities where drinking and driving is one of the leading causes of death for teenage males.[50] The related concern is Goody Goody Gum Drops' suggestion that abuse of alcohol by others restricts children's freedom to enjoy local public space. In New Zealand, 30 per cent of children regularly report feeling unwelcome in their neighbourhood.[51] Richard Louv has expressed concern that children are experiencing psychological and physical suffering as nature becomes something they are learning to 'watch, consume, wear' or 'ignore' rather than experience first-hand.[52] However, seen in the light of Michael Sandel's argument that we need public space as sites to cultivate shared citizenship, loss of access to wilderness is also part of a wider restriction on children's democratic rights to freedom of assembly, in ways that reduce opportunities for young citizens to develop virtues of collective action and develop a sense of mutual affiliation.[53] In closing, the discussion turns to ask how might a more politicised approach help us to think differently about children's environmental education?[54]

Rethinking environmental education: are rainforests even relevant?

Tania Schusler and colleagues argue that environmental education in English-speaking countries is dominated by a moralistic and instrumental view of teaching which aims to 'modify learners' lifestyle behaviours', for example, encouraging children to recycle and reduce their energy consumption rather than think critically about political power, or ask questions like who has what and why.[55] While recycling might be a good idea, the authors complain this instrumental view of learning as behaviour change doesn't necessarily help children to address the 'social determinants of environmental problems'. They call for more environmental education within a 'democratic paradigm' to help children understand and learn the skills of intentional, collaborative and strategic public action.[56] Other writers like Barratt and Barratt-Hacking, Chawla and Cushing, Orr, Kahn, Uzzell and Rathzell, Jensen and Schnack, Tseveren, and Panayotatos and Scott similarly argue that children need support to learn to think both critically and politically about their situation, identifying how power is exercised in decision making and learning to practice and implement strategic actions to affect change in their communities.[57]

David Sobel expresses some concern, however, that we should be very cautious to avoid presenting children with overwhelming issues too early. He argues that if children are confronted with big issues such as loss of rainforests, which they have no ability to affect in a meaningful way, it will only serve to heighten fear and disconnection from nature, which he calls ecophobia: 'a fear of ecological problems and the natural world'.[58] Sobel argues:

> Fear of oil spills, rainforest destruction, whale hunting, acid rain, the ozone hole and Lyme disease. Fear of just being outside. If we prematurely ask children to deal with problems beyond their understanding and control, prematurely recruit them to solve the mammoth problems of an adult world, then I think we cut them off from the possible sources of their strength. I propose there are healthy ways to foster environmentally aware, empowered students. We can cure the malaise of ecophobia with ecophilia – supporting children's biological tendency to bond with the natural world.[59]

Sobel recommends leaving the study of rainforests and similar tough issues to the middle school years. His mantra is 'no tragedies before fourth grade', where tragedies are defined as complex problems beyond the geographical and conceptual scope of the child. Sobel suggests that children's ethical concern and ecological appreciation increases after age 12 as they begin to conceive of an abstract universe of relations.[60] Sobel justifiably cautions us that children can feel disempowered and overwhelmed if difficult issues are thrust upon them without support and skills of ethical and moral reasoning.

We can take Sobel's concerns on board while recognising the reality too that many children already face very difficult or sad issues. The ecological world of too many children in New Zealand includes domestic violence, poor living conditions and family debt.[61] These problems are compounded by exposure to environmental risks (including climate-change-related flooding, coastal erosion or earthquakes in the case of Christchurch children).[62] In these situations, as child psychologist Gill Valentine reminds us, the contextual and relational aspects of children's competence also matters. Valentine argues children learn to think about difficult issues when supported by adults and experienced peers as mentors.[63] When children are helped to address difficult issues in the context of intergenerational learning, they are better placed to face very big or very sad issues that worry them. Valentine's suggestion resonates with observations by Roger Hart that children benefit from the support of adults and older peers to learn to deal effectively with their most difficult problems.[64]

As institutions, schools are also supported to become more effective sites of environmental learning when they have close relationships with their local communities.[65] Schools which engage in community projects to foster common goods contribute in a wider way to recreating community as 'the glue and the goal of democratic life'.[66] Community learning needs vary widely. Kate Burningham and Dianna Thrush's thoughtful report *Rainforests are a long way from here* alerts us to the possibility that young citizens growing up in communities of multiple deprivation may be alienated, if learning activities are framed in ways that they do not see as being relevant to their lives.[67] The comment 'rain forests are a long way from here', made by a respondent in their research, highlights the gulf between the priorities of international environmental campaigns and some low-income urban communities. In low-income communities, Burningham and Thrush argue, small local concerns, such as dog fouling and litter, matter a great deal, and the success in tackling these issues can have a big impact. By comparison, bigger issues like loss of rainforests are less relevant. Burningham and Thrush also observed that in poor urban communities in the United Kingdom, local environmental concerns were often inextricably tied up with wider social and economic goals. Similarly, in the United States, Dana Lanza argues that the questions of environmental justice which concern children in low-income communities are not often easily included in the mainstream environmental debates about access to wilderness. She worked with children growing up in a neighbourhood near a former military ship yard and noted that these children were struggling to find safe, uncontaminated play spaces.[68]

In a world of increasing mobility and growing differences of wealth, having access to a quality local environment matters. Children everywhere need informal opportunities to explore outdoor places. These opportunities support personal development, creative problem-solving skills, and help children to make first hand connections and observations about environmental issues.[69] As Robyn Eckersley argues, like Ratty in the riverbank in the *Wind in the Willows*, we all need local places with which we identify before we can build empathy with the places of others.[70] For many children, particularly children in indigenous communities, access to valued local places is often fundamental to cultural identity.[71] For many Māori children we interviewed, having access to cultural places was an essential part of being Māori: 'I belong to [mountain]', 'I belong to [river or region]', 'I belong to my *iwi'* [tribe]'. Feeling a strong affinity for a tribal environment was vital to the citizenship of these children. Viewed in this context, it is important we think about the political, social and cultural context of environmental education and the needs of children within their valued local environments.[72]

Beyond the opportunity to develop affinity for a local place, formal environmental education (as substantive knowledge learning) helps young citizens understand the changes going on around them.[73] In the wake of the earthquakes one teacher observed that, while some children wanted reassurance and to forget about the aftershocks, another child needed to know the exact magnitude of every one as a way of coping. A common complaint among the young and adults alike in the first months after the quake was the fear that 'I can't trust the ground I walk on'; in this situation more information gives some sense of control.

Substantive knowledge is reinforced when it is based on informal, first-hand experience of personal observation. From Rousseau's *Emile*, to the child development research of Piaget, or Dewey's study of children's citizenship, many have argued that children learn best when their learning is supported by observations and experiences of their material world, structured learning objectives, and culturally nuanced, individualised support and feedback.[74] Environmental educator William Scott reminds us that science literacy matters, but, to be really effective, education must keep children's learning needs in the central spotlight.[75] Sadly, however, children's learning needs are struggling to retain centre stage in many English speaking neoliberal democracies, as national education policies and curricula are restructured to emphasise the teaching (and testing) of universal skills for a global economy. The risk in this case is that children are provided with fewer opportunities to think creatively, to experiment, to reflect, or to connect with other people in local environments about issues that interest or concern them.[76] Ken Robinson describes the problem in the following way:

> ... policy makers typically narrow the curriculum to emphasize a small group of subjects, tie schools up in a culture of standardized testing and limit the discretion of educators to make professional judgments about what and how to teach ... politicians of all persuasions are curiously united in this respect ... it is rare to hear politicians of any party raise questions about the absolute importance of academic standards or standardized systems of education.[77]

Given the pressure on schools to teach children universal skills for a global market economy, the prospects look bleak for developing a new ecological agenda which nurtures creative and critical thinking in environmental education. In the United Kingdom, for example, the Minister of Education has recently called for a move away from teaching about the 'politics' of climate change to re-emphasise the scientific 'facts', arguing the curriculum is growing too 'crowded' and that teaching climate debates should be at the discretion of teachers.[78] In the New Zealand setting, despite an independent network of Enviroschools, the Ministry of Education has focused the national secondary school curricula on 'developing knowledge, understanding, and skills ... to compete successfully in the modern, ever changing world'.[79] In the United States, 'environmental educators face strong pressures not to advocate any political position'.[80] In this context, it will be increasingly difficult for schools to teach a politicised view of environmental education that encourages children to challenge dominant views of the state and economy. Teachers will need strong support from colleagues, professional development and international networks to foster best practice.[81]

Yet, without political awareness, environmental education risks becoming nothing more than a new expression of 'environmentality'.[82] Rather than learning to think critically – let alone confront – illegitimate exercises of political power that fuels unsustainable development, young citizens are encouraged to become willing volunteers and obedient recyclers. At the same time, unless citizens understand environmental processes, citizenship education will continue to be little more than a set of facts about voting and civic leadership, in which 'the environment' is portrayed as just one of a number of competing concerns communities need to contend with, rather than an issue integral to our common security and well-being.

However, there are exciting creative experiments which help us rethink environmental and citizenship learning to challenge dominant or received views. Eizenberg, for example, describes community gardens as possible sites of 'contesting space'.[83] Like Carlsson and Jensen, and Uzzell, Eizenberg argues that community gardens can become sites to connect schools with their wider communities in new ways.[84] Working to set up and maintain community gardens can teach children wider skills about effecting political change and addressing local food insecurity and poverty.[85] For many schools, a local garden which involves neighbours as well as school children can be the first practical step towards community activism for wider political change.[86] As we observed in Chapter 4, when children collaborate with other citizens of all ages, they learn valuable democratic skills of cooperation, community planning and collective resistance to illegitimate decision making.[87] This observation echoes Paulo Freire's vision of critical pedagogy in which children learn to understand their individual problems in collaboration with others: an important a step towards learning to think critically about transboundary environmental challenges.[88]

In summary, we need to rethink environment education for a new generation, and to pay closer attention to the concerns of children. As English-speaking democracies age, the problems of an 'adult attention deficit disorder' will become worse. To ensure that environmental education remains relevant to children's needs, we need to listen more carefully to the issues which trouble children and consider new forms of injustice across generations, communities and urban spaces.

Notes

1 Elliott and Urry 2010.
2 Richard Louv cites research suggesting there has been a decline of 50 per cent in the proportion of North American children aged nine to twelve who spend time in outdoor activities such as beach play, hiking, fishing and gardening (Hofferth cited in Louv

2005, p34). Louv also argues that a child's day has changed, resulting in less discretionary leisure time and increasing confinement as children play in smaller areas (Louv 2005, pp34–5). He suggests one of the key drivers for this in the United States has been housing subdivision (Louv 2005, p29). Most dramatically Play England estimates that in London each child has access to an area no bigger than a kitchen table as outdoor play space that they can call their own (Voce 2009). See also Veitch *et al.* 2006.

3 Freeman and Tranter 2011; Gleeson and Sipe 2006; Bauman 2011.
4 Malone 2007; Cadzow 2004.
5 Glesson and Sipe 2006, p1; see also Louv 2005.
6 Glesson and Sipe 2006; Hart 1997, pp65–7; Green and Hayward forthcoming.
7 See Layard and Dunn 2009, pp1–9; Wilkinson and Pickett 2009, pp23–4. For a discussion of the pressure of the baby-boom generation, see Willetts 2010. For a review of the essential capabilities that children and adults need to live a 'dignified' and 'flourishing' life, see Nussbaum 2011.
8 Hansen 2009, pp271–7.
9 Leichenko and O'Brien 2008, pp 9–12.
10 Lanza 2005.
11 Burningham and Thrush 2001; Cambridge Primary Review 2009; Chawla 1992; Lanza 2005; Valentine 2004.
12 Plan International 2011.
13 Harper *et al.* 2009.
14 Katz 2004.
15 Jackson 2011; Spoonley *et al.* 2004.
16 Augé 1995, p5.
17 Flanagan 2008a.
18 Bauman 2003.
19 For discussion of hyper-consumption and children, see Schor 2004; Mayo and Nairn 2009; Kasser *et al.* 2010.
20 Domjen 2011.
21 Sandel 2009.
22 Ibid., p26.
23 Ibid., pp266–7.
24 Ibid., p266.
25 Freeman and Tranter 2011, pp150–1.
26 Ibid., see pp29–30 for a comparative discussion of children's access to outdoor play space. The authors suggest children from lower socioeconomic communities have comparatively wide-roaming range compared to children in higher income communities.
27 Oliver *et al.* 2011; Freeman and Quigg 2009; Voce 2009; Murtagh *et al.* 2011; Louv 2005.
28 Louv 2005; Voce 2009.
29 Tranter and Pawson 2001; Kearns *et al.* 2003; Mitchell *et al.* 2007.
30 Oliver *et al.* 2011, pp1–12; Valentine 2004; Green and Hayward forthcoming.
31 Valentine 1996, 2004.
32 Katz. 2004, p243.
33 Neil Smith 1996, p211, cited in Katz 2004, p243.
34 Hayes 2011; Bauman 2011.
35 Miller 2011.
36 Hayward 2010a; Green and Hayward forthcoming.
37 Council of Europe 2010; Green and Hayward forthcoming.

38 Bauman 2011; Green and Hayward forthcoming.
39 I was struck by the difference between this perception of home as a place of social interaction for these New Zealand children and a study completed with colleagues from Resolve at the same time of the home activities of young British adults. The latter study which revealed a significant number of young adults in the sample reported feeling isolated and lonely in their living arrangements: see Hayward *et al.* 2011b.
40 Rural children reported some pre-planning due to travel distances involved.
41 SPARC 2001. This ten year benchmark study was repeated in 2011, showing participation in sport declines in teenage years.
42 Pettman 2005, p52.
43 Louv 2005, pp 34–5.
44 Families Commission 2008.
45 Willetts 2010, pp10–23.
46 Freeman 2010.
47 Despite low-level fear about immigration from China, in reality the Tree School roll has remained entirely European/*Pākehā*: see Chapters 6 and 7.
48 Alatini 2009.
49 This finding differs from reports by Freeman (2010) and Freeman and Tranter (2011) which noted that children in low income Dunedin communities were less aware of the quality of their environment.
50 New Zealand Transport Agency 2011.
51 Ministry of Youth Development 2011.
52 Louv 2005, p2.
53 Green and Hayward forthcoming.
54 Saylan and Blumstein 2011 also call for rethinking environmental education from a political perspective: see especially pp72–94.
55 Schusler *et al.* 2009, p111.
56 Ibid.
57 Barrett and Barrett-Hacking 2011; Chawla and Cushing 2007; Hart 1997, pp91–107; Hart 2008; Jensen and Schnack 2006; Orr 2011; Rathzel and Uzzell 2009; Stone and Barlow 2005; Tsevreni and Panayotatos 2011; Kahn 2010; Scott 2011; David 2007.
58 Sobel 1996, p5.
59 Sobel 1996, p6.
60 Ibid., p28.
61 CPAG 2011.
62 Walker *et al.* 2010.
63 Valentine 2004, p105.
64 Hart 1997, p65.
65 Hart 1997; Honig 2009.
66 Honig 2009, p44.
67 Burningham and Thrush 2001.
68 Lanza 2005.
69 Barrett and Barrett-Hacking 2011.
70 Eckersley 2006.
71 Adger *et al.* 2011.
72 Scott 2011; Rathzel and Uzzell 2009.
73 Bishop and Scott 1998.
74 Hattie 2009, pp20–6.
75 Scott 2011.

76 Louv 2005; Cambridge Primary Review 2009.
77 Robinson 2001, p15.
78 Paige 2011.
79 Williams forthcoming.
80 Chawla and Cushing 2007, p448.
81 OECD 2009.
82 Barry 2005.
83 Eizenberg 2004.
84 Carlsson and Jensen 2006; Uzzell 1999.
85 McKay 2011.
86 Schusler 2011, p112.
87 Barratt-Hacking *et al.* 2007.
88 Freire 1985, p194.

6   Embedded justice

Learning ecological responsibility

'In the little world in which children have their existence', says Pip in Charles Dickens' *Great Expectations*, 'there is nothing so finely perceived and felt as injustice'.

(Sen 2009, pvii)

Amartya Sen opened his landmark discussion of justice by reflecting on the intense way children think about fairness. Citing Dickens, Sen argued that many adult citizens can vividly recall childhood experiences of injustice. I was reminded of the intensity of children's sense of justice and injustice when confronted recently by our own daughter's strong reaction to the news that protestors might be cleared from an Occupy site in the United States by the use of force:

> Water cannons?! Mum, mum did you hear that? They just said on the news that they might use water cannons on those student protestors, I can't believe that! That's just like what they did in the US civil rights movement. That's terrible!

Through Rachel's outrage, we've been learning about justice and the civil rights movement with fresh eyes. The efforts of teachers at her high school have raised her sights and those of her classmates above their daily struggle with earthquake aftershocks in Christchurch, to feel empathy and connection with Black-American students protesting in another country at another time. In this process, these teachers have helped awaken what John Barry described as a youthful 'critical awareness' of the political, economic, social and cultural drivers of injustice.[1]

Just citizens are made, not born. Citizen capabilities theorist Martha Nussbaum[2] asks how we can support students to become 'responsible democratic citizens who might think and choose well about a wide range of issues of worldwide significance?'[3] In this chapter, I extend Nussbaum's question further in the context of ecological citizenship to ask: How can we support the capability of young citizens to reason about justice in their local communities, and to think more widely about their responsibilities to others (humans and non-human) in a common world? In the discussion that follows I define embedded ecological justice and review the way children talked about distributive justice (the fair distribution of good and bad things), procedural justice (inclusive and accountable decision making) and political responsibility (our obligations to put things right) in this study. In discussion, I review the ways children learn about justice from the perspective of child development theory. In conclusion, I argue that New Zealand children are helped to think about ecological justice in schools and communities where the substantive content, school culture and wider institutional arrangements of the child's school, and the community practice just reasoning.

Embedded ecological justice: what is it and why does it matter?

'Embedded justice' refers to our everyday reasoning and actions that we take to enhance equality and fairness. Sen speaks of practical reasoning as 'ways of judging how to reduce injustice and advance justice'.[4] In a complex world of competing views and values, citizens need to be able to think through a situation carefully to determine what should be done. This is a different view of justice from one that assumes there is a perfect or 'a priori' universal principle which we should use to guide our actions. Sen's view is an Aristotelian-inspired idea of justice, in which well-being or 'eudaimonia' is achieved, when citizens are helped to reason to the best of their ability.[5] Our experiences of embedded injustice also add depth, intensity, or what Sandel describes as 'grist', to our ability to reason about justice.[6]

In determining what to do, we may be informed by prior agreements, constitutions and rules, for example, agreements that protect the rights of minorities and vulnerable communities. Embedded justice also requires citizens to actively *practice* just decision making by participating in, reaffirming, interpreting, applying and extending decisions about fairness and equity in daily life. To act with practical justice or 'phronesis' is to consider what we can and should do in real-world situations to remove injustice.[7] As educator Emma Worley reminds us, if young citizens are to act with practical reasoning, they will need a variety of skills and supports to learn to think beyond their 'immediate wants' to consider the needs of other people and the non-human world.[8]

The idea of embedded justice is central to ecological citizenship. Dobson notes that environmental space and access to resources is currently very unevenly shared out. In this context we are required to consider how resources are distributed and, where appropriate, to work towards the redistribution of environmental space, reducing the size of our environmental footprint.[9] Rethinking how we distribute resources also requires us to consider the processes we use to make our decisions. Who has a voice in decision making? Should we consider the rights of nature? If so, how? If our decisions have implications for distant communities or future generations, what are our responsibilities to those communities?

These latter questions about responsibilities for justice are central to the vision of ecological citizenship.[10] Dobson argues that a virtuous ecological citizen is internally motivated to live sustainably because of her concern for justice. An ecological citizen doesn't take action to reduce her carbon footprint simply out of pity for Pacific people who will suffer in a changing climate, or because she expects others to do the same. A good ecological citizen is motivated to do the right thing because she acknowledges she occupies ecological space in a way that compromises or forecloses the ability of others or future generations to 'pursue options that are important to them'.[11] She may be a compassionate, empathetic and concerned person, but as an ecological citizen she acts out of a sense of obligation to others and takes responsibility to address the harm she has caused.[12]

The idea of embedded ecological justice is demanding as it does not blame others nor suggest we take action because of a prior agreement or rule. Instead, citizens are required to think about how their obligations and concerns for justice require them to act in their everyday life. The idea of justice as responsibility is developed further by Iris Young in her posthumously-published work *Responsibility for Justice*.[13] Young argues that all agents (not only individual citizens, but communities, companies, boards of directors, shareholders and nation states) 'who contribute to the structural processes that produce injustice share a political responsibility for remedying that injustice'.[14] Like Dobson, Young's idea of responsibility does not end at a national border. For example, as consumers of products, we have an obligation to the workers who produced those goods wherever they are located, to ensure they are treated with justice, and that materials for the product were sourced sustainably. Young acknowledges critics may balk at this expanded notion of justice: surely I paid for what I bought, isn't that enough? How can I reasonably be expected to do anything more? Young argues, however, that we can and should be criticised where we do not use our agency (our ability to think critically and act independently) to bring about justice. We should be held to account when we do not take enough action or take ineffective action. Moreover, Young argues we have 'an obligation to criticise others with whom we share this responsibility'.[15]

Many, but not all of the environmental challenges we face involve questions of justice. Sen argues a disastrous event, like a flood, famine or earthquake, may be a tragedy, but it is not an injustice unless something could have been done to have prevented it.[16] His comments underscore the reasons ecological citizens might be especially concerned by the arguments in *Storms of my Grandchildren* by climatologist James Hansen.[17] Hansen stresses that many things can and must be done if we want to prevent very severe storms from becoming normal events in the lives of our children and future generations.[18] In their writing, both Sen and Hansen remind us that embedded justice is both an intellectual and practical struggle for equitable and fair distribution of material resources, community voice and accountability in decision making. Ecological citizenship requires a deeper understanding of our obligations and political responsibilities to each other and the non-human world.

In summary, a just ecological citizen is one who thinks critically about their responsibilities and then takes action to address injustice. Given that citizens are located in a chain of interactions between people, their institutions or organisations and the non-human world, it is likely our most effective actions will be coordinated actions. Seen in this light, helping children think about embedded ecological justice is a challenging task. It involves supporting children to understand and reason about the fairness of the way benefits and dis-benefits are distributed. It also involves helping children to ask if the decision-making process was inclusive and accountable, and to understand the obligations that we have to put things right to the best of our capabilities.[19] There are wider questions for adults too, in particular: how can we support children to exercise their capability for just reasoning?

Rethinking ecological justice from a child's perspective

In a ground-breaking commentary on children, justice and the environment, Sharon Stephens expressed frustration that children's experiences and concerns about justice are too often rendered invisible in contemporary democracies, even by community movements that advocate environmental justice for marginalised people.[20] Given a growing recognition that children experience some of the most severe impacts of environmental degradation and social oppression, it is disappointing that several years later researchers are still complaining there is little research about how children experience justice and how teachers and schools can best support children's justice learning.[21]

Taking an embedded approach to ecological justice when working with children challenges our adult-centred priorities. If we take the ecology of a child's world seriously, we cannot draw hard and fast lines between the natural and the human world, nor between macro- and micro-scale events. For many young children, their everyday concerns about justice will be the 'little' and immediate questions of fairness that troubled Pip in *Great Expectations*, issues involving day-to-day interactions in playgrounds or with siblings, their concern for pets or the use of classroom resources. For other children, the issues of justice could be matters of life and death. In New Zealand, too many children struggle with unsafe or abusive family environments. Internationally, some children are confronted with conditions of work that amount to slavery, or with polluted play spaces and lack of access to education.[22] The effects of injustice which children experience at the micro level (their well-being or strain in their family) may be exacerbated by macro-level injustices, including a changing climate. Children can – and should – be encouraged to think about their concerns in wider ways.[23] However, the 'little' questions of justice that also trouble a child cannot be pushed to one side while we save the planet.[24]

In the New Zealand study, children spontaneously raised a range of questions about distributional justice, procedural justice and issues of responsibility. In the first instance, in 24 of 25 focus groups, children commented about issues of distributive justice, particularly the access to or loss of valued play spaces, including the closure of the neighbourhood swimming pool, the 'squeezing' of playgrounds and the potential of highway developments to limit their ability to bike and move around freely. Children in the lowest-decile city school were concerned with issues of vandalism and lack of government funding for their play environment and their learning. These latter children were also acutely aware that other schools were able to go on school trips, and felt that underfunding impacted negatively on their learning. In the smallest and poorest school, which was rural, children were aware their town was not as wealthy as other communities and debated the justice of fishing quotas, as the following conversation illustrates. Here the children discuss fishing and seafood harvesting rules in their tribal *rohe* [food gathering] area:

INTERVIEWER:	Is there any other issue you want to have a say on?
SNOOPP DOGG:	That you are allowed to take more than 10 *paua* [shell fish].
INTERVIEWER:	Yeah the quotas?
ARNOLD SWARTIZNIGGA:	Yip the quotas.
INTERVIEWER:	What do you think about the quotas?
BIG GUNZ:	That we shouldn't be allowed to take as much *kahawai* [fish] as we want.
SNOOPP DOGG:	Nah that's a good one!
BIG GUNZ:	Nah cause what if we eat it all, that's bad.
INTERVIEWER:	So they are there for a reason aye?
BIG GUNZ:	Yeah to keep us alive.
SNOOPP DOGG:	But there is thousands and thousands.
BEYONCÉ:	But there is thousands of marlins and you're not allowed to take more than 15.
SNOOPP DOGG:	But you can take 15 if you want 15 [giggles].
BIG GUNZ:	But then you get taken to jail from the MAF [ministry of fisheries].
SNOOPP DOGG:	You get a fine, and you get the stuff that you're using taken off you. Watch it on *Coast* [a television programme]. Watch man!

(Kura School)

In addition to these concerns, all the children at the Tree School and the Music School debated questions of procedural justice, expressing their concern with the way decisions were made about the ban on climbing trees at the Tree School, and the rule that prevented younger children reading books of their choosing in a school library at the Music School. In the following conversation, a child also lightly touches on an issue of domestic injustice:

INTERVIEWER:	Are there any other things you'd like to have a say on?
TAILS:	We should have a say in what books we're allowed to read, cos at our library there's stuff for like 11+, like the Princess Diaries and stuff. Everyone already reads them, and then they have them and you're not allowed to get them out if you're 10. And then all the other libraries have them so you can get them out whenever you want.

ROBIN: With books, talking about books, I can read books that are for 10
                  year olds but I'm not really allowed to read them. I can read
                  them, I'm fine reading them, but I'm not allowed to read them.
TAILS: People should be allowed to have a say in what they do at home.
                  I won't say who, but sometimes people aren't allowed to do
                  things, sometimes people aren't allowed to do anything.
                                                                  (Music School)

The question of justice at home was raised in the context of children discussing
being smacked (see Chapter 3). Children also talked about their sense of responsibility for human and animal rights, worrying about the conditions of labourers
in China or the rights of animals kept in cages. Children in all four of the highest
income school communities expressed personal responsibility for the environment, and a few children questioned 'Big factories ... the big, manufacturing
ones, that have the big chimney's and have the big clouds of smoke coming out
of them.' However, none of the children at the high-income schools commented
on the quality of their own local environment. In contrast, children at the two
lowest income schools debated inequality, were vividly aware their environment
was of poorer quality than that of other communities. The Small World School
talked about graffiti, litter and broken school play equipment. This was striking
given one of the most affluent schools in the study was only a few city blocks
away from the Small World School. Children in the lowest income rural school
valued their outdoor environment, but commented on their lack of opportunities
and community resources.

A challenge for those interested in promoting sustainability is to support young
citizens' ability to see and reason about embedded justice from the perspective of
other peoples with different experiences, and to encourage children to think about
justice as political responsibility rather than blame. The following discussion is
quoted at length as an example of the complex way some children thought about
climate change as questions of blame and distributional injustice, and the difficult
challenge facing children as they reason about justice.

INTERVIEWER: And what sort of impacts do those things [climate changes] have?
SID: Food, resources.
LEWIN: The fresh water will be running out.
SEZ: There will be a lot of wars over water ... and food and stuff. And
                  there wouldn't be much land.
HAMFISH: There will be heaps and heaps of people on one piece of land
                  because all the sea will rise up and there won't be much land.
LEWIN: We will have to build high rise apartments so that people can just
                  live.
LEWIN: And then with all the space that we have we will have to plant
                  food and stuff like that.
HAMFISH: There will be heaps and heaps of people that will be dying.
SEZ: Some people just think well hopefully it's not going to happen
                  when I'm still alive so I don't really care.

INTERVIEWER:	Who has to do something?
SID:	Us.
INTERVIEWER:	By us do you mean everyone on the planet?
SEZ:	We can't just do it as just like twenty people or something. It has to be everyone.
HAMFISH:	I blame the Chinese.
	[group laughs]
INTERVIEWER:	Is that just because they are polluting more than say we are?
HAMFISH:	Yeah. They pollute for almost 75 per cent of the world.
M:	So do America.
HAMFISH:	Yeah America does it as well.
M:	They have the advanced technology.
LEWIN:	I reckon that um like the bigger countries like China ... and the big businesses ...
SID:	... Countries that have more people in it. Have more ... they pollute more because they need to use more ...
INTERVIEWER:	Ok you've got New Zealand, a really small country but it might be polluting more than your average Chinese person, but China is just so large that it naturally pollutes more?
M:	Well I reckon it's everybody not just China and stuff ... you can't just pin it on them.
INTERVIEWER:	So you can't just blame one country or one group of people?
M:	Yeah ... you probably could if you biked everywhere and didn't use electronics or anything.
SEZ:	Like there will be like run out of CO_2, because the trees make CO_2.
HAMFISH:	I reckon what they should do is make a law, a law that says if you don't recycle and do all this stuff here you will get jail time and if you are really bad you might get the death penalty!

(Tree School)[25]

The varied issues of children's ecology broadly conceived by the children themselves remind us, as Dobson has commented, that the relationship between environmental and social justice is neither clear nor simple, and will require careful thought and debate on a case-by-case basis to guide our action in our most difficult environmental debates. Helping children to empathise with the plight of others and reason more widely about the significance of local events is an important step in building wider political understanding, effective action and resistance to illegitimate assertions of power. As Roger Hart argues: 'when children begin to observe their environment and to ask questions about why things are the way they are, they may be quickly elevated to a higher social and indeed political consciousness'.[26] How can we help children think more widely about justice in their everyday lives?

How children learn about justice: from Piaget to Vygotsky

Childhood experiences of justice and injustice are influenced by a range of factors including teaching intervention, community support and peer group modelling.

Many environmental writers, activists and educators have commented on the way that direct experiences of feelings of outrage or indignation contributed to their growing environmental awareness. On the basis of her research with environmental educators in minority communities, for example, Louise Chawla argues that there are: 'two distinct paths into environmentalism: a concern for the environment in and of itself, or a concern for social justice'.[27] In her interviews with activists, Chawla noted how many spoke of their 'anger when they discovered that their working class community was exploited by a polluting industry or their shock when they saw pictures of people in other countries who lived in conditions of abject poverty or famine'.[28] Chawla observed that: 'people often rooted both types of concern in childhood'. She quotes extensively from Roger Hart's reflections on his own childhood:

> I think I was about ten years old when I first became aware of social class differences and their implications. I had observed a team of painters daubing pastel colours on the council houses one street away from our house and I ran home excitedly to discuss with my family what colour we should choose for our house. I thought we would finally be able to change the grass green colour of our doors and windows to something distinctively of our own. My mum laughed. I stood in shock as she explained that we could have no choice in the matter. I vehemently argued that we could. I had seen the men using different coloured paint – all she needed to do was ask. I was wrong, and the next day I stood, hands in pockets and shoulders hunched, as I watched the men throw the assigned paint colour on our section of terrace housing. Perhaps it was that day that my class consciousness began. I remember my outrage in realizing that some people could choose to paint their house whatever colour they wished while others had no choice at all.[29]

Hart's refection's are similar to Simon Dalby, a Canadian professor of environmental sciences. He opened the Global Environment and Human Security conference in Oslo in 2009 with a similarly vivid description of his own memory as a young child looking forward to the return of the swallows. He was always impressed that these small birds flew all the way from Africa into his suburban backyard in Ireland, returning every year to nest in the eaves of a garden shed. One day he came home from school to discover the aging shed had been knocked down. That night, and for some time after as he tried to sleep, he could hear the swallows flying around and around his house, calling and looking for their nesting area. He wonders if his interest in the rights of non-human nature began from his feelings then of something akin to 'intense guilt'.[30]

Reflecting on justice as childhood outrage and intense responsibility reminds us that the embedded justice doesn't stop with thinking critically. These feelings motivate us to act, sometimes taking 'oppositional action' to rectify injustice.[31] Encouraging children to think critically and act justly, including perhaps engaging in civil resistance, is very challenging. It tests our assumptions about how children learn about justice, and what kinds of just actions are appropriate for children to think about, let alone undertake.[32] The most influential approaches to our understanding of how children learn to reason about morality and act with justice has been Piaget's 'stage theory of moral development'. Influenced by the philosophy of Rousseau, Piaget argued that children pass through stages of thinking about their world and how rules are made, beginning from about age five to about seven with a period described as 'moral realism' in which children often believe 'that rules are created by wise adults and therefore must be followed and cannot be changed'.[3] In this period children believe, Piaget argued, in 'immanent justice', that if a rule is broken it will always be punished.[34] A second stage begins about the years of eight to early adolescence, in which children demonstrate 'moral relativism', that is, they show 'understanding that rules are created by people to help them get along'.[35] The implicit biological determinism in Piaget's assumptions is tempered to some extent in that he acknowledges children develop advanced levels of reasoning 'through interaction with peers and observation'.[36]

Piaget's arguments have been challenged by a series of studies that suggest even very young children will question adult rules under some conditions, such as situations where there is greater family priority on democracy, or when a child feels deep injustice, for example, over disposal of a treasured possession.[37] Nevertheless, the idea that children's moral reason progresses through stages has been highly influential. Kohlberg in particular picked up and developed these ideas in his study of how young people learn to reason about complex dilemmas in which there is no easy or right answer. Kolhberg proposed three broad stages children must follow sequentially. These included a pre-conventional level (where reasoning is controlled by obedience to authority), a conventional level (in which moral decision making is based on social norms, including interpersonal expectations and relations) and post-conventional levels of moral reasoning (in which older children develop their own reasoning, based either on social contract principles of expectations and rights or on universal ethical principles).[38]

Like Piaget, Kohlberg's model has been criticised for ethnocentrism, and for celebrating individualistic and universal forms of reasoning associated with Kant and Rawls.[39] Critics argue the quest for objective principles of justice fails to recognise how children develop ethical codes of conduct or use reasoning based on religious principles of care, duty and collective responsibility.[40] Feminist theorists such as Gilligan, and cultural theorists like Turiel, remind us that children also learn justice through interaction with others, and may follow norms other than those set out by Kohlberg.[41] The capabilities philosophy of Martha Nussbaum suggest children's ability to reason about justice is enhanced under conditions of security, health and human well-being, and with skills to read and engage in public reasoning.[42] Nussbaum implies that learning about justice is not a linear process. A child develops her skills for justice with an imagination for empathy, accelerated by feeling loved, and having the opportunity to learn to put herself in another's shoes – both vital precursors for being able to reason about justice.[43]

In contrast to Piaget and Kohlberg's universalist approach to children's understanding of justice, Vygotsky argues that children learn to reason with environmental support including cultural interactions, social observation and discussion with adults and efficacious peers.[44] Vygotsky's argument that children learn about justice through interaction with others underscores the importance of adult intervention to support children as they learn to think about and challenge injustice or the illegitimate assertion of power in local communities. Economist Amartya Sen takes up the idea of adult responsibility for justice. He suggests sustainable justice requires adults to consider future generations, and to make decisions on the basis of whether our choices will enable future generations to have the same freedom – and capability to use and safeguard that freedom – as current generations do. He suggests that, with support to nurture their capacity for just reasoning, citizens can come to understand that to pursue what they value they must also care for non-human nature and future environments.[45] Sen's vision, like Vygotsky, is of a practical, wise citizen supported by their community to exercise their capability to reason fairly about difficult choices they face.[46]

Vygotsky uses the term 'scaffolding' to describe the support and practice young citizens need as they begin to tackle more complex problems.[47] If children are left to their own devices, it is unlikely that they will develop the ability to connect and empathise with others. Vygotksy's perspective suggests that in situations where children are which simply presented with a range of options and allowed to debate these for themselves, it is doubtful they will learn democratic values of tolerance and respect, or engage in the passionate debate needed for just ecological reasoning. Liberation educators Horton and Friere similarly argue, for example, that in an unjust world, when teachers teach with apparent 'neutrality', they perpetuate the injustice of dominant forces.[48] They agree that children benefit from opportunities to engage in political life, practicing moral reasoning and democratic action, with guidance and mentoring. This argument implicitly suggests a more demanding role for schools in teaching justice, but in reality what role can schools play in developing visions of justice for a fairer, common world?

Embedded justice: the role of the democratic community school

Classrooms are political places, teeming with issues of injustice. Schools play a role at three levels in teaching justice: through the substantive content of lessons; in the wider school culture; and through the institutional structure and accountability of the school in its community.

Substantive justice

In the first instance, with regard to the substantive content of what children learn about justice, philosopher James Bohman rightly cautions us to be vigilant and sensitive to the way children engaged in moral debates can be overwhelmed or dominated by adults or authority figures.[49] There are many thoughtful discussions about the creative ways that children can practice moral reasoning, from role plays to writing reflections, from media interviews to field work.[50] As Vare and Scott note, there is a significant difference between learning substantive content, and learning to think critically about social injustice, or ways of living morally in an uncertain future.[51] The latter types of environmental learning are enhanced if children understand the natural world and its processes. What children are learning *matters*. If children are taught simply to recycle and to become obedient volunteers or careful scientists, we risk undermining the ability of young citizens to see and challenge the underlying injustice of environmental degradation, or to connect in empathy with struggles of other groups against oppression and poverty.

As all teachers know, what teachers think they are teaching is often not what children are learning.[52] While many schools argue they teach civic virtue, the reality for teachers is that they may find themselves backing away from controversial moral debate. There are many reasons for this, not the least that teachers often feel very vulnerable teaching questions of justice and injustice.[53] Schools are busy places, and learning about justice takes time. It is often easier to target the behaviour of students through creating environments in which children are nudged to do the 'right thing', or encourage children to parrot 'received rules' and norms rather than explicitly learning skills of reasoning, thinking and free deciding through public debate as citizens.[54] Seen in this light, some critics argue that the substantive content of many environmental education programmes is simply a form of green governmentality, or 'environmentality' in which children are encouraged to internalise a set of rules of behaviour that justify minimal state intervention, but do not learn to think about the moral reasons for acting in any particular way.[55]

Joel Westheimer's thought-provoking critique of citizenship education in North America could just as easily apply to many examples of environmental education. Westheimer interviewed and observed children learning to think about justice with regard to food banks: 'If participatory citizens organise the food drive, and personally responsible citizens donate the food, the social justice orientated citizen asks why people are hungry then act on what they discover.' Yet, as Westheimer also notes:

> Currently the vast majority of school programmes that take the time to teach citizenship are the kinds that emphasize either good character (including the importance of volunteering and helping those in need) or technical knowledge of legislatures and how government works. Far less common are schools that teach students to think about root causes of injustice or challenge existing social, economic and political norms as a means of strengthening democracy.[56]

Education aimed at fostering values of voluntarism, charity and obedience is not the kind of substantive justice education required for a strong, ecological democracy. To sustain such a democracy, each new generation needs opportunities to learn to think critically and independently and to grapple with everyday 'social policy decisions'.[57] Supportive adult intervention can create safe space and new opportunities for children to think critically and to challenge 'dominant narratives' about what is just and right (see discussion in Chapter 7).[58]

Unfortunately, however, too few young citizens have opportunities to debate justice in the classroom, as a curious political silence descends in a curriculum focused on imparting universal skills to meet the needs of employment for global markets rather than learning to reason justly in local communities. Children are readily taught the names of plants and the lifecycle of various plants and animals, but there is a reticence in many classrooms to debate questions about who benefits from the patents over indigenous plants or other environmental resources and why. Yet effective teachers model moral reasoning.[59] Ecological citizenship with its robust and demanding view of justice requires teaching support to help children to learn to reason about what is the right thing to do, rather than simply weigh up the costs and benefits of a decision in a market. It is also a view of education which echoes the vision of citizen schools, advocated by Miles Horton and Paulo Friere, where teachers demonstrate political clarity. This does not mean every lesson is a lesson in justice. As Horton comments, a biology teacher 'still has to teach biology'.[60] Instead, as Horton and Friere argue, students may benefit from opportunities to hear their teacher 'express his or her choice'.[61] In an unjust world, supporting children to make judgments about doing the right thing also requires teachers and other adults to help children see views from the margin, and to challenge existing balances of power in the classroom and wider community.[62]

Public school cultures and institutional practices for justice

Beyond the substantive content of lessons, schools can help – or hinder – children's understanding of justice as a result of the way children experience school culture and institutional practices. In Kohlberg's work on moral reasoning, he called for 'just community schools', in which classrooms are participatory and collective in atmosphere, and where the staff is supported to model moral reasoning and inclusion in their actions.[63] It is disappointing, but understandable, when classroom justice debates are muted. Instead of challenging local businesses on their environmental and social track record, Khan argues, a local business is all too often presented as a necessary and legitimate part of contemporary society,[64] and, in New Zealand's case, quite possibly a sponsor of the school. The possibility that business might force out or marginalise the voice of other citizens is less frequently debated. Children are also encouraged to understand what justice means when they feel the culture of the school and classroom gives them a voice. This was touched upon by a student who complained sometimes if a student is 'naughty' the teachers react 'then they can just be real annoying to you and stuff, like just pick on you, kind of like, but it's a *teacher*'.

Children were often very pragmatic about the ways adults exercise justice and injustice in their treatment of children: 'most adults try – but they usually just pretend they're listening'. However, children's capability for pragmatism does not absolve adults from exercising ecological justice and acting to support children when they face an injustice or express a concern about an issue beyond their powers of agency.[65] For example, working in low-income communities, Dana Lanza notes that children in her community are routinely exposed to environmental injustices on a daily basis through highly-polluted play areas. As a result of her students' experiences, she changed the focus of her environmental teaching to help pupils address these issues.[66] Children in poorer communities are many times more likely to suffer from respiratory illness and more likely to be exposed to environmental hazards like toxic waste. In these settings, Lanza notes children, like adults, need opportunities to reason and plan action, building on small but meaningful gains in places they love or identify with.

However, research by Diana Hess[67] raises further concern that children who need justice education and learning support are most often those children who are least likely to get this kind of education. Hess argues that it is schools in high socio-economic areas that tend to teach moral reasoning about controversial issues most often. She worries that under these conditions citizenship education will simply perpetuate political inequality, because the 'most powerful forms of civic education are more likely to be doled out to the very students who are already on the top of the political heap'.[68]

For children learn to reason about justice effectively, the institutional arrangements that influence *how* justice is taught often matter as much as *what* children are taught. In this regard, state education is a particularly important democratic institution. Sandel argues the 'inadvertent' civic education that takes place when young people from different economic classes, religious backgrounds and ethnic communities come together in common institutions is vital for children's developing sense of democracy and environment.[69] The intuitive appeal of state schools, as Sandel described them, makes sense. Yet for every inclusive, just 'cool' state school, there are other state schools which perpetuate injustice and bullying. How can schools ensure that the justice learning that goes on within their school is not simply inadvertent or haphazard, but purposeful, explicit, thoughtful and ecologically sensitive?

Nora Rathzell and David Uzzell have observed the environmental education and teaching practice in schools in Europe, and have concluded that having formal, regular opportunities to encounter others through a range of planned community interactions across generations improves students' confidence in debating issues of justice and deepens their understanding of the concerns of others.[70] Elsewhere, Uzzell also notes that families with a democratic liberal ethos play a critical role in encouraging children's confidence to seek out and listen to others. Like Sandel, he concludes that free state education, with planned community interaction, matters for creating a learning context that encourages empathy and justice.[71]

Teachers have a difficult task to keep children safe, creating a listening, inclusive learning environment that accepts all students, while also challenging oppressive or restrictive world views. One way is to provide an environment in which children have multiple opportunities to act with justice in role play situations, so they can experiment with different perspectives and identities in debate. Education theorist Vygotsky advocates the value of theatre and plays as ways in which children can reason about the justice of difficult situations, while retaining some control of what is shared and the timing and pace of that sharing.[72] Using puppet plays and storytelling, for example, can be simple but powerful ways in which difficult questions of justice are debated in ways that are less personalised or threatening to children (see Chapter 7).

The work of both Vygotsky and Friere also remind us that children learn to debate and reason about justice through their experiences of their own cultural worlds, by talking to others of different ages, and their peers.[73] The more opportunity for reflection and shared understanding with others of all ages enriches reasoning and can add to the children's sense of being supported as they begin to think through difficult decisions, rather than being increasingly isolated in a community. As Hannah Arendt argues, teaching about justice is effective when children are not isolated or 'broken off' or 'banished' from the world of all adults, but are afforded opportunities to learn from others of different ages and experiences.[74]

Communities for justice

What wider lessons might children learn about justice when growing up in neo-liberal states? Michael Sandel has argued that: 'one of the most striking tendencies of our time is the expansion of markets and market-orientated reasoning into spheres of life traditionally governed by non-market norms'.[75] In this process, Sandel argues, market thinking has crowded out opportunities for other ways of reasoning. If moral decision making is constantly reduced to questions of the most cost-efficient option, we risk truncating children's natural inclination to debate and reason about the values implicit in our decisions. Sandel fears our pursuit of the self-interest of the greatest number of people erodes the opportunity to foster a common citizenship. In addition, Richard Layard argues that in today's highly-mobile societies, children need more support to develop internalised reasoning about morality, because there are fewer community prompts or opportunities to debate the common good.[76]

As children grapple with embedded justice, interactions with other generations provide important support, helping a child learn to reason about moral issues, demonstrate altruism, and express empathy. To learn about ecological justice, children need opportunities to see adults and efficacious peers thinking thoughtfully about their environment and engaged in reasoned decision making to decide what is the right thing to do. But again this process of observing justice in a local community is not automatic. Local communities can 'hothouse' and perpetuate injustice. In the case of the Tree School children, their frustration appears to have been heightened by a wider concern that their community was experiencing too many changes (urban development and loss of play space), and that their parents faced struggles with local decision making that was unresponsive and unrepresentative. Intolerance to other ethnic groups, especially the 'Chinese', was a disturbing undercurrent of debate in a school with an almost entirely *Pākehā/* European roll.

Andrew Dobson has reminded us that, as ecological citizens, it is important we can recognise that the needs and rights of others have claims on us: claims which we should consider. It is not necessary or possible to know or understand all the people who may be affected by our actions. If we have no direct experience of others who are different from ourselves, and know little of their needs and concerns, it is very difficult for us as citizens to become 'other regarding'. Empathy for others requires nurturing and support, and careful challenge of assumptions by teachers. Without this, debates about justice quickly slip into blaming and finding 'baddies'. We cannot entrust lessons of ecological justice entirely to the haphazard world of local community politics. Children also need well-planned teaching interventions to appreciate sustainability as issues of fairness and equity of resource use within and between generations, in different parts of the world and as justice to animals.[77]

Ecologically, just communities are not just green communities, they are communities which challenge the underlying justice of day-to-day decision making. Open, inclusive and accountable processes of reasoning are vital if we are to shed light on the injustices of complex chains of production, or if we are to think through ways to put things right. Children need teachers and institutions (schools, families, churches, tribes and sports clubs) to support them as they practice exercising their capability for justice. In the following extract from a focus group discussing a traditional Korean paper game, we hear children wrestling with the justice of immigration, race relations, and resource use and distribution:

TINA: Um, like Kajil said, some people are really mean around here, like cos they have no friends and do *dgakgi* …

EVERYONE: Mmm, *dgakgi*!

POPCORN: *Dgakgi* is this little origami stuff that [names of other kids from outside of this group, specifically Asian students] got addicted to, and always play at lunch and they can't stop.

KAJIL: Um, about that *dgakgi* comment, it's really taking away the paper of the school. It's getting hard because the teachers have to buy paper all the time and it's um really taking off the money they need for the junior school safety matting, for buying new paper because paper these days is getting really expensive.

(Small World School)

This conversation reveals the big cultural tensions that can be embedded in 'little' questions of justice. In this situation, different ethnic groups and communities of children (fee paying students and local residents) are learning and playing together in one small group. Teaching justice requires us to help children to think through the wider implications of the problems they face, and support their ability to engage in moral reasoning and just decision making. However, teaching children to think and act justly does not absolve adults from taking action to relieve suffering. Extrapolating from tension of access to resources in the classroom, we are reminded that children are disproportionately affected by much wider resource issues and environmental change. Nine out of ten children growing up today are doing so in areas of the world where they will experience severe resource constraints and environmental degradation as the consequence of climate change and resource extraction by developed economies. Exhausted children cannot be expected to challenge the systemic injustices we have created and perpetuated, or to champion the issues alone. Teaching children growing up in neoliberal economies ways to reflect on their community responsibilities for wider injustice does not absolve adults in those economies from taking action. Ecological citizenship demands adults take moral responsibility and action for the situations that children face.

Given children are amongst the communities most affected by environmental degradation and the social oppression of adults, adults also have an obligation to work with and challenge those organisations and agents who have the power to improve outcomes for children. Philosopher Asuncion Lera St Clair described these groups as having the most 'response-ability' to address the concrete issues that blight young lives.[78] When children observe adults reflecting, debating and acting to put things right to improve environmental suffering and relieve social injustice, they witness powerful lessons about how to practice just ecological citizenship. Yet it is not enough to know how to act with justice as an individual. To effect democratic change in their wider community, children also need support to learn the skills of democratic reasoning to convince others. The discussion in the next chapter asks: How we can we support children as they learn to discuss issues and reason democratically in a changing world?

Notes

1 Barry 2006, p22.
2 Nussbaum 2010.
3 Ibid., pp27–28.
4 Sen 2009, pix.
5 Aristotle cited in Sandel 2009, p194
6 Sandel 2009, p29.
7 Worley 2011.
8 Ibid.
9 Dobson 2003, p101.
10 Dobson 2003, p120; see also Barratt-Hacking *et al.* 2007.
11 Ibid.
12 Ibid.
13 Young 2011.
14 Ibid., p142.
15 Ibid., p144.
16 Sen 2009, p4.
17 Hansen 2009, pp244–60.
18 Hansen 2010 also argues it is unjust to arrest young protestors who oppose coal-powered fuel plants. Hansen argues it is ethically irresponsible given the impact that burning fossil fuels will have on the climate of the young and the unborn.
19 This view of agency does not absolve adults from taking action, but it does require adults to support children to develop their capability to act.
20 Stephens 1996.
21 Kelly and Brooks 2009.
22 Sen 2009; Pogge 2002.

23　See Sandel 2009 (p29) for a discussion about embedded justice. Plato was famously scornful of an embedded approach to justice. In his *Republic*, Socrates expressed disdain for those prisoners trapped in caves, who can only ever see the play of shadows on the wall. Plato implies it is only when we leave the prisons of our everyday lives, those made by our rituals, routines and assumptions that we can see life as it really is.

24　Bartlett 2008.

25　For an extended discussion of how children in this focus group discussed climate justice, see Kirk 2008b. Kirk notes that no children at this time discussed climate adaptation. There was little or no media discussion of climate adaptation or justice issues at the time of study. See also Adger *et al.* 2006.

26　Hart 1997, p25.

27　Chawla 1999, p17.

28　Ibid.

29　Ibid., p26.

30　Simon Dalby, December 2011, personal communication.

31　Barry 2005, p43 fn17.

32　Kelly and Brooks 2009.

33　Kail 2010, p382.

34　See an extended discussion about Piaget's immanent view of justice in Kail 2010, p382.

35　Kail 2010.

36　Ibid.

37　Ibid., p382.

38　Ibid., pp383–4.

39　Kail's extended discussion is a useful summary of the literature: Kail 2010, pp375–405

40　Kail 2010, p386.

41　Cited in Kail 2010, pp387–9.

42　Nussbaum 2011; see also Freire 1985.

43　Nussbaum 2010, pp109–10.

44　Vygotsky 1978.

45　Sen 2009, p252; see also Nussbaum 2011.

46　Sen 2009; Evans and Marcynyszyn 2004.

47　Vygotsky 1978.

48　Horton and Freire 1990, p104.

49　Bohman 2011.

50　Rickinson *et al.* 2009.

51　Vare and Scott 2007.

52　See Rickenson *et al.* 2009 for a thoughtful discussion on what learners learn.

53　Aiken 1997. For discussion of the position of teachers, see Ingersoll 2003. Teachers are employees, and classrooms are their workplace. Parents can be vociferous critics, and teaching practice is often determined not only by classroom teachers but by school boards, government policies and employers.

54　Thaler and Sunstein 2008; Worley 2011.

55　Barry 2005; see also Darier cited in MacGregor 2006, p115.

56　Westheimer 2008, p8.

57　Westheimer 2008, p7.

58　See Ladson-Billings 2009.

59　Kail 2011, p389.

60　Horton and Freire 1990, p104.

61　Ibid.

62 Kumashiro 2009.
63 Kohlberg cited in Kail 2010.
64 Kahn 2010, pp8–10.
65 Worley 2011; see also Atkins *et al.* 1998.
66 Lanza 2005.
67 Hess 2009.
68 Ibid.
69 Sandel 2009, p264.
70 Rathzel and Uzzell 2009.
71 Uzzell 1999.
72 Vygotsky 1978; Rathzel and Uzzell 2009.
73 Vygotsky cited in Kail 2010, pp180–4; see also Freire 1985.
74 Arendt 1954 (2006), p178.
75 Sandel 2009, p265.
76 Layard 2005; Layard and Dunn 2009.
77 Barry 2005, pp43–4 fn19.
78 Lera St. Clair 2010.

7 Decentred deliberation
Storytelling and democratic listening

Mister! He said with a sawdusty sneeze,
I am the Lorax. I speak for the trees.

(Dr. Seuss 1957, *The Lorax*)

'... Well, goodbye. I have enjoyed our conversation very much, I assure you.'
'Conversation indeed!' said the Rocket. 'You have talked the whole time yourself.
That is not conversation.'
'Somebody must listen,' answered the Frog, 'and I like to do all the talking
myself. It saves time, and prevents arguments.'

(Oscar Wilde 1888, *The Remarkable Rocket*)

Many democratic theorists now advocate a 'turn' to deliberation in decision making,[1] but deliberative democracy is more than just learning how to debate.[2] Deliberative democracy requires skills to listen across deep differences of life experience and value, and the ability to challenge illegitimate power through discussion. In a complex and diverse world, Amartya Sen reminds us we no longer have the luxury of 'lazy' or 'disengaged tolerance', it is no longer sufficient to simply say 'you are right in your community and I am right in mine'; somehow, we have to find ways to develop democratic solutions for a common future.[3]

Moreover, as both Dr. Suess and Oscar Wilde remind us so vividly in their respective children's stories, effective deliberation about the environment requires more than talk. We need ways to represent the interests of non-human nature in public conversation. Seuss and Wilde also underscore the vital importance of listening to viewpoints which are not in accord with our own understandings of the world.

In this chapter I review the way leading advocates of deliberative democracy differ over the *purpose* of deliberation (what are we intending to do?), the *participants* of deliberation (who should deliberate?), the *practice* (how should we deliberate?), and the *place* (where and when should we deliberate?). I briefly consider consequences of these perspectives for ecological citizenship, before turning to consider storytelling as one way we can help young citizens learn to create shared spaces for conversation, and enhance their skills for radically decentred democratic listening, to improve public deliberation across different world views.

Rethinking deliberative democracy: why, who, how, where and when?

To begin, why should we deliberate? Why not just vote? There are three different arguments put forward to justify public debate as the means of making decisions. The first rests on the idea that hearing from a wide range of viewpoints improves the quality of our decision making. In this rational approach, public participation is valued for instrumental reasons, as a way to enhance our understanding of a problem. Listening to all viewpoints helps ensure that vital local community knowledge, experience and insight is brought to bear on the difficult situations we face. Furthermore, when citizens have been consulted and feel that their views were heard, they are more likely to agree that the process was fair and are more likely to support the legitimacy of the decision, even if the outcome was not the one they advocated.[4]

A second line of reasoning justifies a deliberative approach on the grounds that public conversations form a stronger sense of community, or create a common interest or consensus. From this point of view, deliberation has the potential to transform our collective viewpoints, uncover shared values, or discover a previously-unimagined possibility through the power of conversation.[5] Both of these lines of reasoning inform much of the current turn towards deliberative politics.[6] Many advocates of deliberation have expressed frustration at traditional decision making, where the outcome is arrived at by vote counting. Voting effectively aggregates individual choices or preferences, but as a method of collective decision making, casting a vote does not necessarily require a citizen to consider the views of others, or to reflect critically on their own assumptions, let alone change their minds or find a new solution. Moreover, if we can only vote for predetermined choices, it is possible the outcome of our decision process might be less satisfactory than a situation where new options are discovered through public reasoning. When we engage in public conversations about our visions for a shared future, it is possible that we will discover ideas not previously thought of. While argument and discussion is not always guaranteed to improve decision making, it is valuable for the way new ideas can be formed through open conversation.[7]

In their classic work on deliberation, Amy Gutmann and Denis Thompson argue for a process of reasoned discussion to legitimate decisions, where agreement is reached through the force of the better argument.[8] In this approach, informed by the Habermasian 'ideal' or universal speech situation, citizens are encouraged to speak in ways that others can accept and find reasonable. While there is much merit in recognising that we should respect others and frame our arguments in ways that help others understand our experiences, not everyone agrees the purpose of deliberation is to reach consensus, or that it is possible for each speaker to present their views using 'a mild voice of reason'.[9] Some people, particularly minority communities, may need to express deep outrage, as they frequently find their concerns are inadequately expressed using the rules, rituals and processes of dominant Western debate.

In this light, a third, urgent reason to nurture a more deliberative democracy is to create conditions to enable citizens learn to coexist and connect across deeply-held differences without violence.[10] This is a more radical tradition of deliberative theory. It reminds us that politics is relatively easy when we all agree more or less on the terms of debate and how we should conduct that debate. Where democracy gets really difficult is when we do not agree about how to engage with each other and feel passionately about our differences of opinion.[11] In this situation, those teaching young citizens will need significant skill to help children negotiate very deep differences of life experience and values.

In the radical deliberative tradition, the aim of deliberation is not to reach con-sensus per se, but to create shared public space for on-going democratic dialogue, seeing our differences as an important, creative resource for informing democratic decision making. The aim of radical deliberation is to create a respectful, shared public life in which our differences of opinion are celebrated rather than seen as problems we have to overcome. John Dryzek and Iris Young are two advocates of this vision of deliberation across difference. Both remind us that, by its very nature, politics often involves irreconcilable differences of value. Consensus is not always possible.[12] People often engage in politics when they are motivated by deep passion, or emotion or cultural experience. As a result, the issues that people most want to talk about are not always easy to articulate in the format of rational reasoned argument.

Aiming for consensus on the basis of the better argument may simply privilege those whose voices are advantaged in public debate, and silence views which may be intensely important to minorities.[13] For Māori as an indigenous community, for example, the issues at stake might be best expressed by a *hui* [meeting], or through sharing stories, or communicating through *waiata* [music], dance or *karakia* [prayer].[14] In this context, Iris Young's work is important, as she reminds us that democratic deliberation requires more than argument. Effective deliberation may need greeting rituals, rhetoric and joke telling to encourage effective listening. Young's work calls on us to respect different methods of communication. Her arguments resonate with the comments of a child in the Community-*Kura* School, who spoke of her granddad getting up early in the morning to do *karakia* [prayers and religious evocation] as a way of making changes in her community, and show-ing he was in charge. This child's reflection reminds us that people may have very different assumptions about how communication should occur.[15] In New Zealand, greeting rituals of *haka* [challenge], *mihi* [spoken tribute] and *hongi* [greeting by pressing noses, sharing of breath] are often used to establish connections with oth-ers before conversing as respected adversaries or friends.

Finding ways of communicating and coming together across different life experiences is a significant task for young citizens in every democracy. For more effective deliberation to occur, young citizens may first have to create new public spaces in which they can interact. Physically getting together and finding ways to talk and listen may be a significant challenge. In these cases, rather than rushing for consensus, deliberative strategies and institutions that enable young citizens to recreate a sense of community, providing space and time to develop their own view points and listen to others, may be the more vital first steps towards building a sustainable common future. Politics involves struggle between groups trying co-exist. In the New Zealand study, it was striking that even in small communities children do not always interact with others from different backgrounds in their community (see Chapter 5). It is very hard to understand another person's point of view if you do not encounter them. Consider, for example, the Tree School where children from a school community that was entirely European/*Pākehā*, and where many children expressed fears about immigration from China:

INTERVIEWER:	Are there any issues that you'd like to have a say about?
JESSICA:	Homer, what were you going to say?
HOMER:	The government should give credit to people who manufacture things in New Zealand, because businesses go to China. It's not that good.
BUBBLE O' BILL:	Um, not too long ago some poisons came in from China and they might lead to … Oh, there's another thing, I went to our fish and chip store and we had like 15 cockroaches in our fish and chips, because we waited for like an hour.
GOODY GOODY GUM DROPS:	I know someone who found a rat, they saw some teeth in their meal.
BUBBLE O' BILL:	Yeah? In the Chinese store?
GOODY GOODY GUM DROPS:	Yeah, but you're not meant to tell anyone. My brother went down to go and get some Chinese food at the Chinese shop, he found rat's teeth in it and then he found like eyes and stuff.
INTERVIEWER:	Jessica?
JESSICA:	Well this isn't about rats and fish and chips or anything like that. But in China, I don't really agree with people that work there because they hardly get paid and they work like every day. And that's why we get all the stuff from there, because it's so cheap cos they've got so much money. And I don't really think New Zealand should really get that stuff cos it means that it's supporting it.

(Tree School)

In the Tree School, children wanted to think about different view points, but their deliberation was constrained by having little opportunity to learn to listen respectfully to others from different backgrounds. By contrast at the Small World School, children had their world views regularly challenged by each other as this extract illustrates. In this conversation, the children had all arrived in New Zealand in the past 5 to 6 years from six different countries. Here they were looking at their community map:

INTERVIEWER: So what kinds of things do people from around here do with other people?

POPCORN: I wrote people cooperate and they share and care with each, for each other.

BEN TENISON: Some people steal stuff.

BRITNEY: People, um, do different things.

INTERVIEWER: What kind of things, do you think?

TINA: Some people waste paper [referring to a previous debate about Korean children using up 'school' paper for playground games].

KAJIL: Some people eat different things.

BRITNEY: Lots of Koreans, um, always have noodles.

MARY: I don't! [group giggles]

BRITNEY: I said *lots* of Koreans.

(Small World School)

These two conversations reflect two very different conversations at state schools only a distance of a few kilometres apart. The children had very different opportunities to experience deep cultural differences. In the high-income Tree School there was much fear of immigration from China, but no immigrants from any country attended the school; all identified as European and all the children we interviewed were born in New Zealand. In contrast, much of the Principal and teacher effort at the Small World School was directed towards creating a sense of shared community across 40 nations. In this context, creating spaces to enable children's connections with each other and their family through daily interactions was essential, and had to precede any opportunity to listen to speeches and join in school meetings. The Principal and teachers commented that the intention behind the creation of an international garden representing all the countries at the school was in large part to bring parents together with children and teachers. This activity was a community event spread over several months, involving families who hosted shared meals, and was a trigger for more sports and other cultural events. Children reported enjoying the event and, as an activity, it added to a wider sense of cohesion reported later in the widely-shared sentiment that: 'there's heaps and heaps of … different country people in our school and that makes us really cool cos we're a cool school'.

A model of deliberation which strives for consensus or rushing into deliberation too quickly risks silencing the voices of minority children who may feel pressured to put aside deeply-held cultural practices or concerns for the sake of contributing to public debate, where the terms of that debate are framed by the majority culture.[16] In this light, it seems wishful thinking to suggest we can uncover a shared interest in sustainability. We may be members of one planet but our more immediate democratic task as citizens may be to create opportunities to interact and listen to each other respectfully, with no expectation we will eventually be able to agree. Tough decisions are difficult to make with no experience of shared interaction.

Learning to listen democratically

A significant criticism levelled at the practice of deliberation as a process of reasoned argument is that this practice risks silencing the 'voice' and concerns of children, minorities and non-human nature.[17] Listening to nature is a motif that flows through Rachel Carson's work.[18] Her desire to also encourage children to listen to non-human nature is captured when she writes in *The Sense of Wonder*:

> Hearing can be a source of even more exquisite pleasure but it requires conscious cultivation. I have had people tell me they had never heard the song of a wood thrush, although I knew the bell-like phrases of this bird had been singing in their back yards every spring. By suggestion and example, I believe children can be helped to hear the many voices about them. Take time to listen and talk about the voices of the earth and what they mean – the majestic voice of thunder, the winds, the sound of surf or flowing streams. And the voices of living things: No child should grow up unaware of the dawn chorus of the birds in spring. He will never forget the experience of a specially planned early rising and going out in the predawn darkness ... In that dawn chorus one hears the throb of life itself.[19]

Like Seuss, Wilde and contemporary thinkers Clark, Dobson and Latour, Carson reminds us here that the interests and concerns of the physical world are not easily heard in traditional models of public deliberation.[20] Moreover, when democratic deliberation focuses on the process of talking alone, Andrew Dobson argues we risk underestimating the transformative power of listening.[21] To change our minds, let alone effect political transformation on a broader scale, we need to listen as well as talk. However, listening takes time, and for minority groups in particular, this process of explaining their world view to another, and trying to ensure that dominant groups listen, can be very draining on limited resources.

Learning to listen effectively is a democratising skill for citizenship. The children in the New Zealand study were often acutely aware of the times when they felt they were listened too. For example, many children at the Tree School expressed frustration over not being listened to by teachers during protests about their right to climb trees, commenting after their protests that: 'They [the staff] never brought it up again and they try their hardest not to bring it up.'

Achieving effective listening may take effort and protest. However, opportunities to connect school and community in shared conversation are also valuable ways to nurture democratic listening skills. Many children we interviewed had observed the practicalities of public deliberation and were interested in the practise of public debate, as this discussion reveals:

SAM: The School Board of Trustees, they make changes in our school.
AMANDA: But how?
BLAZE: They talk with the principal and everyone.
FLEXI: They talk to the teachers.

Figure 7.1 'We want leaders who listen': Christchurch protest at the closure of an outdoor pool

Credit: Bronwyn Hayward.

SAM: They talk with the whole town!
BLAZE: And they have meetings.
SAM: Yes meetings.
SAM: Meetings are on Wednesdays usually.

(Farm-Sea School)

While these children at the Farm-Sea School understood how important deliberation was to making decisions in their small town, one of the most significant challenges they also commented on was the need to decentre debate in ways that encouraged adults to listen to them and helped people outside their community understand their concern to protect their local beaches. How can young citizens be supported to have their concerns heard in decision making across space and time, so that their local conversations do not become isolated and irrelevant to wider debate?

Learning to decentre deliberation

In this section I define decentred deliberation and discuss why it matters for ecological citizenship. Decentred deliberation is a term democratic theorist Iris Young used to refer to public conversations that cross local, regional and national spaces, and over time.[22] Given that political power is increasingly global and decentred, Young argued our citizen challenges and responses to power ought to be decentred too. Her arguments are highly relevant for children and young adults learning to engage in intergenerational decision making about sustainability.

Young argues that deliberative democracy too often frames democratic deliberation as a public conversation amongst a specified group of stakeholders, or members of a geographically-defined community or region.[23] These approaches assume a *centred* view of deliberation, where a single body talks together to make decisions at a particular time and place. However, as Iris Young points out, these approaches to deliberation miss the point. Because our most difficult problems are global or *decentred*, our civic responses should be decentred as well. Young expressed frustration with deliberation where groups are brought together as a 'single body' to talk in 'a single encounter'.[24] Given global power, effective citizenship will need to find ways to connect with others or to make linkages, to speak and interact across difference, if global power is to be held to account. Local stories and struggles matter, but, to be heard, local deliberation needs to be exposed to wider scrutiny and supportive alliances forged across space and time.

Writing before the Occupy movement or the Arab spring and the rise of Facebook, Iris Young's body of work on deliberation has nevertheless left us a rich legacy of ways to think about how to decentre deliberation. Young drew on the Habermasian vision of democratic deliberation as a process 'embedded' in dense social interactions, relationships and networks. These dense relationships are too complex to be moved easily in one direction or another.[25] To understand decision making in our new, mass democracies, Young argues we need to move on from always trying to focus our attention on the debate of a single group or forum, even a national legislature. Instead, we should 'understand de-centered deliberative democracy as occurring in multiple forums and sites connected to one another over broad spans of space and time' so that a body of new ideas and opinions can form.[26]

How can we support children as they learn to decentre their arguments, linking strategically with others? Zygmunt Bauman cautions us that young citizens using social media to communicate with others can be very exposed to peer pressure and oppressive surveillance.[27] Social media forums can also be isolating experiences in which we talk only to those with similar views and interests or of similar ages.[28] Or as Rachel Brooks suggests, the internet can also offer a space for young women in particular to talk without having to disclose their name, address or other personal details, creating a feeling of virtual anonymity which 'works well for young adults who want to organize and communicate with others, and create a "space" for oneself to engage in a decentered conversation'.[29]

A role for adults in this complex new media environment is to support young citizens as they learn to manage individual exposure, and express and form passionate views, recognising that they may wish to change their views at a later date. Simply having tools to communicate electronically does not enhance our ability to communicate democratically. Left to our own devices, we do not necessarily learn to deliberate in ways that are always empowering, inclusive and just on-line or off-line. However, the opportunity to hear what is being said by others, and have our own views subjected to scrutiny can help ensure that local voices do not become irrelevant, and that injustice perpetuated in local communities does not go unheeded.[30]

Schools play many roles in decentring and connecting youthful conversations. On the one hand, classrooms are places of hierarchical control which can silence debate; on the other, when young people are confident their teacher 'likes' them (that is, values their opinion), a classroom can become a creative space to begin wider conversations about the common good.[31] In a thoughtful paper, Swedish educationalist Tomas Englund argues that the conditions which nurture effective deliberative democracy are dependent on a wider system of public, state funded schools.[32] These schools help children to encounter others and to develop meaningful connections for mutual learning. He notes the way that a whole variety of communication methods support children as they learn to connect across difference, including music as well as speech encounters. For example, in the case of the Music School in the New Zealand study, children appreciated their choir as a place where they 'mixed up with other kids and we really have fun'. Five children in other focus groups mentioned the Christchurch music festival, a city event where all schools come together in an annual mass choir across the city. Englund argues that state schools should encourage children to encounter others in a variety of ways, and to learn to reason, to change views and to recreate a sense of community.

A network of democratic public schools may support more inclusive debate, yet James Bohman also reminds us that, in interdependent global communities, some powerful groups are able to 'set terms' for others.[33] In this context, young citizens will also need to learn to network with other schools, not only to connect and create a shared community but to learn to strategise to resist the illegitimate exercise of power by distant others.[34] Several of the children at the Community-*Kura* School, for example, were acutely aware of the need to develop strategies to help them connect with others through joint action by school councils, *hui-ā-tau* [tribal meetings], and joining other schools to protest the closure of their local pool.

In another example, during the research, many children were keen to connect the conversations they began in the focus groups with others. As a result, after the focus groups, seven groups asked interviewers to help them set up student forums or connect to community radio stations to make their own radio programmes

Figure 7.2 Storytelling encourages active listening and decentred deliberation

Credit: Bronwyn Hayward.

about issues that mattered to them (which included planning and transport changes in their local area, and climate change). One of these projects involved children interviewing elderly residents and their grandparents about places they had loved as children growing up in the community. This simple example of intergenerational conversation about urban space was decentred on public radio, and the children were very keen to ensure it was heard widely by all their family and friends.

We can also think about decentring deliberation through communication methods that encourage more active listening, such as storytelling.[35]

Decentring deliberation: the role of storytelling

Iris Young argues that a criterion of good deliberation is that it is connected or linked to discussions in other places.[36] Young used the term 'linkage' to describe the way that third parties can help mediate or connect sites or occasions of discussion. When the conversations of groups and organisations are linked, Young argued, communication becomes more politically efficacious and its outcomes are normatively legitimated. Young argued that without mediated conversations, 'a space of public opinion will not consolidate'.[37] Linkages involve people who act as third parties in conversations, helping effective listening, transformation and connection. In a child's world these linkages may be teachers, journalists, local community advocates, youth workers, coaches, or any one of the many often unsung heroes who help bridge, coordinate, network, connect and translate, to build empathy for children in public conversation and, in turn, help children understand the views of others. Many young people struggle to get their voice heard in local planning and decision making. In this process, the actions of others can help or hinder children and young citizens as they try to overcome barriers of isolation, exclusion or irrelevance. For example, individual actors can intervene formally, or informally, to connect local talk with other communities' discussions.

The most effective process of decentring or linking conversations often begins with the simple step of storytelling. Sharing stories is an important deliberative technique that reminds us of several crucial aspects to effective democratic deliberation. First, stories help colour and bring to life the embedded reality of individual lives, not only helping advance an idea to a wider audience, but also putting the audience in a context which improves our ability to listen and to really hear and understand what others are saying. Second, stories help us take imaginative leaps to recreate ourselves and think about our world in new ways that can help us rethink time, place and purpose. Rethinking ourselves, rather than just aggregating preferences in traditional vote counting, helps us transform our thinking.

Philosopher Bonnie Honig notes a fascinating distinction made by Michael Oakshott between origin stories ('in the beginning') and once-upon-a-time stories. In the first, there is a grand narrative, in the latter, there are many contingencies of time and place that enable us to explore and think about other ways of being and living.[38] But all stories put places and experiences in context, and many cultures cope easily with the idea of multiple origin myths.[39] Climate, for example, is often described as a scientific observation, yet in reality individuals experience climate as weather, a lived, local daily experience. It is weather that we understand and enjoy or fear.[40] Storytelling enables us to make sense of the world around us, including changes in weather and longer term shifts in climate. In A. A. Milne's *Winnie the Pooh*, the stories and illustrations by E. H. Shepard capture a keenly-observed and dynamic local eco-system, and help children make sense of the world. The 100 Acre Wood is, in reality the 500 acre Ashdown forest of East Surrey in the United Kingdom. It is captured in the words of Milne and in carefully drawn botanical illustrations of Ashdown forest by E. H. Shepard. The stories are entertaining, but they can also help children make sense of a changing world, as the example of the stories of Piglet's experiences in the big flood and the big wind illustrates:

> It rained and it rained and it rained. Piglet told himself that never in all his life, and he was goodness knows how old – three, was it, or four? – never had he seen so much rain. Days and days and days.[41]

So A. A. Milne begins his story 'In which Piglet is entirely surrounded by water', a story in which our hero, Piglet, soon discovers that being alone as the waters rise makes him feel '... a little Anxious ... to be a Very Small Animal Entirely Surrounded by Water'.[42] In another story in the same series, Piglet does 'a very grand thing', as our small hero experiences the big wind in ways that are also potentially empowering for children in a changing climate.

Children can easily become overwhelmed with the scale of changes facing them, but in these stories Milne builds up a sense of shared endeavour, and scaffolds the learning for children who can identify with the perils and fears of a Very Small Animal. Faced with an autumnal wind so strong that Piglet's ears 'streamed behind him like banners as he fought his way along', Piglet worried, 'supposing a tree fell down, Pooh, when we were underneath it?' 'Supposing it didn't', said Pooh after careful thought. In this story the listening connects with and acknowledges fear, felt in another time and place, and observes a way of responding that is not blind optimism, but choosing to think in a different way.

Vygotsky reminds us that imagination is the first step in a process of emancipation in which children learn to act to create new possibilities.[43] In both the Winnie the Pooh stories, children are decentred through imaginative storytelling, to a different time and place where they can connect with the struggles of a Very Small Animal like Piglet. Storytelling in this way can be a very powerful illustration of ways to regulate emotion and rediscover agency, and forge new shared narratives in the aftermath of disaster, as people struggle to make sense of new conditions.[44] There is a difference, however, between helping a child to decentre an experience and connect with others, and the loss of authentic local voices and insights. While sharing stories provides a way to reflect collectively and connect or empathise, a process of sharing a narrative can also be captured in a global market in ways which can easily lose the critical potential for local deliberation. In the commercialised Disney cartoon version of Winnie the Pooh, the Ashdown forest was lost from view, reframed as the Tangly Wood, a dark and dangerous cartoonish place for children, where we lose the local features of the forest which were captured in the carefully observed local details of a beautiful, dynamic woodland ecosystem. The detail of E. H. Shepard's illustrations captured Milne's text, for example, as when describing the big flood:

> The dry ditches ... had become streams, and the little streams were rivers ... and the river had sprawled out of its own bed and was taking up so much room everywhere, that Piglet was beginning to wonder whether it would be coming into his bed soon.[45]

Furthermore, the power of a good story, like Dr. Seuss' *The Lorax*, reminds us that, even when highly-marketed, the disruptive, challenging messages of a good story that asks 'who speaks for the trees?' can help children to unlock imaginative potential for understanding the broader narratives, as well as building children's empathy and appreciation of environmental issues. Using stories to connect to others in this way can help create new discourses about change. This is a valuable lesson for children, and is particularly important in situations where power is dispersed and beyond the action of individual agents, or where hegemonic debate makes some alternatives seem impossible. It is in these moments that storytelling can unlock democratic imagination for new thinking.

Stories can also support political agency and activism over time. Faced with very difficult debates and battles that are not easily reconciled or unlikely to be resolved within a generation, children can easily become overwhelmed. In this situation, as many indigenous communities know, storytelling, myths and cultural rituals can be very important to maintain a struggle over time. One solution is to share myths and retain the rituals of oral tradition of much older stories, where it is not only the story or song, but who told it, to whom, where, and when that adds to its significance. In New Zealand, like many indigenous cultures, there are strong myths, legends and stories which have local and global resonance. For example, Warren Pohatu has captured the story of Rata and the Birds, an ancient story which links to the people's ancestors in Hawaiiki well beyond Aotearoa New Zealand's borders. Telling this story reminds listeners of the great migrations and connections of indigenous peoples of the sea, not people of small atolls as often described in well-meaning northern environmental campaigns, but the narratives of people who identify with great ocean-going exploration traditions.[46]

Young's concept of linkage has a rich potential to stimulate thinking about how young citizens might learn to decentre deliberation. We have already seen wide uptake of multimedia or digital networks: to reinforce and deepen these, can we develop other ways to link conversations though bonds of kinship or friendship, or spiritual connections, including tribal memory? Elsewhere I have discussed the potential for Aboriginal song lines and Māori *waiata* [song], *poi/haka* [cultural dance] and carvings or weavings in *marae* [meeting places]; all link past deliberation to talk of the present and future.[47]

In the future, how will New Zealanders tell stories to make sense of the climate changes that face children, as ancient *kauri* trees move further from Northland where they are currently, as the rain falls less often in the dry east coast of the South Island, and the communities of the north in New Zealand are faced with more severe storms? Stories help us connect our individual or local struggles, share experiences and learning, and help us make sense of the changes going on in our world. Stories improve active listening, creating possibilities for public space to be created. But what of stories that are inaccessible by words? Elsie Locke, the New Zealand children's novelist, reminds us that children's imaginations can also be nurtured by doing, as well as telling and listening, by looking under the leaves: the idea of exploring nature and thinking differently about the world around us.[48]

To be successful, deliberation may need to involve local groups of children, speaking and interacting together first to establish their own common interests. There are limits to the impact that small groups of any age can have in politics in the absence of resources or institutional and social supports. To become effective, citizen deliberation also requires links with other groups in civil society and key actors. Peer-to-peer conversations are important in establishing shared interests, but, in a struggle to hold power to account, we also need to create spaces for intergenerational alliances and conversation. As one student put it: 'Well to get something done mum always talks to my dad if there is something wrong and I always talk to my mum if there is something wrong with me and then, like, if it's like, something serious my mum will *do* something.'

Evaluating the effectiveness of decentred deliberation

In a world of centred power, how do young citizens learn to judge whether their deliberation is having any effect? Adults are often keen to create forums to hear the voice of children, yet in the process these forums can privilege the adult listeners, who then produce well-meaning documents and audio-visual materials drawing on children's opinions to legitimate adult decision making. At the same time, the wider opportunity for other children to hear what is said, to comment, or to debate the findings and comments is lost.[49] Too often, despite our best intentions, children continue to be seen but not heard in public conversation in English-speaking democracies. Moreover, given the surprising absence of physical public spaces where children can encounter each other for shared conversation, informal and formal youth forums become even more important – school assemblies, national public broadcasting of popular television programmes, shared YouTube and Facebook phenomena matter as vital sites for youthful, civic conversation.

Iris Young argued that the purpose of decentred deliberative democracy is 'primarily critical; to provide norms and criteria' through which the legitimacy of the decision-making process and many of its policy outcomes can be questioned and improved'.[50] Adults can support this process by ensuring that institutional arrangements for youthful deliberation are effective. To evaluate the effectiveness of deliberation, we can use the criteria Young drew on in her *Kettering Review* paper.[51] The first criteria Young identified were the principles of reasonableness and publicity. Did the children feel the opportunities they had to speak out and listen to others were reasonable? Did citizens young and old taking part in the deliberation over time acknowledge that others may be listening or reading about their discussion and concerns and attempt to persuade these people?[52] Young also suggests we could ask whether any arguments associated with particular groups dominated over time. If, she argues for example, the arguments constantly seem to be voiced by white middle class men, 'this can be a sign of political inequality' in deliberation.[53] This problem is even more acute in the case of children's debate. In a review of school deliberation and citizenship programmes, Kahne and Middaugh argue,

> Far from drawing on civic education as a potential tool for ameliorating civic and political inequality, schools are making matters worse. In a nutshell, the very individuals who now have the least influence on political processes – the people whose voices schools most need to inform and support in order to promote democratic equality – often get fewer school based opportunities to develop their civic capacities and commitments than other students.[54]

Youthful citizens need opportunities to connect with others and support as they learn to debate and effect change.[55] As the experience of youth street protests in 2011 illustrated, at some point, however, any community discussion must be connected to wider debate if it is to be persuasive to others and not irrelevant. The way that various sites of discussion can be linked across space and time could be: vertical (perhaps connecting schools with the civic sphere or sites of authoritative decision making in the city and region), horizontal (connecting local schools with other youth forums) and temporal (to ensure that our shared responsibilities for past injustices and our obligations to future generations are met by all generations).[56]

We could describe children's citizenship experiences, where there are multiple linkages connecting dispersed sites of local talk, as strongly decentred. In this situation, children would have many ways to connect their conversations to others in their school and beyond, beginning to hear and connect with conversations in homes and workplaces, scientific organisations, across political boundaries, over generations.[57] Hannah Arendt reminds us that education must connect children to public conversation and, by extension, public life:

> Education is the point at which we decide whether we love the world enough to assume responsibility for it and by the same token save it from the ruin which, except for renewal, except for the coming of the new and the young, would be inevitable. And education, too, is where we decide whether we love our children enough not to expel them from our world and leave them to their own devices, nor strike from their hands their chance of undertaking something new, something unforeseen by us, but to prepare them in advance for the task of renewing a common world.[58]

The schools in which children reported the widest engagement in public life were the middle-income Community-*Kura* and Small World Schools. In the high-income schools, children were involved with a range of structured clubs and activities, but it was the middle-income schools where children reported the widest range of community networks, both formal and informal (see Chapter 5). In helping to decentre deliberation, parents, teachers and coaches can act as individual agents or representatives of institutions. They may not always act democratically. Adults and older children may exclude, co-opt or limit the voices and choices of children. The concern of Susan Fainstein that intermediary agents can be 'exclusionary, hierarchical and authoritarian is even more relevant in the context of deliberation with children'.[59] Adult actors can facilitate listening to youthful dialogue or derail children's protest. At the Music School, for example, children planned a playground strike to protest library lending rules and school being 'boring', but were 'talked out of it' by the playground teacher. However the children at that school remained very frustrated about age restrictions on borrowing school library books. In comparison, many children at the Community-*Kura* School who protested about the closure of the local pool with the support of their teachers and parents appeared confident that activist tactics of disruption can be powerful ways of attracting attention to a cause.

These two examples remind us that children's deliberation needs the support of active adult 'moral agents' if children are to have their voices heard; a school teacher, a local charity or a coach can often act informally to bridge discourses between school, family, and even international organisations. Beyond the school environment, children also need other institutional agents and advocates to help decentre deliberation and support their voices. In New Zealand, the Commissioner for the Environment described individuals who retain institutional and community memory as 'keepers of the long view'.[60] Keepers of the long view include community members, storytellers, residents and activists. Their advocacy can be helpful for increasing the resilience of children, retaining memories of past generations and keeping issues for future generations in the public mind.[61]

As children learn to speak out to challenge authority, their arguments can be very threatening for the authority of families, schools and other community institutions. Chapter 3 discussed the way some children said they felt unable to speak out because they would get a smack at home or because dad was too drunk to listen. Their micro-level experience of power in debate resonates with the experience of children at schools who discover that schools – like families – may not always be ideal sites for free and inclusive democratic debate. Children learn valuable lessons of public discussion through debating competitions, school councils and school assemblies, but when students want to debate very difficult issues that threaten the rules of the institution, schools normally respond to maintain the status quo and traditional forms of authority. In these situations, young citizens may need to join with groups and organisations outside the school to find valuable sources of alternative support as they learn to express their concerns. In this context, John Dryzek reminds us that non-governmental movements can serve as important spaces for alternative thinking and debate.[62] We can extrapolate from his argument to understand the micro-level experience of schools where radical deliberation (which threatens to undermine school authority or traditional views, for example) might be more easily nurtured outside the classroom.

Given the significant obstacles facing children in their efforts to be heard, the linkages of trans-governmental institutions like UNICEF, Save the Children Fund and the OECD are also vital ways to decentre adult, national debates, helping put local concerns in a wider context and subjecting local decision making to international scrutiny. Iris Young's discussion of linkage unlocks imaginative possibilities for countering the isolating or exclusionary effects of local centred deliberation as it impacts on children. At present there is a Commissioner for Children in New Zealand, but no voice for future generations. In the United Kingdom, new groups like the Alliance for Future Generations has proposed an Ombudsman for Future Generations[63]. These proposals help decentre debate for children, enabling the wide range of ecological issues that matter to them to be heard in democracies where baby boomers dominate the ballot box. But adults also have a responsibility to actively support young citizens in other practical ways. I turn now to revisit the difficult ecological issues which confront young citizens, and to describe the ways adults can use their own 'social hand print' and political imagination to support children and address issues of intergenerational injustice.

Notes

1 Dryzek 1990 (1994).
2 Griffin 2011.
3 Sen 2009, px.

4 See an extended discussion of citizen deliberation in Fischer 2003, pp205–20; see also Dryzek 2009.
5 Bobbio 2010.
6 Much of the contemporary interest in deliberation has been driven by the work of theorists Jurgen Habermas, James Cohen, James Bohman, John Dryzek, Iris Young and Amy Gutmann. See, for example, Habermas 1996.
7 For a review of literature that discusses the way deliberation can polarise and harden rather than transform opinion, see Bobbio 2010.
8 Gutmann and Thompson 1996.
9 Bessette 1997.
10 Gutmann and Thompson 1996, 2004.
11 Hulme 2009.
12 Young 1990; Dryzek 1990 (1994).
13 Young 1990, pp33–65.
14 Hayward 1995.
15 Mouffe 2002; Honig 2009.
16 See Young 1990, pp39–63; also Wilson and Yeatman 1995.
17 Clark 2011.
18 Consider the title of her most well known book *Silent Spring*: here silencing of birdsong was a symbol of great injustice (Carson 1962 (2002)).
19 Carson 1965 (1998), pp84–5.
20 Clark 2011; see Dobson 2010a for an extended discussion of speaking and listening to nature drawing on Latour 2004.
21 Ibid.
22 For a discussion of Iris Young's perspectives on decentered deliberation in an environmental context, see Young 2006b, p4; Hayward 2008a.
23 Over the past twenty years, mainstream democratic thinking, especially in area of environmental planning, has not so much taken a 'deliberative turn' as run into a neoliberal cul de sac. I discuss this idea in a tribute to the late Iris Young, a passionate, reasoned yet radical deliberative thinker, teacher and activist: see Hayward 2008a.
24 Young 2006b, p44 and Hayward 2008a.
25 Young 2006b, p44.
26 Young 2006b, p43.
27 Bauman 2011.
28 Moreover, in following how local children use social media to protest against local governments in Britain who were using Mosquito alarms, I was struck by the way these social forums can be quite isolating for young citizens. For example, the European Council called on governments to ban the Mosquito but, because the Facebook forums of young people had no advocacy group or connection to formal policy making, they did not hear of the event and missed a chance to build on EU debate: see Green and Hayward forthcoming.
29 Harris 2004, p161, cited in Brooks 2009.
30 Young 2006a; Hayward 2008a.
31 Hattie 2009, p28.
32 Englund 2011.
33 Bohman 2004, p50.
34 Young 2004 also shares the concerns of Bohman (2004), O'Neil (1996) and Weale (1999).
35 Dobson 2010a.

36 Young 2006a.
37 Young 2006b, p52.
38 Honig 2009, pp36–7.
39 Margolin 2005, p72.
40 Jasanoff 2010.
41 Milne 1927 (2001), p117.
42 Ibid., p118.
43 Vygotsky 1978, p99.
44 Kail 2010, p322. However, I learned myself the cultural limits of shared narratives as I once tried to relate this story to a Scottish meeting of environmental educators, who patiently listened before politely reminding me I was in effect sharing a story from England in Scotland, and – worse – the meeting itself was being held in a hall that Beatrix Potter, the English naturalist and children's writer, had often stayed in on holiday, so if I must use an English story in Scotland, why did I not use one of hers? The importance of shared narrative was noted by one of our young interviews who commented after the study, 'the Harry Potter books defined my childhood'.
45 Milne 1927 (2001), p118.
46 Kolomatangi cited in Hayward 2008c.
47 Berkes 1999; Kahukiwa 2006.
48 Locke 1975.
49 Hart 1999; Hayward 2008a.
50 Young 2006b, p48.
51 Young 2006b.
52 Ibid., p53.
53 Ibid.
54 Kahne and Middaugh 2009, p31.
55 Young 2006b; Young 2007.
56 Young 2006b, p43; Young 2007, p178.
57 Pateman 1970 (1990); Mansbridge 1999; Dryzek 2000; Weale 2002; Bohman 2007.
58 Arendt 1954 (2006), p198.
59 Fainstein 2007, p385.
60 Young, D. 2007.
61 Healthy Communities Coalition 2005; Lefale 2003.
62 Dryzek 1990 (1994), pp87–9.
63 Alliance for Future Generations 2011.

8   The social handprint

[T]he public has no hands except those of individual human beings ... the essential problem is that of transforming the action of such hands so that it will be animated by regard for social ends.

(Dewey 1927, cited in Barber 1984, p. 133)

As John Dewey and Benjamin Barber remind us, a healthy democracy requires active citizens, but individual action alone is insufficient to effect democratic change. In this chapter I consider the wider lessons of the New Zealand case for our understanding of the paradox of citizenship as personal responsibility, and the limits of a SMART approach to environmental education. I offer the social handprint as a way to think about the alternative SEEDS of ecological citizenship for children and adults. In closing, I reflect on the dramatic impact of the earthquake which followed this study and now confronts Christchurch children with complex, ongoing environmental and democratic changes.

Despite living in one of the most radically reformed neoliberal democracies in the world, many children interviewed in this study reported a refreshingly un-branded and physically un-bounded childhood. However, the New Zealand case also forcefully reminds us that encouraging children to take personal responsibility as citizens, to play outdoors and to resist consumer branding is beside the point if we ignore the wider socio-ecological problems that worry them. Yes, many New Zealand children we interviewed still play outside. Yes, many children were growing up in communities rich in social capital, where buying consumer products was not a substitute for authentic personal relationships. Yes, many of these children attended schools incorporating active outdoor education. And yes, New Zealand children under the age of 14 years are now amongst the most ethnically diverse national cohort in the world – a remarkable demographic transformation. These are achievements to be celebrated. And yet New Zealand children also struggle with the highest rates of youth suicide, and some of the highest rates of youth unemployment, accidental injury, ill health, poverty and domestic abuse in the OECD.[1] New Zealand children are growing up in a country that has experienced some of the highest rates of income inequality and greatest differences in the material well-being of older adults and young, poor children in the OECD.[2]

Viewed in this light, much of our emphasis in citizenship and environmental education seems beside the point. What is so great about encouraging children to play outdoors if we ignore the significant emotional and health risks that many children are exposed to from domestic violence indoors or inadequate and damp housing in a changing environment?[3] Why provide opportunities for children to protest or have their say if we are not prepared to listen to their concerns and change our ways? What is the value in encouraging children to recycle and reduce waste if many New Zealand children simply go on to become unemployed or out of education, more so than in any other country in the OECD?[4] What is moral about encouraging children to take personal responsibility for their lives and the future of the planet while the community passes the costs of escalating carbon emissions, superannuation and unsustainable resource use onto this generation and the ones that follow through a complex series of investment decisions with short term benefits that exacerbate long-term vulnerability in a changing world?[5]

While it is commendable that many children are learning to take personal responsibility for their citizenship and their planet, are their parents and grandparents sharing this responsibility? In New Zealand's recent social and economic history, there have been periods of shared prosperity during which accelerating rates of social inequality and environmental degradation were slowed. Yet in New Zealand today, as in many nations, the gulf is now widening between a privileged adult elite with continued access to environmental, social and economic resources, and young, poor, ethnically-diverse and increasingly urban citizens.[6]

The New Zealand experience is a cautionary tale. It underscores the limits of the SMART practices of thin environmentalism: Self-help agency, Market participation, A priori justice as faith in the social contract, Representative democracy and Technological transformation. Too often the vision of SMART environmentalism leaves the drivers of environmental injustice unchallenged. Worse still, some green solutions shift more costs onto children through poorly-conceived environmental projects that only help the already advantaged.[7] Young citizens cannot live sustainable lives in communities where the institutional structures and processes of decision making are discriminatory, exploitative or unjust. Surely we have a collective adult obligation to nurture children as citizens in the same way that we respect our elderly? Re-creating a sustainable world starts with adult action to address the complex problems that influence the ecology of childhood.

We compound injustice to children when we preach about individual behaviour change and, in the process, erode the collective language, democratic tools and imagination young citizens will need to achieve, maintain and re-create a more just and sustainable world. In this regard, however, there is also good news in the New Zealand case, offering, as it does, some insights into the fine-grained and nuanced way it is possible to make a meaningful difference to the lives of a new cohort of citizens. Adults can and must take collective action to address intergenerational ecological injustice. This study highlights the way extended families, local sports coaches, protest experiences and community schools can help nurture the SEEDS of a stronger ecological education, supporting children as they learn new citizenship skills of: Social agency, Environmental education, Embedded justice, Decentered deliberation and Self-transcendence.

The recent, remarkable resurgence of youth political engagement internationally suggests we have been too quick to dismiss the democratic imagination of young citizens. Youthful energy and passion is a motor for social and political change. Despite the pressures of consumer lifestyles and financial insecurity, many young citizens in neoliberal democracies remain interested in the future of their community and questions of social justice.[8] Many want to 'make a difference'.[9] We squander these civic aspirations at our peril. Yet pro-environmental and democratic values are not the inevitable result of youth activism, material prosperity or regular access to nature.[10] A turn towards ecological citizenship will require significant institutional and community support.[11] Shifting our emphasis in citizenship and environmental education away from SMART environmental experiences to the SEEDS of ecological citizenship better supports young citizens as they confront the task of re-creating a common world.[12]

I return then to a question that opened this book: How can we nurture children's capabilities for ecological citizenship? The results of this study and wider research into children's political learning should give us pause for thought. Too often, children who have the least influence on the political process also have the fewest opportunities to develop the skills of effective citizenship. Many education programmes unwittingly marginalise the children who stand to gain most from the chance to serve on a school council or take part in a community activity with supportive peers and adult mentors.[13] In the New Zealand case, some children spoke confidently about their citizenship experiences, but others were less sure, reporting varying degrees of *non-citizenship* associated with the FEARS experiences of Frustrated agency, Environmental exclusion, Authoritarian decision making, Retributive justice and a Silenced imagination. These experiences are exacerbated under conditions of child poverty, domestic abuse, adult alcoholism or community intolerance.[14]

Some children were eager to consider alternative green futures. Many children who experienced SMART environmental citizenship were drawn from the highest-income school catchments and participated in gifted and talented education programmes. These children could reason thoughtfully about environmental change. Some were prepared to imagine large-scale technological risk to achieve desired environmental outcomes. However, it was striking that few children espousing SMART principles of thin environmentalism questioned the underlying issues of injustice that contributed to environmental degradation. It was also noticeable that many children from high-income, urban communities took part in a range of structured afterschool activities; consequently they had fewer opportunities to encounter others in informal afterschool play. Networks of informal social capital were less significant in the community maps of children in the highest income urban schools. These children took part in many structured afterschool clubs and tuition activities, and some mentioned shopping, but they rarely commented on informal afterschool street play or the quality of their (pleasant) local environments, referring only to these aspects of everyday community life with respect to special holiday and weekend experiences.

In contrast, this study lends support to the research of others who suggest it is children attending the culturally-diverse, middle- and lower-income, state-funded schools who are often doing the 'real work' of maintaining democracy and recreating a shared vision of a common and sustainable world.[15] Pupils from the Small World School and the urban Community-*Kura* School, for example, reported micro successes in their day-to-day struggles to connect with others: 'There's heaps and heaps of different country people in our school and that makes us really cool cos we're a cool school.' This process was not always easy, as highlighted by children's comments about the problems of sharing resources amongst ethnic groups or dealing with bullying. However, in these schools, children had opportunities to encounter others with different world views. In the Small World School, for example, many children enjoyed regular informal interactions between the school and families from 40 nations. In the bilingual Community-*Kura* School, children expressed pride in the opportunity to learn Māori as an indigenous language, to feel they were listened to by significant adults, and to undertake a variety of collaborative and intergenerational projects within and beyond the school. At both schools children volunteered a wide variety of their own formal and informal social networks.

Perhaps most significantly, a social norm of active citizenship was reinforced in all state-funded, community schools. Here children had opportunities to observe adults and peers taking part in public life through school fundraising, a local pool protest, serving on the school board or in tribal, local and national politics. In short, despite neoliberal roll back of the social contract and loss of state support for many aspects of youth citizenship, many children attending state schools still reported confidence in collective action as a means to achieve change.[16] In this light it was not environmental education *per se*, but learning conditions where children feel included and valued, and where norms of empathy and civic engagement are encouraged, which nurture SEEDS of strong ecological citizenship. Informal environmental affinity and formal environmental education matters, but this New Zealand study echoes the findings of research by Chawla and Cushing, Tsevreni, Uzzell and others, who suggest children's pro-environmental values are best supported in conditions of democratic learning where children feel valued, and can practice skills of listening to others and debating issues they care about within a supportive, multigenerational community.[17]

However, not all young citizens were confident about their ability to participate in their community or felt equally included as citizens. Some young citizens in seven focus groups reported feeling excluded or fearful in their local communities as a result of bullying or adult alcoholism; some new migrants, especially fee paying students, knew few people who could make changes in their community. Family violence was also commented on by three children. For example, when asked by a friend if he could 'protest' against his mum, Bob replied: 'If I did she'd just give me a smack ...' This conversation and two others reported comments about being smacked or 'getting the belt', provided a brief, moving insight into children negotiating adult power in a family setting. Bob's comment that his mum 'doesn't care' about new legislation protecting New Zealand children from being beaten is a stark reminder that legislative rights are a powerful source of support for children, but legislative change alone is not enough: supporting children as citizens also requires individual and community commitment.

New Zealand has experienced a high growth in income inequality at times over the past twenty years. Children in the two lowest income schools were very aware of the differences between the quality of their environment and that of other children, revealed in jokes about graffiti and vandalism: '[t]here is actually one thing that we don't have that other schools do have … two hoops! We only have one! Yeah someone broke the other … [basketball] hoop'. In this context, strong networks of social capital appear to help children cope with the unfairness of inequality. In the smallest and poorest rural *Kura* School, for example, children appreciated their local rural environment and felt strongly supported by *whānau* [wider family] relationships on tribal land, creating a sense of *whānaunātanga* [mutual support], speaking positively about the 'opportunities' that a local tribal trust provided for school trips and children's activities.[18]

At the Tree School children also reported conflicted attitudes to citizenship. The children at this high-income rural school all reported feeling that their valued places, ways of life and rights to have a say were under threat from urban development, immigration from China, or that they were not being heard in decision making. Many children expressed frustration that neither they – nor their mums and dads – were being listened to by decision makers in the school, community clubs or local council, which were dominated by 'higher ups' or people who 'stayed and stayed' and therefore dominated local decision making. Teachers at this school suggested older children who objected to lack of voice in decision making engaged in low level bullying towards young children because they had 'been there the longest'. Moreover, while the community faced pressure from urban sprawl, the ethnic diversity of the school roll remained entirely European/*Pākeha*.

These varied experiences of young citizens remind us that, left to their own devices, children are unlikely to learn about the values of democracy. Nor is affinity to environmental places enough to nurture a sense of social justice. The problems that confront young lives can easily overwhelm even the most resilient child. Children cannot be expected to address the environmental and social challenges we have bequeathed them without significant support. David Orr has argued for new models of citizenship which engage hand, head and heart to encourage young citizens to reflect on their values (heart), to think critically as they form their ideas (head) and to take actions (hand).[19] I suggest that perhaps it is adults who most need to engage their heads and hearts as they use their hands as ecological citizens to support young citizens.

From footprints to handprints: rethinking the agency of ecological citizenship

In 1996, Wackernagel and Rees published their ground-breaking Ecological Footprint model, a tool that graphically represents the physical space required to meet the needs of a given population through manufacturing, distribution, consumption and waste.[20] The authors hoped the ecological footprint would provide a simple, '... yet potentially comprehensive' account for the 'flows of energy and matter to and from any defined economy', converting these into 'the corresponding land/water area required from nature to support these flows'. The footprint illustrates the way per capita energy and material consumption is increasing at rates beyond the limits of the ecological system.[21]

The ecological footprint model has proved a powerful tool for enhancing public awareness about the way that processes of production and consumption impact on the physical world, sparking other ways of measuring human consumption, including carbon or water footprints.[22] The footprint model has also inspired new handprint models of environmental citizenship. Environmental handprints have developed in response to the suggestion that, if my ecological footprint represents 'my negative impact on the environment', my handprint 'represents what I can do about it'.[23] Inspired by the ecological footprint, yet frustrated by a lack of progress on environmental degradation and sustainability, many activists have turned to the concept of a handprint, arguing it is 'up to us all to change our footprint and apply an active handprint'.[24] In this argument, citizens are frequently urged to *reduce* their ecological footprint and *increase* their handprint. Used in this way, handprints are an emerging tool for raising public awareness and mobilising individuals to take action. Yet handprints are ambivalent political symbols. On the one hand, these images represent a welcome return to the Aristotelian concept of active citizenship. On the other, handprint images may merely reinforce unexamined assumptions of self-help citizenship and personal responsibility.

The following three examples illustrate ways that handprint thinking is currently being used in environmental education, the green economy and community activism. First, handprints are used increasingly in environmental education. 'Hands for change' is one of the most developed examples. Launched at an International Environmental Education Conference in 2007 and refined at a conference in Kuala Lumpur in Malaysia in 2008, this programme aims to raise awareness about sustainability and assist individuals to assess the efficacy of their actions to address ecological degradation and social injustice.[25] Hands for change includes an online web tool which asks questions such as: 'Do you make conscious efforts to conserve/save water? ... Do you eat locally grown fresh food? ... Do you ever share any of your income or resources with other people (not your family or employees) or charitable organisations?'[26] While such questions have the potential to encourage children to reflect on the impact of their individual lifestyles, they overlook the way wider institutions, cultural norms and social practices also constrain and enable opportunities for citizens to act. Moreover, if used uncritically, the handprint calculator may simply reinforce assumptions about the value of individual action. For example, this quiz rewards more points for individual efforts to achieve sustainability than actions taken on a community, state or international level, overlooking the times when collective action is a more effective solution.[27]

Handprint thinking is also used in discussion about the green economy. For example, the company Carbon Handprint UK argues: 'Your carbon footprint is your effect on our planet, your handprint is what you do about it.'[28] Their website

Figure 8.1 Child protesting climate change with a CAFOD handprint placard, London
Credit: Bronwyn Hayward.

encourages consumers and businesses to 'enlarge' their handprint by engaging in a range of actions from off-setting Christmas shopping to adopting an 'Eco-code' in the work place and developing cleaner green technology.[29] Despite a promising focus, discussion about consumer and corporate handprints in the green economy rarely challenges the role of industry in creating conditions of ecological injustice. Moreover, these handprint models rarely question whether technological transformations are realistic or sufficient, given the scale of the problems we face.[30]

Third, handprint imagery is often used to mobilise public action, and is increasingly used by environmental organisations. The UK campaign to 'Restore the Earth' and the Catholic peace and justice organisation CAFOD both used handprint symbolism to help mobilise large protests prior to the Copenhagen climate conference. The CAFOD handprint placards were accompanied by the slogan 'our climate is in our hands'.[31] Handprint images celebrate and motivate citizen action, but in neoliberal democracies our public commitment to shared purpose or endeavor can be relatively weak. Individual handprints are an ambivalent symbol of political action. The image of the individual handprint captures autonomous individual agency. The challenge is to find a way to engage the hard-won and highly-prized value of liberal autonomy as freedom to effect *collective* action. Handprint campaigns are laudable, and yet in visually equating 'my citizenship' with 'my handprint' we risk suggesting sustainability is a problem that can be addressed by specific actions undertaken by a loose coalition of individuals coming together at single point in time. This approach deflects attention from the need for strong, sustained and coordinated social action to confront the systemic causes of environmental injustice. The emphasis on what I can do with my hands, risks leaving unchallenged, the injustice I can't reach, the long 'chain of human suffering' embedded in our daily experience of production and consumption processes.[32]

In the context of trans-boundary threats, including a changing climate, water scarcity, loss of biodiversity and financial insecurity, the green mantra to 'think global, act local' is not always helpful. Rallying citizens to take individual, local action, risks isolating these individuals and rendering their struggles irrelevant to wider debate. There is also a risk in celebrating the power of local action that we overlook the ways that the actions of individuals are constrained and mediated by a wider context, including their social institutions, cultural norms and economic institutions.[33]

Handprint thinking also risks constraining our vision of a shared responsibility for environmental justice, to a narrower idea of 'blame'. Handprints are often thought about as incriminating evidence at the scene of a crime. This centred approach to justice – blaming some people and absolving others – is unhelpful if it encourages us to play ecological detective, identifying 'who dunnit' in environmental crimes rather than addressing the wider issues, such as how something came to be done, and what responsibility we should take collectively to avoid a repetition of the problem. We need to remember our interdependence and our collective responsibility.[34] Clear accountability in decision making is important, but centring the blame for problems when things go wrong on a 'bad mayor', a 'nasty industrialist' or a 'greedy banker' is not. Blaming individuals shifts our focus from the wider structural causes of environmental and social injustice.[35] Effective ecological citizenship demands a wider vision of justice. We need to think about ways we can support the 'response-ability' of citizens and our political institutions to enable effective remedial action and avoid injustice being repeated.[36]

In reality, a more effective form of political action may be one which targets multiple levels of local, national and international decision making using a range of activities, protest strategies, lobbying and alliance building to improve horizontal communication and coordination between groups.[37] In an era of global environmental change, effective, collective citizen action will require careful thought about the way we use our hands to effect change to ensure we are not simply displacing or obfuscating the problems, let alone making things worse. Before rushing to leave our handprint, we need time to reflect on the possible consequences of our actions, listening carefully to all voices, including children. Educationalist John Elliot has argued after Arendt that taking action is important, but taking time to pause and engage in dialogue is also critical.[38] Exposing our actions to scrutiny by non-governmental organisations, the media and formal review for intergenerational justice are ways to encourage a lighter, effective touch.[39] Dialogue and listening are prudent strategies if we wish to develop 'determinative morality', or a vision of what we ought to do, not just what we ought not do.[40]

This kind of critical thinking is far removed from unexamined notions of SMART environmentalism as self-help citizenship in which individuals are encouraged to solve environmental symptoms, but leave underlying questions of ecological justice unchallenged. It resonates with approaches to environmental education known as action competence or ecological pedagogy.[41] The later approaches take a critical and reflective approach to teaching as social justice. Inspired by the liberation tradition of Freire and Horton, eco-pedagogy is reminiscence of the social learning experienced in the civil rights, peace and feminist struggles.[42] In using handprint imagery in teaching, we can reflect on the way our activities and practices have temporal and spatial consequences, a link Bandura suggests has been disconnected through globalisation and export economies. Bandura argues it is difficult for citizens to comprehend the indirect effects of our actions on countless distant others.[43] Viewed in this light, we could envisage social handprint models as ways to reinvigorate debates about our collective obligations to ameliorate the harm our social and economic policies, practices and actions have caused others, including future generations and the non-human word.[44]

Reimagining our social handprint

For all its limitations, a handprint remains a powerful symbol, reminding us that we will leave an impact on our world, and that our decisions and actions will matter over time. When we take action, will it be in ways that are empathetic, compassionate and collaborative? Or will our impact be heavy-handed and domineering? Will our environmental handprint thinking be limited to individual action, or can we think about the way communities, corporations and nation states are collectively responsible for social and environmental change? Can we use the symbolism of human hands to help us rethink the legacy of citizenship in new ways? Can we use handprint imagery to symbolise citizenship as human connectedness and interdependency in a changing world? Is the image of 'holding hands' a more appropriate depiction of our mutual vulnerability and our need to collaborate to achieve common goals? Can we as citizens – young and old – 'hold hands' to take collective, thoughtful, just action for ecological change, symbolised as a *social* handprint?

The difficult challenges we now face require a new political imagination for citizenship, one in which the idea of personal responsibility in a cosmopolitan world is tempered with communitarian empathy. Seen in this light, I argue children need ecological citizenship education that provides the SEEDS experiences of Social agency, Environmental education, Embedded justice, Decentred deliberation

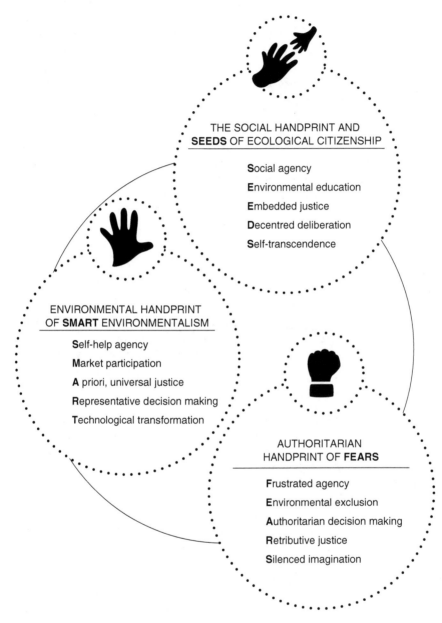

THE SOCIAL HANDPRINT AND
SEEDS OF ECOLOGICAL CITIZENSHIP

Social agency

Environmental education

Embedded justice

Decentred deliberation

Self-transcendence

ENVIRONMENTAL HANDPRINT
OF **SMART** ENVIRONMENTALISM

Self-help agency

Market participation

A priori, universal justice

Representative decision making

Technological transformation

AUTHORITARIAN
HANDPRINT OF **FEARS**

Frustrated agency

Environmental exclusion

Authoritarian decision making

Retributive justice

Silenced imagination

Figure 8.2 Summary: What kind of citizen handprint will you leave behind in a changing
          world?

and Self-transcendence as essential elements of a new vision of ecological citizenship.
The alternative model of a social handprint I sketch here is a first step to
considering representations of this citizenship. In suggesting our aim should
be to make our handprints smaller and lighter, and that our heroic aspirations as

ecological citizens should be tempered by humbleness, I am not calling for a loss of citizen courage. It takes courage to connect with others, to make ourselves vulnerable by enlarging our field of compassion. However, some thinkers have wisely cautioned overconfidence in widespread political or social transformations, reminding us that humbleness is valuable given the limits of what we know.[45] Viewed in this light, our aim should be not to always *increase* our handprint, but to ensure we take collective action in ways that are reversible rather than heroic, and ensuring our actions have the consent of those we presume to assist.[46]

Given the reach and grasp some citizens have in political life, ecological citizenship should be exercised with care. Aided by global communication, strengthened by financial investment and international infrastructure, the capability of some (usually northern and often older male) citizens to define the problem, identify solutions and leave indelible handprints on the futures and pasts of distant others is undesirable. Well-meaning social action campaigns like *Restoration of the Earth*, for example, used handprint imagery to motivate citizens to 'restore the great ecosystems around the planet; forests, oceans, freshwater, tundra, corals and the soils'.[47] Yet mobilising a campaign of northern citizens to secure iconic landscapes may inadvertently marginalise the concerns of small, southern indigenous communities. As Tongan philosopher Malakai Kolomatangi has commented, such campaigns can unwittingly reinforce a new image of Pacific peoples as vulnerable communities of small atolls, not people of the sea and explorers of vast oceans.[48] Kolomatangi's concerns about the power of citizens of the global north to redefine southern communities are underscored by UNICEF research with children of the Pacific, which suggests some children now feel a heightened anxiety about their immediate survival, and feel isolated and unsupported.[49] In this light, ecological citizenship takes a demanding view of our collective responsibility to connect with others to address injustice. To exercise ecological citizenship requires wisdom and humility, recognising we may not always know what is best to do in the face of dangerous global environmental change. We should aim to leave a light touch, mindful of the limits of our knowledge and informed by concern for the needs of others.

New ideas about citizenship are developing rapidly through decentred dialogue and youthful protest[50] exercised spontaneously, yet also in concert with distant others.[51] In their scepticism of traditional authority and enthusiasm for liberal autonomy, a new generation of citizens is experimenting with ideas of 'leaderless' political transformation.[52] The Occupy, UK Uncut and Spanish Indigados movements are examples of loosely-coordinated horizontal actions to resist powerful hierarchies in an increasingly globalised world of communication.[53] These movements have powerful but ambivalent potential. In one sense, the emergence of spontaneous global protest suggests a new vision of citizenship as networked social agency.[54] In this context, the imagery of a social handprint can celebrate our collective potential as citizens to collaborate across space and time to hold decision making to account and to imagine alternative futures.

Yet the non-hierarchical and spontaneous nature of loosely networked protest can also be easily coopted, and the energy of networked citizenship can peter out in the absence of stronger bonds of shared purpose and coordinated planning. Young citizens alone cannot foster a more inclusive democracy, let alone challenge the power of accumulated capital.[55] New tools of social media can enhance communication or isolate citizens, rendering young citizens vulnerable to greater surveillance or peer pressure.[56] Youthful activists face powerful opposition. As new expressions of citizenship emerge, how can we best support young citizens without getting in their way or thwarting their opportunities to lead and recreate a new future? Can we rethink our own social handprint as an older generation, for example, as that of trustee, guardian, mentor, cheerleader or witness? Here the capabilities approach of Martha Nussbaum helpfully reminds us of our potential to use our hands to create the conditions for young people to develop skills of democratic citizenship and a deeper appreciation of non-human nature.[57]

The combination of collective responsibility for action and confidence of citizens to effect change can be a powerful and disruptive force in politics.[58] In his book *Kettled Youth*, Dan Hancox ends quoting a text he received from a student after a protest: 'thought occurred – we just might win this'.[59] Here Hancox captures the power that imagining a different trajectory has on our visions of the future. Raising the confidence of groups about their political efficacy has the potential to change future trajectories and challenges expectations.[60] In a globalising world, however, even the most highly-networked young citizens will struggle to effect change in the face of diffuse financial, military and political power. In this context, we will need many hands, working at multiple levels, to reinforce collective bonds and effective social agency. It is in this vision and experience of collective mobilisation that the baby boom generation can offer positive support to a new generation of youthful protestors. As younger citizens learn the techniques and tools of democratic collaboration and resistance, the experience of the feminist, indigenous, civil rights and anti-slavery movements provide powerful examples of successful social action.[61] The impact of these movements improved the living conditions and aspirations of millions of women and girls in particular, many of whom flourished with education, employment and democratic voice.[62]

Young citizens are advantaged when they can learn by drawing on cultural memory through intergenerational dialogue and practical experience.[63] Collaborating with older citizens in shared projects helps young citizens as they learn to identify appropriate ways to use their resources to engage in democratic resistance. Opportunities to participate in decision making with older efficacious peers or adults also enhance a child's sense of purposive action in a changing world.[64] Yet, as adults, we need to think carefully about appropriate ways to support young citizens, so we do not stifle the emergence of new forms of political energy.[65]

Environmental education that encourages conversations, connections and listening across our differences of place and time can enhance youthful citizen skills and capabilities to effect change.[66] Local, diverse, state-funded schools were identified in this study as vital public spaces for cultivating the SEEDS of ecological citizenship. Opportunities to encounter others of all ages, in safe, inclusive, democratic learning environments were suggested as ways to nurture critical thinking and practical action for social agency. 'Citizen Schools' have been suggested as another way in which teachers and students can learn to work with communities to examine and challenge the systemic forces that influence the conditions of young lives.[67] Uzzell, for example, argues children benefit from close school and community relationships, and authentic opportunities for community problem solving.[68] However, today there are fewer opportunities for schools to develop citizen education programmes, let alone forge more informal community links. Schools are required to teach to narrowly-defined curriculum achievement measures. Opportunities for informal, spontaneous interactions in local places with others who share different views are diminished rather than enhanced in this context. Individual teachers may also feel understandably isolated or vulnerable if they encourage students to question the justice of political decisions in a classroom discussion or community activity.[69] Similarly, parents who wish to nurture democratic values in an unjust world may feel equally alone. Yet it is the networked actions of citizens everywhere, and their democratic imagination, that will create and sustain conditions of change.

However, the experiences of indigenous communities also reminds us that no amount of 'action' can ever 'put right' some suffering, loss or injustice.[70] In these situations, citizens also need skills to listen empathetically and with compassion. For example, the Australian '*Sea of Hands* campaign for reconciliation' aims to foster greater understanding of a shared public citizenship responsibility for past injustices of war, colonisation, domination and genocide.[71] This campaign reminds us actions do not always speak louder than words. Bearing witness and listening, for example though formal truth and reconciliation tribunals, is also important.[72] In this light, we urgently need to reevaluate the way environmental education can support values of inclusive, active democratic citizenship. The really difficult environmental problems we face reflect deep value differences that require more listening and more community interaction, not less. Young citizens need more support as they learn to cooperate and plan for a common future where we cannot agree.[73] Further, children's citizenship is supported when they are exposed to models of adult interaction that engage with others as respected adversaries rather than enemies or antagonists.[74] The SEEDS experiences of ecological citizenship include a spiritual quality of self-transcendence as well as self-conscious civic action. Rachel Carson describes this self-transcendence as a sense of wonder. Carson's work speaks about the limits of human understanding and the value of learning to transcend our own worldviews to empathise with non-human nature.[75] I argue we also need to nurture a child's sense of wonder about democracy, nurturing empathy for others, and an appreciation of the extraordinary potential of ordinary people acting in collaboration to create a more compassionate and sustainable world. To achieve democratic change, however, young citizens will need more than a sense of wonder: they need education and the support of adults, as they learn to hold decision-makers to account, to resist illegitimate power, and to collaborate imaginatively with others to achieve a more sustainable common, future.

The value of a democratic imagination in a changing world

The political handprint which is emerging in a new generation is a social one. As young citizens take to the streets and e-media, many are determined to make a difference through networks of collaborative, non-hierarchical action.[76] Our role as teachers, parents and community activists of all ages is to support young citizens as they discover their democratic imagination and capacity for collective action. To be effective in the face of complex problems and far-reaching power, ecological citizens need more than electronic technology. Citizens will also need the skills of empathy, critical thinking and the ability to reason about difficult issues of justice. To broaden understanding of new and complex environmental problems, we can also learn lessons from social movements that encourage thinking beyond self-interest.[77]

The challenges faced by the world's youngest citizens are both similar and different from the political struggles which defined the baby boom generation. Over thirty years, dominant discourses of economic growth and individual responsibility have become global and hegemonic, crowding out opposing ways of seeing the world. In this context, environmental philosopher Loraine Code has argued that our most important task as teachers, parents and colleagues is to support our students and children to 'think their way out of an entrenched imaginary', which emphasises mastery of the natural world and self-reliance, to discover our interdependence and to create new opportunities to cohabitate.[78] For a new generation to realise a new vision of citizenship as mutual interdependence on a finite planet, we will need many sites of struggle and conversation which connect to foster new narratives of collaboration and community.[79]

In his early observations of children immersed in imaginative play, educational psychologist Vygotsky made a telling observation. When a child engages in imaginary play, Vygotski argues, it is '… not a fortuitous fact in a child's life, but is rather the first manifestation of the child's emancipation from situational constraints'.[80] Vygotsky reminds us that it is in her imagination that a child learns to exercise her potential power for agency, forming ideas and acting upon them. It is also in imaginative play, Vygotsky argues, that children can learn to refrain from acting on immediate impulses. Observing situations where a child creates an imaginary game and imposes rules to guide action, Vygotsky argues a child is simultaneously enjoying creative spontaneity and discovering freedom within self-determined limits. Child development theory has focused largely on understanding freedom as personal autonomy.[81] Yet Vygotsky's insightful reflection on the power of the imagination opens up the possibility for us to consider the creative as well as practical conditions citizens will need to achieve a more just, democratic and sustainable future. Can we reimagine a similar sense of collective freedom in ecological citizenship, as we learn to live spontaneously within collectively agreed limits or rules?

Growing up under neoliberalism and recession, many costs are passed to the millennium generation and the ones that follow, as cuts are made of essential public services children depend upon and our global economies seek new, unsustainable ways to 'recover'. In this setting, greater environmental awareness can help support young citizens, but the networked actions of parents, teachers, grandparents and peers, together with state-funded, inclusive schools. are also essential to sustain the democratic imagination of young citizens. These actors and the institutional support of diverse, inclusive state schools emerged in this study as essential sites for nurturing the SEEDS of a new, ecological citizenship. In closing, I reflect on the playful and thoughtful observations of children talking about their prospects for effecting change:

INTERVIEWER: What do you want people to take from this study?
ROBERTA: They, the government wouldn't listen to us; we'd need to get adults involved …
LEONARDO DA VINCI: I just hope that people will listen or read this thingy and I'd like them to just understand that we have a mind and we can think, it's just most of our thoughts include lollies [sweets/candy]! [laughs]
TROY: Not always! …
MILEY: We can't do as much as adults but we can learn stuff and remember for when we are adults, [then] we might be able to do a bit more than adults are doing now.
                                                  (Community-*Kura* School)

Do we have to wait until 'Roberta', 'Leonardo da Vinci', 'Troy' and 'Miley' grow up before adults 'get involved' and start doing 'a bit more' than we are doing now? In our collective adult attention deficit disorder, we have over looked the ecological concerns of our children. When will adults act to address the environmental, economic and social insecurities we caused and which are blighting the prospects of children?[82] What kind of action will we take to address their concerns, and what kind of social handprint will we will leave behind for future generations? Will it be the heavy hand of FEARS experiences of authoritarian decision making, the injustice of the invisible hand of SMART experiences of thin environmentalism, or the light touch of ecological citizenship, which nurtures the SEEDS of Social agency, Environmental awareness, Embedded justice, a Decentered democratic debate and Self-transcendence?

Epilogue

On 4 September 2010, shortly after the interviews for this study were completed, the city of Christchurch experienced a 7.1 magnitude earthquake. A few months later, on 22 February 2011, Christchurch children and their families were subjected to a second shallow and more devastating 6.3 magnitude aftershock which killed over 180 people. Homes and school buildings were destroyed or 'munted', thousands of children moved schools and cities for a temporary period; some have not returned. Several children we interviewed were in the worst affected central city at the time of the aftershock; some lost family members or friends.

Figure 8.3 Christchurch children playing in a crack in the road after the 4 September 2011
        earthquake

Credit: *The Press* Fairfax NZ Ltd.

Yet in the rush to rebuild a 'sustainable' green city centre to retain business in a
shaky province, we have lost sight of the needs of our children. Children's lives
have been dramatically disrupted, yet little media attention has been paid to date
to their struggles. A spike in reported domestic violence is one disturbing indicator of the ongoing grief, stress and exhaustion experienced by many families.[83]
Principals and teachers have been at the forefront of efforts to support and sustain
their communities, reporting both strain and community regeneration.

In the scale of a disaster, the limits of personal responsibility become obvious to everyone. It was the social agency and youthful energy of high-school and university students on Facebook who organised a campaign involving 10,000 young volunteers to help clean up Christchurch. Their efforts inspired my community as many other creative community responses sprang into life.[84] What is disturbing, however, was how quickly we let down the children and young people of Christchurch democratically in the months that have followed the disaster.

The government reaction to the earthquakes was to suspend the constitution for several weeks, and to grant wide-ranging powers to a new Minister for Earthquake Recovery, to replace the city's struggling local council with a 'command and control' model of bureaucratic governance for the next five years. Despite the significant efforts of teachers in state-funded school communities to sustain vital social networks, the New Zealand government has announced a surprising intention to introduce a business model for new charter schools into the lowest income and worst-affected earthquake communities.[85] These steps remind us that the conditions that are required to sustain a democracy cannot be taken for granted, but have to be recreated by each generation.[86]

New Zealand children currently receive inequitable social support compared to older citizens, and many are exposed to significant environmental risk. In this context, local state schools are a vital support for their citizenship. Rachel Carson implicitly reminds us it is not only birds that are silenced as we degrade our environment; it is the imagination of our children.[87] Yet nurturing a democratic imagination can be a powerful and disruptive force for an alternative future. I close with this conversation between two 9-year-old girls reflecting on their experience of a community protest to retain their local pool. In their conversation we hear the SEEDS of a new generation of civic activism:

ASHLEY: You feel very important and special, and you've got this kind of vibe inside you, cause you feel like you're getting heard and everyone in the world knows – cause you're shouting so loud and you're putting your heart towards something.

ROSE: Maybe if the whole school go together with another school, and then we all wrote letters, absolutely all of us, and then we all send them to the government, our council, and then we could get signs and protest and stuff, and we'd have more people and there would be lots of letters – and they wouldn't know what to do!

INTERVIEWER: So then maybe they'd have to listen?

ROSE: Yup.

(Community-*Kura* School)

We may not agree with Rose's confidence that adults will listen, but if we want to create a more environmentally just and common future, we should nurture the power of her democratic imagination.

He mihi nui tenei ki te hapori kura nana tenei rangahau i whakaae, ara, ki te k tūmuaki i ngā kaiako, ki ngā matua, a, kei tua atu i enei, ki ngā tamariki whakamiharo. Tēnā koutou katoa te tautoko i ta mātou mahi. Sincere thanks to the schools that supported this project, and most importantly, to the frank and inspiring children for sharing your communities.

Notes

1 Children's Social Health Monitor 2011; CPAG 2011; OECD 2009b.
2 Davies *et al.* 2010.
3 Boven *et al.* 2011, p15.
4 OECD 2011b; Collins 2010.
5 Bertram and Terry 2010; Oram 2009; Nissen 2011; O'Brien *et al.* 2009.
6 OECD 2011b, Willetts 2010.
7 For a discussion of environmental problems facing children in developed economies, see Cureton 2011 and Flanagan 2008; for an example of the way well-intended environmental education and market partnerships can inadvertently privilege the already privileged, see Ghosh 2011.
8 Kasser *et al.* 2010.
9 Hayward *et al.* 2011b.
10 Inglehart 1997; Uzzell 1999.
11 See Roderick Watts and Constance Flanagan's (2007) thoughtful discussion about the value of liberation psychology and a developmental approach to understanding how youthful action to address social injustice can enhance collective and individual wellbeing.
12 Arendt 1954 (2006), p193.
13 Youniss and Middaugh 2009, p31; Schusler *et al.* 2009; Barratt-Hacking *et al.* 2007.
14 Laugeson 2011.
15 Not all state-funded public schools are equally effective seedbeds of citizenship: see Kohn 2011; Naussbaum 2010, especially pp27–46.
16 Hart 2008.
17 Similar observations have been reported by Tsevreni (2011), who argues children in Greece regularly learn a 'shallow' form of environmentalism based on scientific reasoning, at the expense of their ability to develop a strong relationship with their community, critical thinking and independent action. Malone (2007) argues that Australian children growing up experiencing restricted opportunities for varied community interactions are deprived of opportunities to build skills as critical, competent, independent and resilient learners. See Chawla and Cushing 2007; Uzzell 1999.
18 Dalton 2008.
19 Orr 2005a (p98), 2005b.
20 Wackernagel and Rees 1996, pp51–2.
21 Ibid., p1.
22 Druckman and Jackson 2009; Wiedmann and Minx 2007; Hoekstra and Chapagain 2007.
23 Transition Edinburgh University 2009; CEE 2008a.
24 Transition Edinburgh University 2009.
25 As the handprint has developed it has become a more promising collective approach: see the results of a competition amongst 22 primary schools for reducing school handprints (*Ceenario* 2011). Gunawardene 2008.
26 CEE 2008b.

27 CEE 2008b.
28 Carbon Handprint UK 2009.
29 Carbon Handprint UK 2009.
30 Jackson 2009, pp77–86; O'Riordan 1976, pp86–110; Druckman and Jackson 2009.
31 CAFOD 2009.
32 Dobson 2007, pp174–5; Barry 2005; Pogge 2002; Young 2006a, 2006b; Bauman 2011.
33 For discussion of contemporary youth politics, see Mason 2011. For reflections on the tension between structural and individual agency, see Giddens 2009, pp50–7; Jackson 2008; Seyfang 2005.
34 Young 2011.
35 Hayward 2008a; Young 2006a, 2006b.
36 Lera St. Clair 2010.
37 See Hayward 2008a for a discussion of Iris Young's concept of linkages between citizen groups and organisations in the context of a changing climate.
38 Elliot 2004.
39 For examples of intergenerational review, see Alliance for Future Generations 2011
40 On determinative morality, see Young 2011; Dobson 2003.
41 Jensen and Schnack 1997.
42 Khan 2010; Hart 1997.
43 Bandura 2007.
44 Pogge 2002, pp30–1; Young 2011; Bohman 2007.
45 Freeden 2009.
46 Ibid.
47 Restore the Earth Movement 2009.
48 Kolomatangi oral comments reported in Hayward 2008a.
49 UNICEF 2011c.
50 I was struck by the way each new generation rediscovers and reinvents its message when witnessing the first of the student protests about university fee hikes in London in 2010: see Hayward 2010b.
51 Bohman 2007; Dobson and Bell 2005; Dobson 2007; Hayward 2008b.
52 Blissett 2011; Curtis 2011.
53 Mason 2011.
54 Ainger 2011.
55 Dryzek 2000, 2006; Jackson 2009.
56 Bauman 2011.
57 Nussbaum 2011, especially pp33–45; Sen 2009, pp18–19.
58 Chawla and Cushing 2007.
59 Hancox 2011.
60 Dobson 2003; Jackson 2009; Leichenko and O'Brien 2008; Jasanoff 2010; Soper 1995.
61 Flanagan 2008.
62 See Flanagan 2008 pp198–200 and Young 2006b for a similar observation of opportunity for networked activism and intergenerational political learning from previous social movements.
63 Hart 1997; see also Flanagan 2008.
64 Ibid.
65 For a thoughtful discussion of youthful activism as 'possibilities for the future', see Flanagan 2008, pp197–206.
66 Jensen and Schnack 1997; Bishop and Scott 1998.
67 Horton and Friere 1990.

68 Uzzell 1999.
69 See Flanagan 2008 for a frank discussion of the difficulties facing teachers who support children as they learn to challenge authority.
70 Walker 2004.
71 Sea of Hands 2008.
72 Dobson 2010a.
73 Mouffe 2002; Young 2006a, 2006b; Honig 2009; Dryzek 2000, 2006; Bohman 2004; Hulme 2009.
74 Mouffe 2002; Dryzek 2000.
75 Carson 1965 (1998).
76 Flanagan 2008a; Costanza 2011; Cole and Durham 2008.
77 Bohman 2007; Dobson and Bell 2005; Dobson 2007; Hayward 2008a.
78 Code 2010, pp30–1.
79 Jasanoff 2010; Young 2006a, 2006b.
80 See Vygotsky's extended discussion of children in imaginative play (1978, pp99–100).
81 Hart 2008, p28.
82 Bohman 2011, p192; see also Liebig and Widmaier 2009.
83 Lynch 2011.
84 See Brett 2011 and Hayward forthcoming for discussion of baking armies and farmer armies, transition town movements and community timebanks, dancing groups, churches and many more who helped recreate a community. For examples of youthful imagination that has fostered a theatre of resistance and sites of creativity in the wake of rapid building demolition, and connections between students facing disasters in Japan and Christchurch, see *Gap Filler* 2011 and *PechaKucha* 2011.
85 Harper 2011.
86 Honig 2009; Wolf *et al.* 2009.
87 Carson 1965 (1998).

Appendix

Focus group prompts

1   What kinds of activities do children from around here do with other people?
2   The groups we often do things with we can call communities.

    a   What does it mean to you to be a citizen of these communities?
    b   Who makes the decisions in these communities?
    c   Do you think that the people that make the decisions in these communities listen to children like you? Why or why not?

3   Are there any issues you'd like to have a say about?

This project received ethical approval from the Education Research Human Ethics Committee, University of Canterbury, New Zealand.

Supplementary climate change discussion prompts

Five schools were prompted for their opinions (Tree School, Farm-Sea School, Faith School, Gate School and Music School).

1   What is your view of climate change? Do you think it's happening?
2   What do you think are the causes of climate change?

    a   What pollution do you think is the most serious for climate change?

3   What effects do you think climate change might have on you now/will it have on you in the future?
4   Who or what do you think is responsible for these causes of climate change?
5   What are some things that can be done to help stop climate change?
6   Who does the most in your community to help with climate change?
7   What can kids your age do to help with climate change? Can you do as much as adults?

Glossary

Hongi   To press noses in greeting, share breath, smell, sniff
Hui   To gather, congregate, assemble, meet
Hui ā-tau   Annual meeting
Iwi   Extended kinship group, tribe, nation, people, nationality
Kapa haka   Concert party, *haka* (to dance, perform) group, Māori cultural group, Māori performing group
Kōhanga reo   Māori language preschool or language nest
Karakia   To recite ritual chants, say grace, pray, recite prayer, chant
Koro   Grandfather, elderly man, or term of address to an older man
Kura kaupapa Māori   Primary school operating under Māori custom and using Māori as the medium of instruction
Marae   The open area in front of the *wharenui* (meeting house), where formal greetings and discussions take place. Often also used to include the complex of buildings around the *marae*
Me tōku whānau   With my family
Mihi   To greet, pay tribute, acknowledge, thank
Pākehā   New Zealander of European descent or exotic – introduced from or originating in a foreign country
Papa kāinga   Original home, home base, village
Tangata   People
Taua   Grandmother (*Ngāi Tahu* dialect)
Whānau   Extended family, family group or to be born, give birth
Whanaungatanga   Relationship, kinship, sense of family connection – a relationship through shared experiences and working together which provides people with a sense of belonging
From Moorfield 2011.

References

Adger, N., Paavola, J., Huq, S. and Mace, M. J. (2006) *Fairness in adaptation to climate change*. Cambridge, MA: MIT Press.

Adger, N., Barnett, J., Chapin III, F. S. and Ellemor, H. (2011) 'This must be the place: underrepresentation of identity and meaning in climate change decision making'. *Global Environmental Politics* 11(2): 1–25.

Aiken, J. (1997) 'Striving to teach "justice, fairness, and morality"'. *Clinical Law Review* 4(1).

Ainger, K. (2011) 'The Spanish Election is a mandate for the indigados'. *The Guardian*, 21 November. Online at http://www.guardian.co.uk/commentisfree/2011/nov/21/spanish-election-mandate-indignados (accessed 12 December 2011).

Alatini, M. (2009) *Analysis of unintentional child injury data in New Zealand: Mortality (2001–2005) and morbidity (2003–2007)*. Auckland: Safe Kids New Zealand. Online at http://www.safekids.org.nz/Downloads/Research/Safekids%20Analysis%20VLR_2.pdf (accessed 8 December 2011).

Alliance for Future Generations (2011) *About the Alliance for Future Generations*. London: Foundation for Democracy and Sustainable Development. Online at http://www.fdsd.org/what-we-do/future-generations/ (accessed 19 December 2011).

Almond, G. and Verba, S. (1963 (1989)) *The civic culture: Political attitudes and democracy in five nations*. London: Sage.

Aqtash, N., Seif, A. and Sheif, A. (2004) 'Media coverage of Palestianan children and the Intifada'. *International Communication Gazette* 66(5): 383–409.

Arendt, H. (1954 (2006)) *Between past and future*. New York: Penguin.

Arendt, H. (1958 (1998)) *The human condition*. Chicago: University of Chicago Press.

Arnstein, S. (1969) 'A ladder of citizen participation'. *Journal of American Institute of Planners* 35(4): 45–54.

Atkins, M., McKay, M., Arvanitis, P., London, L., Madison, S., Costigan, C., Haney, M., Hess, L., Zevenbergen, A. and Bennett, D. (1998) 'An ecological model for school-based mental health services for urban low-income aggressive children'. *The Journal of Behavioural Health Services and Research* 25(1): 64–75.

Augé, M. (1995) *Non-places: Introduction to an anthropology of supermodernity*. London: Verso.

Bagnolia, A. and Clark, A. (2010) 'Focus groups with young people: A participatory approach to research planning'. *Journal of Youth Studies* 13(1): 101–19.

Baker-Cristales, B. (2009) 'Mediated resistance: The construction of neoliberal citizenship in the immigrant rights movement'. *Latino Studies* 7(1): 60–82.

Bandura, A. (1997) *Self-efficacy: The exercise of control*. New York: Freeman.

Bandura, A. (2007) 'Impeding ecological sustainability through selective moral disengagement'. *International Journal of Innovation and Sustainable Development* 2(1): 8–35.

Barber, B. (1984 (2003)) *Strong democracy: Participatory politics for a new age*. Berkeley: University of California Press.

Barber, B. (2004) *Fear's empire: War, terrorism and democracy*. New York: Norton.

Barber, B. (2007) *Consumed: How markets corrupt children, infantilize adults, and swallow citizens whole*. New York: Norton.

Barnardos (2011) 'Our poll results show negative view of children'. *Barnardos UK*, 3 November 2011. Online at http://www.barnardos.org.uk/news_and_events/current_news.htm?ref=74120 (accessed 14 November 2011).

Barnett, J. and Pauling, J. (2005) 'The environmental effects of New Zealand's free-market reforms'. *Environment, Development and Sustainability* 7(2): 271–89.

Barratt, R. and Barratt-Hacking, E. (2011) 'Place-based education and practice: Observations from the field'. *Children, Youth and Environments* 21(1): 1–13.

Barratt-Hacking, E., Barratt, R. and Scott, W. (2007) 'Engaging children: Research issues around participation and environmental learning'. *Environmental Education Research* 13(4): 529–44.

Barry, J. (1999) *Rethinking green politics*. London: Sage.

Barry, J. (2005) 'Resistance is fertile: From environmental to sustainability citizenship'. In Dobson, A. and Bell, D. (eds) *Environmental citizenship*. Cambridge, MA: MIT Press, pp21–48.

Barry, J. (2006) *Environment and social theory* (2nd edition). London: Routledge.

Bartlett, S. (2008) 'Climate change and urban children: Impacts and implications for adaptation in low and middle income countries'. *Environment and Urbanization* 20(2): 501–19.

Bartlett, S., Hart, R., Satterthwaite, D., de la Barra, X. and Missair, A. (1999) *Cities for children: Children's rights, poverty and urban management*. London: Earthscan.

Bauman, Z. (2003) *Community: Seeking safety in an insecure world*. Cambridge: Polity Press.

Bauman, Z. (2011) 'Is this the end of anonymity? From micro-drones to the internet, technology is invading the private sphere – with our encouragement'. *The Guardian*, 28 June. Online at http://www.guardian.co.uk/commentisfree/2011/jun/28/end-anonymity-technology-internet (accessed 12 November 2011).

BBC (2011) *BBC News School Report Survey*. Plymouth: Royal Statistical Society, University of Plymouth. Online at http://news.bbc.co.uk/2/shared/bsp/hi/pdfs/24_03_11_school_report_survey.pdf (accessed 12 March 2012).

Beaumont, E. (2010) 'Political agency and empowerment: Pathways for developing a sense of political efficacy in young adults'. In Sherrod, L., Torney-Purta, J. and Flanagan, C. (eds) *Handbook of research on civic engagement in youth*. Hoboken: Wiley, pp525–58.

Beaumont, E. (2011) 'Promoting political agency, addressing political inequality: A multilevel model of internal political efficacy'. *The Journal of Politics* 73: 216–31.

Bedford, R. (2002) 'International migration in New Zealand: Context, components and policy issues'. *Journal of Population Research* 39(27): 39–66.

Bellamy, P. (2008) 'Immigration chronology: Selected events 1840–2008'. Parliamentary Library Research Paper 2008/01. Wellington: New Zealand Parliamentary Library.

Bengry-Howell, A., Morey, Y., Griffin, C., Riley, S. and Szmigin, I. (2010) '"All together at the same thing for the same reason": A temporary escape from neoliberalism: Intersubjectivity and sociability in a music festival context'. Youth 2010: Identities, Transitions, Cultures, Guildford, UK. 6–8 July.

Benhabib, S. (2006) 'The "claims" of culture properly interpreted: Response to Nikolas Kompridis'. *Political Theory* 34: 383–8.

Berkes, F. (1999) *Sacred ecology: Traditional ecological knowledge and resource management*. Philadelphia: Taylor & Francis.

Bertram, G. and Terry, S. (2010) *The carbon challenge: New Zealand's emission trading scheme*. Wellington: Bridget Williams Books.

Bessette, J. (1997) *The mild voice of reason: Deliberative democracy and American national government*. Chicago: Chicago University Press.

Bishop, K. and Scott, W. (1998) 'Deconstructing action competence: Developing a case for a more scientifically-attentive environmental education'. *Public Understanding of Science* 7(3): 225–36.

Bishop, R. and Glynn, T. (1999) *Culture counts: Changing power relations in education*. Palmerston North: Dunmore Press.

Blaiklock, A., Kiro, C. A., Belgrave, M., Low, W., Davenport, E. and Hassall, I. (2002) 'When the invisible hand rocks the cradle: New Zealand children in a time of change'. Innocenti Occasional Paper, Economic and Social Policy Series. Florence: UNICEF.

Blay-Palmer, A. (2011) 'Sustianable communities: An introduction'. *Local Environment* 16(8): 747–52.

Blissett, L. (2011) 'Adam Curtis, self-organization and UK Uncut: An Ecology of weeds'. Online at http://www.newleftproject.org/index.php/site/blog_comments/adam_curtis_self_organisation_and_uk_uncut_an_ecology_of_weeds (accessed 12 November 2011).

Boal (2000) *Theatre of the oppressed*. London: Pluto Press.

Bobbio, L. (2010) 'Types of deliberation'. *Journal of Public Deliberation* 6(2): article 1.

Bohman, J. (2004) 'Decentering democracy: Inclusion and transformation in complex societies'. *The Good Society* 13(2): 49–55.

Bohman, J. (2007) *Democracy across borders: From dêmos to dêmoi*. Cambridge, MA: MIT Press.

Bohman, J. (2011) 'Children and the rights of citizens: Nondomination and intergenerational justice'. *The ANNALS of the American Academy of Political and Social Science* 633(1): 128–40.

Bookchin, M. (1980) *Toward an ecological society*. Montreal: Black Rose Books.

Bookchin, M. (1990) *Remaking society: Pathways to a green future*. Boston: South End Press.

Boston, J., Dalziel, P. and St John, S. (1999) *Redesigning the welfare state in New Zealand: Problems, policies and prospects*. Auckland: Oxford University Press.

Boulding, E. (1996) *Our children, our partners: A new vision for social action in the 21st century*. Kelvin Grave, QLD: Margaret Fell.

Bourdieu, P. (1998) *Practical reason: On the theory of action*. Palo Alto, CA: Stanford University Press.

Boven, R., Harland, C. and Grace, L. (2011) 'More ladders, fewer snakes: Two proposals to reduce youth disadvantage'. Discussion Paper 2011/1. Wellington: New Zealand Institute.

Brett, C. (2011) 'Christchurch 3 months on'. *The Press*, 22 May. Online at http://www.stuff.co.nz/national/christchurch-earthquake/5037194/Christchurch-three-months-on (accessed 13 December 2011).

Bronfenbrenner, U. (1979) *The ecology of human development: Experiments by nature and design*. Cambridge, MA: Harvard University Press.

Brooks, R. (2009) 'Young people and political participation: An analysis of European union policies', *Sociological Research Online* 14(1). Online at http://www.socresonline.org.uk/14/1/7.html (accessed 20 August 2010).

Brown, K. and Westaway, E. (2011) 'Agency, capacity, and resilience to environmental change: Lessons from human development, well-being, and disasters'. *Annual Review of Environment and Resources* 36: 321–42.

Buck, J. (2009) *The Puzzle of Young Asian Political Participation: A Comparative Discussion of Young Asian Political Participation in New Zealand and the United States*. A thesis submitted in fulfilment of the requirements for a Master of Arts in Political Science, University of Canterbury.

Bunting, M. (2003) 'Passion and pessimism'. *The Guardian*, 5 April. Online at http://www.guardian.co.uk/books/2003/apr/05/society (accessed 21 November 2011).

Burgess, J., Harrison, C. and Filius, P. (1998) 'Environmental communication and the cultural politics of environmental citizenship'. *Environment and Planning A* 30(8): 1445–60.

Burningham, K. and Thrush, D. (2001) '"Rainforests are a long way from here": The environmental concerns of disadvantaged groups'. York: Joseph Rowntree Foundation. Online at http://www.capacity.org.uk/downloads/rainforest_are_long_way.pdf (accessed 12 November 2011).

Burningham, K., Venn, S., Gatersleben, B., Christe, I. and Jackson, T. (forthcoming) *Moments of change*. Guildford: Sustainable Lifestyles research Group, University of Surrey, UK. http://www.ukerc.ac.uk/support/tiki-download_file.php?fileId=1916&display (accessed 1 December 2011).

Butcher, A. and McGrath, T. (2004) 'International students in New Zealand: Needs and responses'. *International Education Journal* 5(4): 540–51.

Buttigieg, C. (2010) *Deliberative Democratic Theory in Action: A community group responds to energy and climate issues*. A thesis submitted in fulfilment of the requirements of a Master of Arts in Political Science, University of Canterbury.

Cadzow, J. (2004) 'The bubble-wrap generation'. *The Age, Good Weekend* supplement, 17 January, pp18–21.

CAFOD (2009) 'Greenbelt: Hands up for climate justice'. Online at http://www.cafod.org.uk/news/uk-news/greenbelt-2009-04-09 (accessed 20 November 2010).

Cambridge Primary Review (2009) 'Cambridge Primary Review: The Final Report'. Online at http://www.primaryreview.org.uk/Downloads/Finalreport/CWE-briefing.pdf (accessed 12 November 2011).

Carbon Handprint UK (2009) 'Your carbon footprint is your effect on our planet. Your handprint is what you do about it'. Online at http://www.carbonhandprint.co.uk/ (accessed 20 November 2010).

Carlsson, M. and Jensen, B. B. (2006) 'Encouraging environmental citizenship: The roles and challenges for schools'. In Dobson, A. and Bell, D. (eds) *Environmental citizenship*. Cambridge, MA: MIT Press, pp237–61.

Carson, R. (1962 (2002)) *The silent spring*. New York: Mariner.

Carson, R. (1965 (1998)) *A sense of wonder*. New York: Harper Collins.

CEE (2008a) *Increase your hand print: Decrease your footprint*. Centre for Environmental Education. Online at http://www.handsforchange.org/handprinttools.html (accessed 12 December 2011).

CEE (2008b) *Hands for change: Handprint calculator*. Centre for Environmental Education. Online at http://www.handsforchange.org/handprintquiz.aspx (accessed 5 January 2012).

Ceenario (2011) 'Paryayaran Mitra in Andhra Pradesh'. *Ceenario: E-newsletter for the Centre of Environmental Education* 46, 1–15 July.

Chawla, L. (1992) 'Childhood place attachments'. In Altman, I. and Low, S. (eds) *Place attachment*. New York: Plenum Press, pp63–86.

Chawla, L. (1999) 'Life paths into effective environmental action'. *The Journal of Environmental Education* 31(1): 15–26.

Chawla, L. and Heft, H. (2002) 'Children's competence and the ecology of communities: A functional approach to the evaluation of participation'. *Journal of Environmental Psychology* 22: 201–16.

Chawla, L. and Cushing, D. (2007) 'Education for strategic environmental behaviour'. *Environmental Education Research* 13(4): 437–52.

Children's Social Health Monitor (2009) *Introduction to the Children's Social Health Monitor*. Dunedin: University of Otago. Online at http://www.nzchildren.co.nz/ (accessed 12 November 2011).

Children's Social Health Monitor (2011) *The Children's Social Health Monitor: 2011 Update*. Dunedin: University of Otago.

Christoff, P. (1996) 'Ecological citizens and ecologically guided democracy'. In Doherty, B. and de Geus, M. (eds) *Democracy and green political thought: Sustainability, rights and citizenship*. London: Routledge, pp151–69.

Clark, A. and Moss, P. (2001) *Listening to young children: The Mosaic approach*. London: National Children's Bureau and the Joseph Rowntree Foundation.

Clark, N. (2011) *Inhuman nature: Sociable life on a dynamic planet*. London: Sage.

Codd, J. (2005) 'Teachers as "managed professionals" in the global education industry: The New Zealand experience'. *Educational Review* 57(2): 193–206.

Code, L. (2010) 'Particularity, epistemic responsibility, and the ecological imaginary'. *Philosophy of Education Yearbook*. Urbana-Champaign: The Philosophy of Education Archive, University of Illinois, pp 23–34. On line at http://ojs.ed.uiuc.edu/index.php/pes/article/view/2997/10749 (accessed 12 March 2012)

Cohen, E. (2005) 'Neither seen nor heard: Children's citizenship in contemporary democracies'. *Citizenship Studies* 9(2): 221–40.

Cohen, J. and Arato, A. (1994) *Civil society and political theory*. Cambridge, MA: MIT Press.

Cole, J. and Durham, D. (2008) 'Introduction: Globalization and the temporality of children and youth'. In Cole, J. and Durham, D. (eds) *Figuring the future: Globalization and temporalities of children and youth*. Santa Fe: SAR Press.

Collins, S. (2010) 'Child poverty rate in New Zealand too high'. *New Zealand Herald*, 10 June. Online at http://www.nzherald.co.nz/nz/news/article.cfm?c_id=1&objectid=10650823 (accessed 1 December 2011).

Colmar Brunton (2008) *Seen and heard: Children's media use, exposure and response*. Wellington: Broadcasting Standards Authority. Online at http://www.bsa.govt.nz/assets/Research/Seen-and-Heard-Part2-Media-Use.pdf (accessed 12 December 2011).

Costanza, R. (2011) 'Needed: The solutions generation'. *Solutions*. Online at http://www.thesolutionsjournal.com/node/991 (accessed 1 December 2011).

Council of Europe (2010) 'Prohibiting the marketing and use of the "Mosquito" youth dispersal device'. Council of Europe: Committee on Culture, Science and Education. 22 March. Online at http://assembly.coe.int/Documents/WorkingDocs/Doc10/EDOC12186.pdf (accessed 8 December 2011).

CPAG (2011) *Left further behind: How policies fail the poorest children in New Zealand*. Auckland: Child Poverty Action Group.

Crain, W. (2005) *Theories of development: Concepts and applications*. Upper Saddle River, NJ: Pearson Prentice Hall.

CRESA (2010) *Access to safe and secure housing for at risk and vulnerable young people*. Wellington: Centre for Housing Research Aotearoa New Zealand.

Crompton, T. and Kasser, T. (2009) 'Meeting environmental challenges: The role of human identity'. Godalming, Surrey: WWF. Online at http://www.wwf.org.uk/wwf_articles.cfm?unewsid=3105 (accessed 12 November 2011).

Cunningham, S. and Lavalette, M. (2004) '"Active Citizens" or "Irresponsible Truants"? School student strikes against the war'. *Critical Social Policy* 24(2): 255–69.

Cureton, S. (2011) 'Environmental victims: Environmental injustice issues that threaten the health of children living'. *Reviews on Environmental Health* 26(3): 141–7.

Curtis, A. (2002) 'The century of the self'. *BBC Four*, 29 April–2 May. Online at http://www.bbc.co.uk/bbcfour/documentaries/features/century_of_the_self.shtml (accessed 22 November 2011).

Curtis, A. (2011) 'How the "ecosystem" myth has been sued for sinister means'. *The Observer*, 29 May. Online at http://www.guardian.co.uk/environment/2011/may/29/adam-curtis-ecosystems-tansley-smuts (accessed 12 November 2011).

Dalton, R. and Doh Chull Shin (eds) (2006) *Citizens, democracy, and markets around the Pacific Rim: Congruence theory and political culture*. Oxford: Oxford University Press.

Dalton, W. (2008) *Indigenous language acquisition and political efficacy: In what ways and to what extent does immersion education or bilingual school affect children's internal political efficacy?: A comparative study*. A dissertation submitted in fulfilment of the requirements for Māori 480: Research Essay, University of Canterbury.

Dalziel, P. (2002) 'New Zealand economic reforms: An assessment'. *Review of Political Economy* 14(1): 31–46.

Daniels, H., Cole, M. and Wertsch, J. (eds) (2007) *The Cambridge companion to Vygotsky*. Cambridge: Cambridge University Press.

David, M. (2007) 'Changing the educational climate: Children, citizenship and learning contexts?'. *Environmental Education Research* 13(4): 425–36.

Davies, Crothers and Hanna (2010) 'Preventing child poverty: Barriers and solutions'. *New Zealand Journal of Psychology* 39(2): 20–31.

Dean, M. (1999) *Governmentality: Power and rule in modern society*. London: Sage.

Devine-Wright, P., Devine-Wright, H. and Fleming, P. (2004) 'Situational influences upon children's attitudes and beliefs about global warming and energy'. *Environmental Education Research* 10(4): 493–506.

Dewey, J. (1916 (1966)) *Democracy and education: An introduction to the philosophy of education*. New York: Macmillan Free Press.

Dewey, J. (1927) *The public and its problems*. New York: Holt.

Dobson, A. (2003) *Citizenship and the environment*. Oxford: Oxford University Press.

Dobson, A. (2005) 'Citizenship'. In Dobson, A. and Eckersley, R. (eds) *Political theory and the ecological challenge*. Cambridge: Cambridge University Press, pp481–561.

Dobson, A. (2006) 'Ecological citizenship: A defence'. *Environmental Politics* 15(3): 447–51.

Dobson, A. (2007) *Green political thought*. London: Routledge.

Dobson, A. (2009) 'Citizens, citizenship and governance for sustainability'. In Adger, N. and Jordan, A. (eds) *Governing sustainability*. Cambridge: Cambridge University Press, pp125–41.

Dobson, A. (2010a) 'Democracy and Nature: Speaking and listening'. *Political Studies* 58(4): 752–68.

Dobson, A. (2010b) *Environmental citizenship and pro-environmental behaviour: Rapid research and evidence review*. London: Sustainable Development Research Network.

Dobson, A. and Bell, D. (eds) (2005) *Environmental citizenship*. Cambridge, MA: MIT Press.

Dobson, A. and Sáiz, Á. V. (eds) (2005) *Citizenship, environment, economy*. Milton Park, Oxon: Routledge.

Doherty, R. (2007) 'Education, neoliberalism and the consumer citizen: After the golden age of egalitarian reform'. *Critical Studies in Education* 48(2): 269–88.

Domjen, B. (2011) 'Sexy ad campaign targeting children sparks anger'. *The Sunday Mail*, 5 June. Online at http://www.news.com.au/entertainment/fashion/sexy-ad-campaign-targeting-children-sparks-anger/story-e6frfn7i-1226069391059 (accessed 8 December 2011).

Donald, H. (2009) *Principled non-voters and postmaterialist theory: An exploratory analysis of young principled non-voters in New Zealand*. A thesis submitted in fulfilment of the requirements for a Master of Arts in Political Science, University of Canterbury.

Douglas, R. (1993) 'The politics of successful reform'. Speech to the Mount Pelerin Society, Australia.

Druckman, A. and Jackson, T. (2009) 'The carbon footprint of UK households 1990–2004: A socio-economically disaggregated, quasi-multiregional input-output model'. *Ecological Economics* 68(7): 2066–77.

Druckman, A., Chitnis, M., Sorrell, S. and Jackson, T. (2010) 'An investigation into the rebound and backfire effects from abatement actions by UK households'. RESOLVE Working Paper 05-10. University of Surrey, Guildford. Online at http://www3.surrey. ac.uk/resolve/Docs/WorkingPapers/RESOLVE_WP_05-10.pdf (accessed 12 November 2011).

Dryzek, J. (1990 (1994)) *Discursive democracy: Politics, policy and political science*. Cambridge: Cambridge University Press.

Dryzek, J. (2000) *Deliberative democracy and beyond: Liberals, critics, contestations*. Oxford: Oxford University Press.

Dryzek, J. (2006) *Deliberative global politics: Discourse and democracy in a divided world*. Cambridge: Policy Press.

Dryzek, J. (2009) 'The Australian citizens' parliament: A world first'. *Journal of Public Deliberation* 5(1): article 9.

Duerden, N. (2010) 'Daddy where will the polar bears live?' *The Independent*, 1 November. Online at http://www.independent.co.uk/environment/green-living/daddy-where-will-the-polar-bears-live-2121710.html (accessed 1 November 2010).

Duggan, L. (2003) *The twilight of equality? Neoliberalism, cultural politics and the attack on democracy*. Boston: Beacon Press.

Easton, D. and Dennis, J. (1967) 'The child's acquisition of regime norms: Political efficacy'. *American Journal of Political Science* 61(1): 25–31.

Eckersley, R. (1996) 'Liberal democracy and the rights of nature: The struggle for inclusion'. In Matthews, F. (ed) *Ecology and democracy*. London: Frank Cass, pp169–98.

Eckersley, R. (2006) 'Communitarianism'. In Dobson, A. and Eckersely, R. (eds) *Political theory and the ecological challenge*. Cambridge: Cambridge University Press, pp91–107.

Eizenberg, E. (2004) 'The production of contesting space: Community gardens and the cultivation of social change'. Open Space Conference, Edinburgh, UK. 29 October. Online at http://www.openspace.eca.ac.uk/conference/proceedings/PDF/Eizenberg.pdf (accessed 12 November 2011).

Elliot, J. (2004) 'The struggle to redefine the relationship between "knowledge" and "action" in the academy: Some reflections on action research'. *Educar* 34: 11–26.

Elliott, A. and Urry, J. (2010) *Mobile lives*. London: Routledge.

Emirbayer, M. and Mische, A. (1998) 'What is agency?'. *American Journal of Sociology* 103(4): 962–1023.

Englund, T. (2011) 'The potential of education for creating mutual trust: Schools as sites for deliberation'. *Educational Philosophy and Theory* 43(3): 236–48.

Evans, G. and Marcynyszyn, L. (2004) 'Environmental justice, cumulative environmental risk, and health among low- and middle-income children in upstate New York'. *American Journal of Public Health* 94(11): 1942–4.

Fainstein, S. (2007) 'Iris Marion Young (1946–2006): A tribute'. *Antipode* 39(2): 382–7.

Families Commission (2008) *The Kiwi nest: 60 years of change in New Zealand families*. Wellington: Families Commission. Online at http://www.nzfamilies.org.nz/research/the-kiwi-nest (accessed 30 November 2011).

Ferguson, S., Blakely, T., Allan, B. and Collings, S. (2005) *Suicide rates in New Zealand: Exploring the associations with social and economic factors*. Report 2: Social Explanations for Suicide in New Zealand. Wellington: New Zealand Ministry of Health. Online at http://www.moh.govt.nz/moh.nsf/0/BEB6627B003586A5CC2570D400809A5B/$File/suicideratesinnewzealand.doc (accessed 1 March 2010).

Finlayson, A. (2010) 'Foreword', 5–6. In UK Sustainable Development Commission, *Improving young people's lives: The role of the environment in building resilience, responsibility and employment chances*. London: Sustainable Development Commission.

Fischer, F. (2003) *Reframing public policy: Discursive politics and deliberative practices*. Oxford: Oxford University Press.

Fischer, F. (2005) *Citizens, experts and the environment: The politics of local knowledge*. Durham, NC: Duke University Press.

Fiske, S., Gibert, D. and Lindzey, G. (eds) (2010) *Handbook of social psychology* (volume 2). Hoboken, NJ: John Wiley.

Flanagan, C. (2008a) 'Private anxieties and public hopes: The perils and promise of youth in the context of globalization'. In Cole, J. and Durham, D. (eds) *Figuring the future: Globalization and the temporalities of children and youth*. Santa Fe: SAR Press, pp197–206.

Flanagan, C. (2008b) *Young people's civic engagement and political development*. The Network on transitions to Adulthood. University Park, PA: Pennsylvania State University. Online at http://www.transad.pop.upenn.edu/downloads/youth%20civic%20engagement%20and%20political%20development.pdf (accessed 12 March 2012).

Flanagan, C. and Sherrod, S. (1998) 'Youth political development: An introduction'. *Journal of Social Issues* 54(3): 447–56.

Foucault, M., Burchell, G. and Gordon, C. (1991) *The Foucault effect: Studies in governmentality*. Chicago: University of Chicago Press.

Franklin, M. (2004) *Voter turnout and the dynamics of electoral competition in established democracies since 1945*. Cambridge: Cambridge University Press.

Freeden, M. (2009) 'Failures of political thinking'. *Political Studies* 57(1): 141–64.

Freeland, C. (2011) 'Wall Street protesters challenge the reagan revolution'. *New York Times*, 14 October, p2.

Freeman, C. (2010) 'Children's neighbourhoods, social centres to "terra incognita"'. *Children's Geographies* 8(2): 157–76.

Freeman, C. and Quigg, R. (2009) 'Commuting lives: Children's mobility and energy use'. *Journal of Environmental Planning and Management* 52(3): 393–412.

Freeman, C. and Tranter, P. (2011) *Children and their urban environment: Changing worlds*. London: Earthscan.

Freire, P. (1970) *Pedagogy of the oppressed*. Harmondsworth: Penguin.

Freire, P. (1975) *Education: The practice of freedom*. London: Writers and Readers.

Freire, P. (1985) *The politics of education: Culture, power and liberation*. New York: Bergin and Garvey.

Gap Filler (2011) 'Christchurch'. Online at http://www.gapfiller.org.nz/ (accessed 13 December 2011).

Ghosh, S. (2011) 'Participation in the Green Power Partnership: An analysis of higher education institutions as partners in the program'. *International Journal of Sustainability in Higher Education* 12(4): 306–21.

Giddens, A. (1986) *The constitution of society: Outline of the theory of structuration*. Berkeley: University of California Press.

Giddens, A. (1998) *The Third Way: The renewal of social democracy*. Cambridge: Polity Press.

Giddens, A. (2009) *The politics of climate change*. Cambridge: Polity Press.

Gleeson, B. and Sipe, N. (eds) (2006) *Creating child friendly cities: Reinstating kids in the city*. Milton Park: Routledge.

Gluckman, P. and Hayne, H. (eds) (2011) 'Improving the transition: Reducing social and psychological morbidity during adolescence'. Wellington: Office of Prime Minister and Cabinet. Online at http://www.pmcsa.org.nz/wp-content/uploads/Improving-the-Transition-report.pdf (accessed 12 November 2011).

Gough, S. and Scott, S. (2006) 'Promoting environmental citizenship through learning: Toward a theory of change'. In Dobson, A. and Bell, D. (eds) *Environmental Citizenship*. Cambridge, MA: MIT Press, pp263–85.

Green, N. and Hayward, B. (forthcoming) '"Anti-loitering", "acoustic dispersal" alarms: The control of children and young people's access to and use of public space'. *Local Environment*.

Greenberg, E. (1970 (2009)) *Political socialization*. New York: Transaction Press.

Griffin, M. (2011) 'Developing deliberative minds: Piaget, Vygtosky and the deliberative democratic citizen'. *Journal of Public Deliberation* 7(1): 1–28.

Grimmond, D. (2011) *1000 days to get it right for every child; The effectiveness of public investment in New Zealand children*. Wellington: Infometrics and Every Child Counts. Online at http://www.crin.org/docs/NZ_Every_Child_Counts_Aug_11.pdf (accessed 12 December 2011).

Gunawardene, N. (2008) 'From footprints to handprints: Treading lightly on the earth'. *Moving Images, Moving People!*, 2 March. Online at http://movingimages.wordpress.com/2008/03/02/from-footprints-to-handprints-treading-lightly-on-earth/ (accessed 13 September 2009).

Gutmann, A. and Thompson, D. (1996) *Democracy and disagreement*. Cambridge, MA: Belknap Press.

Gutmann, A. and Thompson, D. (2004) *Why deliberative democracy?* Princeton, NJ: Princeton University Press.

Habermas, J. (1996) *Between facts and norms: Contributions to a discourse theory of law and democracy*. Cambridge, MA: MIT Press.

Hajer, M. (1995) *The politics of environmental discourse: Ecological modernization and the policy process*. Oxford: Clarendon Press.

Halseth, G. and Doddridge, J. (2000) 'Children's cognitive mapping: A potential tool for neighbourhood planning'. *Environment and planning B* 27: 565–82.

Hamilton, C. (2010) *Requiem for a species: Why we resist the truth about climate change*. Crows Nest, NSW: Allen & Unwin.

Hammond, K., Wyllie, A. and Casswell, S. (1999) 'The extent and nature of televised food advertising to New Zealand children and adolescents'. *Australian and New Zealand Journal of Public Health* 23: 49–55.

Hancox, D. (2011) *Kettled youth: The battle against the neoliberal endgame*. Vintage Digital.

Hansen, J. (2010) *Storms of my grandchildren: The truth about the coming climate catastrophe*. New York: Bloomsbury USA.

Harper, C., Jones, N., McKay, A. and Espey, J. (2009) *Children in times of economic crisis: Past lessons, future policies*. London: Overseas Development Institute and UNICEF.

Harper, P. (2011) 'Claim charter schools not fair on quake students'. *New Zealand Herald*, 7 December. Online at http://www.nzherald.co.nz/nz/news/article.cfm?c_id=1& objectid=10771543 (accessed 12 December 2011).

Hart, D. and Kirshner, B. (2009) 'Civic participation and development amongst urban adolescents'. In Youniss, J. and Levine, P. (eds) *Engaging young people in civic life*. Nashville: Vanderbilt Press, pp102–20.

Hart, R. (1992) *Children's participation: From tokenism to citizenship*. Florence: UNICEF.

Hart, R. (1997) *Children's participation: The theory and practice of involving young citizens in community development and environmental care*. London: Earthscan.

Hart, R. (2008) 'Stepping back from the ladder: Reflections on a model of participatory work with children'. In Reid, A., Jensen, B. B., Nikel, J. and Simovska, V. (eds) *Participation and learning perspectives on education and the environment, health and sustainability*. Emeryville: Springer, pp19–31.

Harvey, D. (2007) *A brief history of neoliberalism*. Oxford: Oxford University Press.

Hattie, J. (2009) *Visible learning: A synthesis of over 800 meta-analyses relating to achievement*. Milton Park: Taylor & Francis.

Hayes, D. (2011) 'England on trial'. *Inside Story*, 16 August. Online at http://inside.org. au/england-on-trial/ (accessed 21 November 2011).

Hayward, B. (1995) 'The greening of participatory democracy'. *Environmental Politics* 4(4): 215–36.

Hayward, B. (2006) 'Public participation'. In Miller, R. (ed) *New Zealand government and politics*. Melbourne: Oxford University Press, pp514–24.

Hayward, B. (2008a) 'Let's talk about the weather: Decentring democratic debate about climate change'. In Hayward, B. (ed.) *The politics of climate change: New Zealand and small Pacific states*. Auckland: Dunmore Books.

Hayward, B. (2008b) 'Nowhere far from the sea: Political challenges of coastal adaptation to climate change in New Zealand'. *Political Science* 60(1): 47–61.

Hayward, B. (2008c) 'Editorial'. In Hayward, B. (ed) *The politics of climate change: Issues for New Zealand and small states of the Pacific*. Wellington: Dunmore Publishers.

Hayward, B. (2010a) 'Bowling with a sponsor: New Zealand children's attitudes to citizenship and climate change mitigation'. 60th Political Studies Association Annual Conference, Edinburgh, UK. 10 March.

Hayward, B. (2010b) 'Where have all the adults gone?' *Open Democracy*, 10 December. Online at http://www.opendemocracy.net/bronwyn-hayward/where-have-all-adults-gone (accessed 21 November 2011).

Hayward, B. (forthcoming) 'Rethinking resilience'. *Society and Ecology*.

Hayward, B. (forthcoming) 'Why citizenship matters more than behaviour change'. In Lawrence, J., Cornforth, A., and Barrett, P. (eds) *Climate futures: Pathways for society*. Wellington: Victoria University Press.

Hayward, B. and O'Brien, K. (2010) 'Social contracts in a changing climate: Security of what, and for whom?' In O'Brien, K., Lera St. Clair, A. and Kristofferson, B. (eds)

(2010) *Climate change, ethics and human security*. Cambridge: Cambridge University Press, pp451–521.

Hayward, B. and Jackson, T. (2011) 'New graduates face a more uncertain future than ever before'. *The Guardian*, 11 June. Online at http://www.guardian.co.uk/sustainable-business/ blog/tim-jackson-british-graduates-green-dreams (accessed 15 November 2011).

Hayward, B., Donald, H., Sheerin, C. and Raikena, A. T. (2006) '*Whakarongomai*! Listen to me! How young people talk about politics'. Dialogue across Difference: Governance in a Multicultural Era Conference, Canberra, Australia. 4–5 December. Online at http:// deliberativedemocracy.anu.edu.au/documents/DAD%20papers/BronwynHayward.pdf (accessed 15 November 2011).

Hayward, B., Donald, H. and Okeroa, E. (2011a) 'Flourishing: Young lives well lived in New Zealand'. In United Nations Environment Programme (ed.) *Visions for change: Country papers*. Paris: United Nations Environment Programme: 56–61.

Hayward, B., Jackson, T. and Evans, D. (2011b) 'UK youth: The conflicts of contemporary lifestyles'. In United Nations Environment Programme (ed.) *Visions for change: Country papers*. Paris: United Nations Environment Programme, pp99–105.

Hayward, J. and Wheen, N. (eds) (2004) *The Waitangi tribunal:* Te Roopu Whakamana I te Tiriti o Waitangi. Wellington: Bridget Williams Books.

Hayward, T. (2006) 'Ecological citizenship: Justice, rights and the virtue of resourcefulness'. *Environmental Politics* 15(3): 435–46.

Healthy Communities Coalition (2005) *50 stories in 50 days*. Franklin, Australia: Franklin Community Health Network.

Heath, S., Brooks, R., Cleaver, E. and Ireland, E. (2009) *Researching young people's lives*. London: Sage.

Hess, D. (2009) 'Principles that promote the discussion of controversial issues in the curriculum'. In Youniss, J. and Levine, P. (eds) *Engaging young people in civic life*. Nashville: Vanderbilt University Press, pp59–80.

Heywood, A. (2004) *Political Theory: An introduction* (3rd edition). Basingstoke: Palgrave Macmillan.

Higgins, J. and Nairn, K. (2006) '"In transition": Choice and the children of New Zealand's economic reforms'. *British Journal of Sociology in Education* 27(2): 207–20.

Hoekstra, A. and Chapagain, A. (2007) 'Water footprint of nations: Water use by people as a function of their consumption pattern'. *Water Resource Management* 21: 35–48.

Honig, B. (2009) *Emergency politics: Paradox, law, democracy*. Princeton, NJ: Princeton University Press.

Horton, M. and Freire, P. (1990) *We make the road by walking*. Philadelphia: Temple University Press.

Hosking, J., Jones, R., Percival, T., Turner, N. and Ameratunga, S. (2010) 'Climate change: The implications for child health in Australasia'. *Journal of Paediatrics and Child Health*, 47(8): 493–6.

Howden-Chapman, P., Hales, S., Chapman, R. and Keskimäki, I. (2005) *The impact of economic recession on youth suicide: A comparison of New Zealand and Finland*. Wellington: Ministry of Health.

Howden-Chapman, P., Chapman, R., Hales, S., Britton, E. and Wilson, N. (2010) 'Climate change and human health: Impact and adaptation issues for New Zealand'. In R. A. C. Nottage, D. S. Wratt, J. F. Bornman and K. Jones (eds.) *Climate change adaptation in New Zealand: Future scenarios and some sectoral perspectives*. Wellington: New Zealand Climate Change Centre, pp112–21.

Howker and Malik (2010) 'The new age of protest: A fresh generation of activists could prove a real threat to the coalition'. *Prospect* 179: 26–31.

Huckle, J. (2010) 'ESD and the current crisis of capitalism: Teaching beyond green new deals'. *Journal of Education for Sustainable Development,* 4(1): 135–42.

Hulme, M. (2009) *Why we disagree about climate change: Understanding controversy, inaction and opportunity.* Cambridge: Cambridge University Press

Hvistendahl, M. (2011) 'Young and restless can be a volatile mix'. *Science,* 29 July, 333 (6042): 552–4.

Igoe, J. and Brockington, D. (2007) 'Neoliberal conservation: A brief introduction'. *Conservation and Society* 5(4): 432–49.

Ingersoll, R. (2003) *Who controls teachers work? Power and accountability in America's schools.* Cambridge, MA: Harvard University Press.

Inglehart, R. (1997) *Modernization and postmodernization: Cultural, economic, and political change in 43 societies.* Princeton: Princeton University Press.

Inglehart, R. and Welzel, C. (2005) *Modernization, cultural change and democracy: The human development sequence.* New York: Cambridge University Press.

Inglehart, R. and Welzel, C. (2010) 'Changing mass priorities: The link between modernization and democracy'. *Reflections* 8(2): 551–67.

Jackson, N. (2011) *The demographic forces shaping New Zealand's future: What population ageing [really] means.* National Institute of Demographic and Economic Analysis, Hamilton: University of Waikato.

Jackson, T. (2008) 'Where is the "well-being dividend"? Nature, structure and consumption inequalities'. *Local Environment* 13(8):703–23.

Jackson, T. (2009) *Prosperity without growth: Economics for a finite planet.* London: Earthscan.

James, O. (2007) *Affluenza.* London: Vermilion.

Jasanoff, S. (2010) 'A new climate for society'. *Theory Culture Society* 27(2–3): 233–53.

Jeffrey, C. (2011) 'Geographies of children and youth II: Global youth agency'. *Progress in Human Geography.*

Jensen, B. and Schnack, K. (1997) 'The action competence approach in environmental education'. *Environmental Education Research* 3(2): 163–178.

Jensen, D., McBay, A. and Keith, L. (2011) *Deep green resistance.* New York: Seven Stories.

John, P., Cotterill, S., Moseley, A., Richardson, L., Smith, G., Stoker, G. and Wales, C. (2011) *Nudge, nudge, think, think: Experimenting with ways to change civic behaviour.* London: Bloomsbury Academic.

Johnson, S. (2012) 'Students vs. the machine: Lessons learned in the student community following the Christchurch earthquakes'. *E-volunteerism* XII(2). Online at http://www.e-volunteerism.com/volume-xii-issue-2-january-2012/feature-articles/1201#comment-309 (accessed 12 March 2012).

Johnston, K. (2011) 'Widening gap between rich and poor'. 6 December. Online at http://www.stuff.co.nz/business/money/6092128/Widening-gap-between-rich-and-poor (accessed 12 December 2011).

Kahn, R. (2010) *Critical pedagogy, ecoliteracy, and planetary crisis: The ecopedagogy movement.* New York: Peter Lang.

Kahne, J. and Westheimer, J. (2006) 'The limits of political efficacy: Educating students for a democratic society'. *Political Science and Politics* 39(2): 289–96.

Kahne, J. and Middaugh, E. (2009) 'The civic opportunity gap in high school'. In Youniss, J. and Levine, P. (eds) *Engaging young people in civic life.* Nashville: Vanderbilt Press, pp29–48.

Kahukiwa, R. (2006) *Matatuhi*. Auckland: Penguin Books.

Kail, R. (2010) *Children and their development* (5th edition). Upper Saddle River, NJ: Pearson Prentice Hall.

Kasser, T., Crompton, T. and Linn, S. (2010) 'Children, commercialism and environmental sustainability'. *Solutions* 1(2): 14–17.

Katz, C. (2004) *Growing up global: Economic restructuring and children's everyday lives.* Minneapolis: University of Minnesota Press.

Keale, C. (2009) 'How many New Zealanders use Trade-me? All of us'. *National Business Review*, 25 February. Online at http://www.nbr.co.nz/opinion/chris-keall/how-many-new-zealanders-use-trade-me-all-us (accessed 30 November 2011).

Kearns, R., Collins, D. and Neuwelt, P. (2003) 'The walking school bus: Extending children's geographies?'. *Area* 35(3): 285–92.

Kelly, D. and Brooks, M. (2009) 'How young is too young? Exploring beginning teachers' assumptions about young children and teaching for social justice'. *Equity and Excellence in Education* 42(2): 202–16.

Kelsey, J. (1996) *The New Zealand experiment*. Auckland: Auckland University Press.

Kerr, D. (1999) 'Re-examining citizenship education in England'. In Torney-Purta, J., Schwille, J., and Amadeo, J. (eds) *Civic education across countries: Twenty-four national case studies from the IEA civic education project*. Amsterdam: IAEEA.

King, M. (2003) *The Penguin history of New Zealand*. Auckland: Penguin.

Kirk, N. (2008a) 'The impact of neo-liberalism on children's attitudes to climate change mitigation'. *Political Science* 60(1): 160–5.

Kirk, N. (2008b) *Children of the market? The impact of neoliberalism on children's attitudes to climate change mitigation*. A thesis submitted in fulfilment of the requirements for a Master of Arts in Political Science, University of Canterbury.

Knight, S. (2009) *Forest schools and outdoor learning in the early years*. London: Sage.

Kohn, M. (2011) 'If you are an egalitarian, why do you send your children to private school?'. *Dissent* 58(2): 57–63.

Krosnick, J. (1991) 'The stability of political preferences: Comparisons of symbolic and non-symbolic attitudes'. *American Journal of Political Science* 35(2): 547–76.

Kymlicka, W. (2001) *Politics in the vernacular: Nationalism, multiculturalism, citizenship.* Oxford: Oxford University Press.

Kymlicka, W. (2002) *Contemporary political philosophy: An introduction*. Oxford: Oxford University Press.

Ladson-Billings, G. (2009) 'Foreword'. In Kumashiro, K. (author) *Against common sense: Teaching and learning toward social justice*. New York: RoutledgeFalmer. ppxvii–xxviii.

Lanza, D. (2005) 'Tapping the well of urban youth activism: Literacy for environmental justice'. In Stone, M. and Barlow, Z. (eds) *Ecological literacy: Educating our children for a sustainable world*. San Francisco: Sierra Club Books, pp213–26.

Larner, W. (2000) 'Neoliberalism: Policy, ideology, governmentality'. *Studies in Political Economy* 63(3): 5–25.

Larner, W. and Craig, D. (2005) 'After neoliberalism? Community activism and local partnerships in Aotearoa New Zealand'. *Antipode* 37(3): 402–24.

Latour, B. (2004) *Politics of Nature: How to bring the sciences into democracy.* Cambridge, MA: Harvard University Press.

Laugeson, R. (2011) 'Fuel poverty in the land of plenty'. *The Listener*, 3725, 1 October. Online at http://www.listener.co.nz/commentary/fuel-poverty-in-the-land-of-plenty/ (accessed 8 December 2011).

Layard, R. (2005) *Happiness: Lessons from a new science.* New York: Penguin Group USA.

Layard, R. and Dunn, J. (2009) *A good childhood: Searching for values in a competitive age.* London: Penguin Books.

Leach, J. (2011) 'The poor perception of younger people in the UK'. London: Intergenerational Foundation. Online at http://www.if.org.uk/wpcontent/uploads/2011/08/The_Poor_Perception_of_Younger_People_in_the_UK_17Aug3.pdf (accessed 21 November 2011).

Leach, M., Scoones, I. and Stirling, A. (2010) *Dynamic sustainabilites: Techology, environment and social justice.* London: Earthscan.

Lefale, P. (2003) 'Indigenous knowledge in the Pacific'. *Tiempo: Global Warming and the Third World* 49. Online at http://www.tiempocyberclimate.org/portal/archive/issue49/t49a1.htm (accessed 12 November 2011).

Leichenko, R. and O'Brien, K. (2008) *Environmental change and globalization: Double exposures.* Oxford: Oxford University Press.

Lera St. Clair, A. (2010) 'Global poverty and climate change: Towards the responsibility to protect'. In O'Brien, K., Lera St. Clair, A. and Kristoffersen, B. (eds) *Climate change, ethics and human security.* Cambridge: Cambridge University Press, pp180–98.

Levine, P. (2011) 'On civic renewal'. Online at http://peterlevine.ws/ (accessed 20 November 2011).

Lewis, N. (2005) 'Code of practice for the pastoral care of international students: Making a globalising industry in New Zealand'. *Globalisation, Societies and Education* 3(1): 5–47.

Leyva, R. (2009) 'No Child Left Behind: A neoliberal repackaging of social Darwinism'. *Journal for Critical Education Policy Studies* 7(1): 365–8.

Liebig, T. and Widmaier, S. (2009) 'Children of immigrants in the labour markets of EU and OECD countries: An overview'. OECD Social, Employment and Migration Working Paper 97. Brussels: OECD Publishing. Online at http://dx.doi.org/10.1787/220823724345 (accessed 1 December 2011).

Lister, R. (2007) 'Why citizenship? Where, when and how children?'. *Theoretical Inquiries in Law* 8 (2): 693–718.

Locke, E. (1975) *Look under the leaves.* Christchurch: Pumpkin Press.

Louv, R. (2005) *Last child in the woods: Saving our children from nature-deficit disorder* (revised edition). Chapel Hill, NC: Algonquin Books.

Loynes, C. (forthcoming) 'Outdoor education: An English tradition?' Online at http://www.thresholdconsulting.co.uk/chris.htm (accessed 1 November 2010).

Lukes, S. (2005) *Power: A radical view* (2nd edition). Basingstoke: Palgrave Macmillan.

Lynch, K. (2011) 'Spike in domestic violence after Christchurch earthquake'. *Christchurch Press*, 9 March. Online at http://www.stuff.co.nz/national/christchurch-earthquake/4745720/Spike-in-domestic-violence-after-Christchurch-earthquake (accessed 12 November 2011).

McCrea, E. (2005) 'The roots of environmental education: How the past supports the future'. Stevens Point, WI: Environmental Education and Training Partnership.

MacGregor, S. (2006) *Beyond mothering Earth: Ecological citizenship and the politics of care.* Vancouver: UBC Press.

McKay, G. (2011) *Radical gardening: Politics, idealism and rebellion in the garden.* London: Francis Lincoln.

MacLeod, C. and Moller, H. (2006) 'Intensification and diversification of New Zealand agriculture since 1960: An evaluation of current indicators of land use change'. *Agriculture, Ecosystems and Environment* 115: 201–18.

McMeeking, S. (2011) 'The role of future generations in durable decision making'. Climate Futures – Pathways for Society, Wellington, New Zealand. 30 March–1 April.

McMichael, A., Campbell-Lendrum, D., Corvalán, C., Ebi, K., Githeko, A., Scheraga, J. and Woodward, A. (eds) (2003) *Climate change and human health: Risks and responses.* Geneva: WHO. Online at http://www.who.int/globalchange/publications/climchange.pdf (accessed 12 November 2011).

McVeigh, T. (2010) 'Backlash over Richard Curtis' 10: 10 climate film'. *The Guardian*, 2 October. Online at http://www.guardian.co.uk/environment/2010/oct/02/1010-richard-curtis-climate-change (accessed 5 December 2011).

Malone, K. (2007) 'The bubble-wrap generation: Children growing up in walled gardens'. *Environmental Education Research* 13(4): 513–52.

Mansbridge, J. (1999) 'Everyday talk in the deliberative system'. In Macedo, S. (ed) *Deliberative politics: Essays on democracy and disagreement.* New York: Oxford University Press, pp211–39.

Margolin, M. (2005) 'Indian pedagogy: A look at traditional Californian Indian teaching techniques'. In Stone, M. and Barlow, Z. (eds) *Ecological literacy: Educating our children for a sustainable world.* San Francisco: Sierra Club.

Marshall, T. and Bottomore, T. (1950 (1992)) *Citizenship and social class.* London: Pluto.

Martinsson, J. and Lundqvist, L. (2010) 'Ecological citizenship: Coming out "clean" without turning "green"?'. *Environmental Politics* 19(4): 518–37.

Mason, P. (2011) 'Twenty reasons why it's kicking off everywhere'. *Idle Scrawl*, 5 February. London: BBC. Online at http://www.bbc.co.uk/blogs/newsnight/paulmason/2011/02/twenty_reasons_why_its_kicking.html (accessed 12 December 2011).

Mathews, F. (ed.) (1996) *Ecology and democracy.* London: Frank Cass.

May, S., Hill, R. and Tiakiwai, S. (2004) 'Bilingual/immersion education: Indicators of good practice'. Final report to the Ministry of Education. Wellington: Ministry of Education.

Mayo, E. and Nairn, A. (2009) *Consumer kids: How big business is grooming our children for profit.* London: Constable.

Meadows, D., Meadows, D., Randers, J. and Behrens, W. (1972) *The limits to growth: A report for the club of Rome's project on the predicament of mankind.* London: Potomac Associates.

Melo-Escrihuela, C. (2008) 'Promoting ecological citizenship: Rights, duties and political agency'. *ACME* 7(2): 113–34.

Middlemiss, L. K. (2010) 'Reframing individual responsibility for sustainable consumption: Lessons from environmental justice and ecological citizenship', *Environmental Values* 19: 147–67

Midgely, M. (2004) *The myths we live by.* London: Routledge.

Milbrath, L. (1984) *Environmentalists: Vanguard for a new society.* Albany: State University of New York Press.

Miller, D. (2011) 'Almost half of all Britons think children are becoming "feral": Shock survey reveals how we're turning our backs on youngsters'. *Daily Mirror*, 4 November. Online at http://www.dailymail.co.uk/news/article-2057028/Almost-half-Britons-think-children-feral.html#ixzz1fKyXRhn7http://www.dailymail.co.uk/news/article-2057028/Almost-half-Britons-think-children-feral.html (accessed 8 December 2011).

Milne, A. A. (1927 (2001)) *Winnie the Pooh: The complete collection of stories and poems.* London: Egmont.

Ministry of Youth Development (forthcoming) *What's important to young people?* Survey Report. Wellington: Ministry of Youth Development.

Mitchell, H., Kearns, R. and Collins, D. (2007) 'Nuances of neighbourhood: Children's perceptions of the space between home and school in Auckland, New Zealand'. *Geoforum* 38(4): 614–27.

Mitchell, T., Tanner, T. and Haynes, K. (2009) 'Children as agents of change for Disaster Risk Reduction: Lessons from El Salvador and the Philippines'. Children in a Changing Climate Research Working Paper 1. Brighton: University of Sussex.

Mol and Spaargaren (2009) 'Ecological modernisation and industrial transformation'. In Castree, N., Demerit, D., Liverman, D. and Roads, B. L. (eds) *A companion to environmental geography*. Oxford: Wiley-Blackwell, pp253–65.

Moncrieffe, J. (2009) 'Introduction: Intergenerational transmissions: Cultivating children's agency?' *IDS bulletin* 40(1): 1–8.

Moorfield., J. C. (2011) Te Aka Māori–*English, English–Māori dictionary and index*. Auckland: Pearson.

Mouffe, C. (2002) 'Politics and passions: The stakes of democracy'. *Ethical Perspectives* 7(2–3): 146–50.

Mulgan, J. (1972) *Man alone*. Palmerston North: Longman Paul.

Murray, P. (2011) *The sustainable self*. London: Earthscan.

Murtagh, N., Gatersleben, B. and D. Uzzell, D. (2011) *Resistance to change regular travel behaviour: Self-identity threat, previous travel behaviour and psychological reactance*. RESOLVE Working Paper Series, 01-11. Guildford: University of Surrey.

Nairn, K. and Higgins, J. (2007) 'New Zealand's neoliberal generation: Tracing discourse of economic (ir)rationality?'. *International Journal of Qualitative Studies* 20(3), 261–81.

Nairn, K., Higgins, J. and Sligo, J. (forthcoming) *The children of Rogernomics: The neoliberal generation leaves school*. Dunedin: Otago University Press.

New Zealand Mental Health Commission (2011) *The National Indicators Report 2011*. Wellington: Ministry of Health.

New Zealand Ministry for the Environment (2007) *Environment New Zealand 2007*. Wellington: Ministry for the Environment. Online at: http://www.mfe.govt.nz/publications/ser/enz07-dec07/ (accessed 15 November 2011).

New Zealand Ministry for the Environment (2011) *Environment report card*. Wellington: Ministry for the Environment. Online at http://www.mfe.govt.nz/environmental-reporting/report-cards/land-use-environmental-snapshot/2010/index.html (accessed 1 December 2011).

New Zealand Ministry of Social Development (2010) *The Social Report 2010*. Wellington: Ministry of Social Development.

New Zealand Transport Agency (2011) *Trapped*. Online at http://www.nzta.govt.nz/about/advertising/drink-driving/trapped.html (accessed 8 December 2011).

Nissen, S. (2011) *Fixing the NZ ETS? Emissions trading as a solution to the 'wicked problem' of climate change*. A dissertation submitted in fulfilment of the requirements for POLS 480: Supervised Research Paper, University of Canterbury.

Norris, P. (2002) *Democratic Phoenix: Reinventing political activism*. Cambridge: Cambridge University Press.

Norris, P. (2011) *Democratic deficit: Critical citizens revisited*. New York: Cambridge University Press.

Nussbaum, M. (2010) *Not for profit: Why democracy needs the humanities*. Princeton, NJ: Princeton University Press.

Nussbaum, M. (2011) *Creating capabilities: The human development approach*. Cambridge, MA: Harvard University Press.

O'Brien, K., Hayward, B. and Berkes, F. (2009) 'Rethinking social contracts: Building resilience in a changing climate'. *Ecology and Society* 14(2): 12.

O'Neil, O. (1996) *Towards justice and virtue*. Cambridge: Cambridge University Press.

O'Riordan, T. (1976) *Environmentalism*. London: Pion.

OECD (2009a) *Society at a glance – Social indicators*. Paris: OECD. Online at http://www.oecd.org/dataoecd/28/2/42672411.pdf (accessed 1 March 2010).

OECD (2009b) *Doing better for children*. Online at http://www.oecd.org/document/12/0, 3746,en_2649_34819_43545036_1_1_1_1,00.html (accessed 1 December 2011).

OECD (2009c) *Teaching practices: Teachers' beliefs and attitudes*. Paris: OECD. Online at http://www.oecd.org/dataoecd/32/9/43541655.pdf (accessed 8 December 2011).

OECD (2011a) 'New Zealand: OECD better life initiative'. Online at http://www.oecd betterlifeindex.org/countries/new-zealand/ (accessed 15 November 2011).

OECD (2011b) *Divided we stand: Why inequality keeps rising*. Online at http://www.oecd. org/dataoecd/40/12/49170449.pdf (accessed 12 December 2011).

Oliver, M., Witten, K., Kearns, R., Mavoa, S., Badland, H., Carroll, P., Drumheller, C., Tavae, N., Asiasiga, L., Jelley, S., Kaiwai, H., Opit, S., En-Yi Judy Lin, Seetsur, P., Barnes, H., Mason, N. and Ergler, C. (2011) 'Kids in the city study: Research design and methodology'. *Public Health* 11: 587–99.

Ong, A. (2004) *Neoliberalism as exception: Mutations in citizenship and sovereignty*. North Carolina: Duke University Press.

Oommen, V. and Anderson, P. (2008) 'Policies on restriction of food advertising during children's television viewing times: An international perspective'. Australian College of Health Service Executives 2008 Conference, Gold Coast, Australia. 29–30 May.

Ophuls, W. (1977) *Ecology and the politics of scarcity: Prologue to a political theory of the steady state*. San Francisco, CA: Freeman.

Oram, R. (2009) 'One giant step backwards'. *Sunday Star Times*, 20 September. Online at http://www.stuff.co.nz/sunday-star-times/business/2880926/One-giant-step-backwards (accessed 1 December 2011).

Orr, D. (1994) *Earth in mind, on education, environment and the human prospect*. Washington, DC: Island Press.

Orr, D. (2005a) 'Recollection'. In Stone, M. and Barlow, Z. (eds) *Ecological literacy: Educating our children for a sustainable world*. San Francisco, CA: Sierra Club Books, pp96–106.

Orr, D. (2005b) 'Foreword'. In Stone, M. and Barlow, Z. (eds) *Ecological literacy: Educating our children for a sustainable world*. San Francisco, CA: Sierra Club Books, ppix–xi.

Orr, D. (2011) *Hope is an imperative: The essential David Orr*. Washington, DC: Island Press.

Our Children's Trust (2011) 'Atmosphere as public trust'. Online at http://ourchildrenstrust. org/legal-action (accessed 14 December 2011).

Pachauri, R.K. and A. Reisinger (2007) *Climate change 2007: Synthesis report*. Contribution of Working Groups 1, 2 and 3 to the Fourth Assessment Report of the Intergovernmental Panel on Climate Change. Geneva: IPCC.

Paige, J. (2011) 'Michael Gove pushes for return to more rigorous GCSE and A-level exams'. *The Guardian*, 18 June. Online at http://www.guardian.co.uk/education/2011/jun/18/michael-gove-exams-gcse-schools (accessed 8 December 2011).

Palmer, G. (1979) *Unbridled power: An interpretation of New Zealand's constitution and government*. Wellington: Oxford University Press.

Pateman, C. (1970 (1990)) *Participation and democratic theory*. Cambridge: Cambridge University Press.

PechaKucha (2011) *PechaKucha 20×20 inspire Japan.* Online at http://www.pecha-kucha. org/ (accessed 12 December 2011).

Pettman, R. (ed) (2005) *New Zealand in a globalising world.* Wellington: Victoria University Press.

Pew Research Centre (2011) 'The generation gap and the 2012 election: Angry silents, disengaged millenials'. Washington DC: Pew Research Centre for the People and the Press. Online at http://pewresearch.org/pubs/2122/generation-gap-barack-obama-mitt-romney-republicans-democrats-silent-generation-millenials-genxers-baby-boomers (accessed 14 November 2011).

Phillips, J. (2009) 'History of immigration: The end of a "white New Zealand" policy'. Te Ara – *The encyclopedia of New Zealand.* Online at http://www.TeAra.govt.nz/en/ history-of-immigration/15 (accessed 22 November 2011).

Piaget, J., Tomlinson, A. and Tomlinson, J. (1929) *The child's conception of the world.* London: Harcourt, Brace.

Plan International (2011) *Weathering the storm: Adolescent girls and climate change.* Surrey: Plan International Headquarters.

Pogge, T. (2002) *World poverty and human rights.* Cambridge: Polity Press.

Pogge, T. (2010) *Politics as usual: What lies behind the pro-poor rhetoric.* Cambridge: Polity Press.

Punch, S. (2002) 'Interviewing strategies with young people: The "secret box", stimulus material and task-based activities'. *Children and Society* 16(1): 45–56.

Putnam, R. (1995) 'Bowling alone: America's declining social capital'. *Journal of Democracy* 6(1): 65–78.

Putnam, R. (2000) *Bowling alone: The collapse and revival of American community.* New York: Simon & Schuster.

Putnam, R. (2007) '*E pluribus unum*: Diversity and community in the twenty-first century'. The 2006 Johan Skytte Prize Lecture. *Scandinavian Political Studies* 30(2): 137–74.

Qualifications and Curriculum Authority (1998) 'Education for citizenship and the teaching of democracy in schools'. Final report of the Advisory Group on Citizenship, 22 September. London: Qualifications and Curriculum Authority.

Rathzel, N. and Uzzell, D. (2009) 'Transformative environmental education: A collective rehearsal for reality'. *Environmental Education and Research* 15(3): 263–77.

Reid, A. and Scott, W. (2006) 'Researching education and the environment: An introduction'. *Environmental Education Research* 12(3–4): 571–88.

Restore the Earth Movement (2009) (http://www.restore-earth.org/) Harry Handprint and Fred Foot Video. Online at http://www.guardian.co.uk/environment/blog/2009/jun/24/ joanna-lumley-climate-change (accessed 12 November 2011).

Rickinson, M., Lundholm, C. and Hopwood, N. (2009) *Environmental learning: Insights from research into the student experience.* Dordrecht: Springer.

Rickinson, M., Lundholm, C. and Hopwood, N. (2010) *Environmental learning: Insights from research into the student experience.* Berlin: Springer.

Robinson, K. (2001) *Out of our minds: Learning to be creative.* Oxford: Capstone.

Rockstrom, J., Steffen, W., Noone, K., Persson, A., Stuart Chapin III, F., Lambin, E. F., Lenton, T. M., Scheffer, M., Folke, C., Schellnhuber, H. J., Nykvist, B., de Wit, C., Hughes, T., van der Leeuw, S., Rodhe, H., Sörlin, S., Snyder, P., Costanza, R., Svedin, U., Falenmark, M., Karlberg, L., Corell, R., Fabry, V., Hansen, J., Walker, B., Liverman, D., Richardson, K., Crutzen, P. and Foley, J. (2009) 'A safe operating space for humanity'. *Nature* 461: 472–5.

Rose, C. (2010) 'Change outcomes issue'. *The Campaign Strategy Newsletter* 66. Online at http://bit.ly/94qTgS (accessed 21 November 2011).

Rose, N. (1996) *Inventing our selves*. Cambridge: Cambridge University Press.

Rose, N. (1999) *Powers of freedom: Reframing political thought*. Cambridge: Cambridge University Press.

Rousseau, J.-J. (1762 (1966)) *Emile*. London: Everyman.

Sandel, M. (2009) *Justice: What's the right thing to do?*. New York: Farrar, Straus and Giroux.

Sapiro, V. (2004) 'Not your parents' political socialization: Introduction for a new generation'. *Annual Review of Political Science* 7: 1–23.

Save the Children (2008) *In the face of disaster: Children and climate change*. London: International Save the Children Alliance.

Saylan, C. and Blumstein, D. (2011) *The failure of environmental education (and how we can fix it)*. Berkeley: University of California Press.

Schor, J. (2004) *Born to buy: The commercialized child and the new consumer culture*. New York: Scribner.

Schusler, T., Kransny, M., Peters, S. and Decker, D. (2009) 'Developing citizens and communities through youth environmental action'. *Environmental Education Research* 15(1): 111–27.

Scott, W. (2002) 'Education and sustainable development: Challenges, responsibilities and frames of mind'. *The Trumpeter: Journal of Ecosophy* 18(1): 1–12.

Scott, W. (2011) 'Sustainable schools and the exercising of responsible citizenship – A review essay'. *Environmental Education Research* 17(3): 409–23.

Scott, W. and Gough, S. (2003) *key issues in sustainable development and learning: A critical review*. London: Routledge.

Sea of Hands (2008) 'Sea of hands, Lincoln's Inn Fields, London UK'. Online at http://www.eniar.org/events/seaofhands.html (accessed 20 November 2010).

Sen, A. (2009) *The idea of justice*. Cambridge, MA: Harvard University Press.

Seuss, Dr. (1957) *The lorax*. New York: Random House.

Seyfang, G. (2005) 'Shopping for sustainability: Can sustainable consumption promote ecological citizenship?'. *Environmental Politics* 14(2): 290–306.

Sheerin, C. (2007) *Political Efficacy and Youth Non-Voting: A Qualitative Investigation into the Attitudes and Experiences of Young Voters and Non-Voters in New Zealand*. A thesis submitted in fulfilment of the requirements for a Master of Arts in Political Science, University of Canterbury.

Shove, E. (2010) 'Beyond the ABC: Climate change policy and theories of social change'. *Environment and Planning A* 42(6): 1273–85.

Smith, Adam (1776 (2008)) *Wealth of nations*. New York: Oxford University Press.

Smith, Anne (2005) 'Children's views of citizenship: Cross cultural perspectives – an introduction and overview of results'. Childhoods Conference, Oslo, Norway. 29 June–3 July.

Smith, J. (2006) *What do Greens believe?* London: Granta Books.

Sobel, D. (1996) *Beyond ecophobia: Reclaiming the heart in nature education*. Barrington, MA: Orion Society.

Soper, K. (1995) *What is nature? Culture, politics and the non-human*. Oxford: Wiley-Blackwell.

SPARC (2001) *Survey results*. Active New Zealand. Online at http://www.activenzsurvey.org.nz/Results/ (accessed 30 November 2011).

Speth, J. (2008) *The bridge at the edge of the world: Capitalism, the environment, and crossing from crisis to sustainability*. New Haven, CT: Yale University Press.

Spoonley, P. (2006) 'A contemporary political economy of labour migration in New Zealand'. *Tijdschrift voor Economische en Sociale Geografie* 97(1): 17–25.

Spoonley, P., Macpherson, D. and Pearson, C. (eds) (2004) Tangata, Tangata: *The changing ethnic contours of New Zealand*. Victoria, Australia: Dunmore Press.

Statistics New Zealand (2004) *Ethnic population projections: Issues and trends*. Online at http://www.stats.govt.nz/reports/articles/ethnic-pop-projections-issues-and-trends.aspx (accessed 1 March 2010).

Statistics New Zealand (2011) *Key findings on New Zealand's progress using a sustainable development approach: 2010.* Wellington: Statistics New Zealand. Online at http://www.stats.govt.nz/browse_for_stats/environment/sustainable_development/key-findings-2010.aspx (accessed 9 November 2012).

Stephens, S. (1996) 'Reflections on environmental justice: Children as victims and actors'. *Social Justice* 23(4): 62–86.

Stevenson, A. (2007) 'What we know about how urban design affects children and young people: The interaction between health outcomes and the built environment'. Discussion Paper, Christchurch City Council. Online at http://www.cph.co.nz/Files/Children-and-Urban-Design.pdf (accessed 15 November 2011).

Stone, M. and Barlow, Z. (eds) (2005) *Ecological literacy: Educating our children for a sustainable world*. San Francisco, CA: Sierra Club.

Strauss, A. (1990) *Basics of qualitative research: Grounded theory, procedures and techniques*. Newbury Park, CA: Sage.

Sunday Star Times (2008) 'Fonterra "should have known"'. *Sunday Star Times*, 21 September. Online at http://www.stuff.co.nz/national/637713/Fonterra-should-have-known (accessed 12 November 2011).

Sustainable Development Commission (2006) *I will if you will: Towards sustainable consumption*. London: Sustainable Development Commission.

Swartz, D. (2002) 'The sociology of habit: The perspective of Pierre Bourdieu'. *The Occupational Theory Journal of Research* 22(1): 61–9.

Tanner, T. and Mitchell, T. (2008) 'Entrenchment or enhancement: Could climate change help to reduce chronic poverty?' *IDS Bulletin* 39 (4): 6–15.

Taylor, N. and Smith, A. (2009) *Children as citizens*. Dunedin: University of Otago Press.

Thaler, R. and Sunstein, C. (2008) *Nudge: Improving decisions about health, wealth and happiness* (2nd edition). London: Penguin.

The Enviroschools Foundation (2011) *Welcome to the Enviroschools Foundation*. Online at http://www.enviroschools.org.nz/ (accessed 1 December 2011).

Thompson, G. (2007) 'Responsibility and neoliberalism'. *Open Democracy*, 31 July. Online at http://www.opendemocracy.net/article/responsibility_and_neo_liberalism (accessed 22 November 2011).

Thoreau, H. (1851 (2007)) *Walking*. Rockville, MD: Arc Manor.

Torney-Purta, J. (1997) 'Review essay: Links and missing links between education, political knowledge, and citizenship'. *American Journal of Education* 105(4): 446–57.

Torney-Purta, J. (2002) 'The school's role in developing civic engagement: A study of adolescents in twenty-eight countries'. *Applied Developmental Science* 6(4): 203–12.

Torney-Purta, J., Schwille, J. and Amadeo, J.-A. (eds) (1999) *Civic education across countries: Twenty-four case studies from the IEA civic education project*. Amsterdam: International Association for the Evaluation of Educational Achievement.

Torney-Purta, J., Lehmann, R., Oswald, H. and Schulz, W. (2001) *Citizenship and education in twenty-eight countries: Civic knowledge and engagement at age fourteen*. Amsterdam: IEA.

Torney-Purta, J., Barber, C. and Richardson, W. (2004) 'Trust in government-related institutions and political engagement among adolescents in six countries'. *ActaPolitica: International Journal of Political Science* 39: 380–406.

Transition Edinburgh University (2009) *Footprints and handprints Edinburgh: University of Edinburgh.* Online at https://docs.google.com/viewer?a=v&pid=explorer&chrome=true&srcid=0BwCRI7B_YICcMzAyMWYxMzktNjNlZS00YTBkLTkzOWEtYTQ2N WNhNTdjNTk5&hl=en_US (accessed 12 November 2011).

Tranter, P. and Pawson, E (2001) 'Children's access to local environments: A case study of Christchurch, New Zealand'. *Local Environment* 6(1): 27–48.

True, J. and Gao, C. (2010) 'National identity in a global political economy'. In Miller, R. (ed) *New Zealand government and politics.* Melbourne: Oxford University Press, pp41–53.

Tsevreni, I. (2011) 'Towards an environmental education without scientific knowledge: An attempt to create an action model based on children's experiences, emotions and perceptions about their environment'. *Environmental Education Research* 17(1): 53–67.

Tsevreni, I. and Elisabeth Panayotatos, E. (2011) 'Participatory creation of a place-based teaching and learning methodology for children's participation and citizenship in the urban environment'. *Child, Youth and Environments* 21(1): 293–309.

UNICEF (2009) *The state of the world's children: Celebrating 20 years of the convention on the rights of the child.* New York: UNICEF.

UNICEF (2010) *Children's vulnerability to climate change and disaster impacts in East Asia and the Pacific.* Thailand: UNICEF East Asia and Pacific Regional Office.

UNICEF (2011a) *State of the world's children: Adolescence – an age of opportunity.* New York: UNICEF.

UNICEF (2011b) *State of Pacific youth 2011: Opportunities and obstacles.* Noumea: UNICEF Pacific. Online at http://www.unicef.org.nz/store/doc/StateofthePacificYouth Report.pdf (accessed 15 November 2011).

UNICEF (2011c) *Children and climate change: Climate change impacts on children in the Pacific: A focus on Kiribati and Vanuatu.* New York: UNICEF.

UNICEF and Plan International (2011) 'The benefits of a child centred approach to climate change'. London: UNICEF. Online at http://www.unicef.org.uk/Documents/Publications/ClimateChange_child_centred2011.pdf (accessed 19 September 2011).

Uzzell, D. (1999) 'Education for environmental action in the community: New roles and relationships'. *Cambridge Journal of Education* 29: 397–413.

Uzzell, D. (2010) 'Psychology and climate change: Collective solutions to a global problem'. Joint British Academy/British Psychological Society Annual Lecture, London. 23 September. Online at http://www.britac.ac.uk/events/2010/babps-climate.cfm (accessed 20 October 2010).

Valentine, G. (1996) 'Children should be seen and not heard: The production and transgression of adult's public space'. *Urban Geography* 17(3): 205–20.

Valentine, G. (2004) *Public space and the culture of childhood.* Aldershot: Ashgate.

Vare, P. and Scott, W. (2007) 'Learning for a change: Exploring the relationship between education and sustainable development'. *Journal of Education for Sustainable Development* 1(2): 191–8.

Veitch, J., Robinson, S., Ball, K. and Salmon, J. (2006) 'Where do children usually play? A qualitative study of parents' perceptions of influences on children's active free-play'. *Health & Place* 12(4): 383–93.

Verba, S., Schlozman, K. and Brady, H. (1995) *Voice and equality: Civic voluntarism in American politics.* Cambridge, MA: Harvard University Press.

Voce, A. (2009) 'The Play England project: Three year review'. Play England Council. Online at http://www.playengland.org.uk/media/101342/0906-play-england-council-adrian-voce.pdf (accessed 21 November 2011).

Vowles, J. (2009) 'The 2008 election in New Zealand'. *Electoral Studies* 28(3): 507–10.

Vygotsky, L. S. (1978) 'Mind in society: The development of higher psychological processes'. In Cole, M., John-Steiner, V., Scribner, S. and Souberman, E. (eds) *Interaction between learning and development*. Cambridge, MA: Harvard University Press.

Wackernagel, M. and Rees, W. (1996) *Our ecological footprint: Reducing human impact on the Earth*. Gabriola Island, BC: New Society.

Walker, M., Whittle, R., Medd, W., Burningham, K. and Moran-Ellis, J. (2010) *Hull Children's Flood Project: Final report*. Lancaster: Lancaster University. Online at http://eprints.lancs.ac.uk/49462/1/FINAL_REPORT.pdf (accessed 8 December 2011).

Walker, R. (2004) Ka Whawhai Tonu Matou: *Struggle without end* (revised edition) Auckland: Penguin.

Ward, C. (1995) *Talking schools: Ten lectures*. London: Freedom Press.

Watts, R. and Flanagan, C. (2007) 'Pushing the envelope on youth civic engagement: A developmental and liberation psychology perspective'. *Journal of Community Psychology* 35(6): 779–92.

Weale, A. (1992) *The new politics of pollution*. Manchester: Manchester University Press.

Weale, A. (1999) *Democracy: Issues in political theory*. London: St Martin's Press.

Weale, A. (2002) *Risk, democratic citizenship, and public policy*. Oxford: Oxford University Press.

Weale, A. (2009) 'Governance, government and the pursuit of sustainability'. In Adger, N. and Jordan, A. (eds) *Governing sustainability*. Cambridge: Cambridge University Press, pp55–75.

Westheimer, J. (2008) 'No Child left thinking: Democracy at risk in American Schools'. Democratic Dialogue Series 17. University of Ottawa, Canada.

Westheimer, J. and Kahne, J. (2004) 'What kind of citizen? The politics of education for democracy'. *American Educational Research Journal* 41(2): 237–69.

Whitmarsh L., O'Neill, S. and Lorenzoni, I. (eds) (2010) *Engaging the public with climate change: Behaviour change and communication*. London: Earthscan.

Wiedmann, T. and Minx, J. (2007) 'A definition of "carbon footprint"'. In Pertsova, C. (ed) *Ecological economics: Research trends*. New York: Nova Science, pp1–11.

Wilde, O. (1888) 'The remarkable rocket'. In Laslett, S. (ed) (1998) The Happy Prince *and other tales from Oscar Wilde*. Bristol: Paragon.

Wilkinson, R. and Pickett, K. (2009) *The spirit level: Why equality is better for everyone*. London: Penguin.

Willetts, D. (2010) *The pinch: How the baby boomers took their children's future – and why they should give it back*. London: Atlantic Books.

Williams, P. (forthcoming) 'Educating for sustainability in New Zealand: Success through environschools'. In Robertson, M. (ed) *Schooling for sustainable development: A focus on Australia, New Zealand, and the Oceanic region*. New York: Springer.

Wilson, M. and Yeatman, A. (1995) *Justice, biculturalism and difference*. Auckland: Allen & Unwin.

Witt, D. (2010) *Ernest Thompson Seton: The life and legacy of an artist and conservationist*. Layton: Gibbs Smith.

Wolf, J., Brown, K. and Conway, D. (2009) 'Ecological citizenship and climate change: perceptions and practice'. *Environmental Politics* 18(4): 503–21.

Wolf, M. (2011) 'Why the world's youth is in a revolting state of mind'. *Financial Times*, 19 February, p11. Online at http://www.ft.com/cms/s/0/6577ca92-3b94-11e0-a96d-00144feabdc0.html#axzz1dFAtLGES (accessed 12 August 2011).

Wood, B. (2011) *Citizenship in our place: Exploring New Zealand young people's everyday, place-based perspectives on participation in society*. A thesis submitted in fulfilment of the requirements of a Doctor of Philosophy, Victoria University of Wellington.

Wood, J. (2011) 'Ecological citizenship as public engagement with climate change'. In Whitmarsh L., O'Neil, S. and Lorenzoni, I. (eds) *Engaging the public with climate change: Behaviour change and communication*. London: Earthscan.

Woodfield, A. and Gunby, P. (2003) 'The marketization of New Zealand schools: Assessing Fiske and Ladd'. *Journal of Economic Literature* 41(3): 863–84.

Woodly, D. (2006) 'Black Youth Book Project: Political efficacy literature review'. University of Chicago. Online at http://www.racialequitytools.org/resourcefiles/woodly.pdf (accessed 10 March 2009).

Wordsworth, W. (1807 (1983)) 'Ode: Intimation of Immortality'. In Curtis, J. (ed.) *Poems in two volumes, and other poems, 1800–1807*. Ithaca, NY: Cornell University Press.

Worley, E. (2011) 'Can we teach moral reasoning? Comment to the RSA, London'. Online at http://comment.rsablogs.org.uk/2011/08/18/teach-moral-reasoning/ (accessed 1 December 2011).

Wray-Lake, L., Flanagan, C. A. and Osgood, D. W. (2010) 'Examining trends in adolescent environmental attitudes, beliefs, and behaviors across three decades'. *Environment and Behavior* 42(1): 61–85.

Young, D. (2007) *Keeper of the long view: Sustainability and the PCE*. Wellington: Parliamentary Commission for the Environment.

Young, I. M. (1990) *Justice and the politics of difference*. Princeton, NJ: Princeton University Press.

Young, I. M. (2000) *Inclusion and democracy*. Oxford: Oxford University Press.

Young, I. M. (2001) 'Activist challenges to deliberative democracy'. *Political Theory* 29(5): 670–90.

Young, I. M. (2004) 'Response to Bohman, Drexler, and Hames-Garcia'. *The Good Society* 13(2): 61–3.

Young, I. M. (2006a) 'The importance of de-centering deliberative democracy'. At American Philosophical Association, Chicago, USA. 26–29 April.

Young, I. M. (2006b) 'De-centering deliberative democracy'. *Kettering Review* 24(3): 43–60.

Young, I. M. (2007) *Global challenges: War, self-determination and responsibility for justice*. Cambridge: Polity Press.

Young, I. M. (2011) *Responsibility for justice*. Oxford: Oxford University Press.

Youniss, J. and Levine, P. (2009) *Engaging young people in civic life*. Nashville, TN: Vanderbilt University Press.

Youniss, J. and Middaugh, E. (2009) 'Democracy for some: The civic opportunity gap in high school'. In Youniss, J. and Levine, P. (eds) *Engaging young people in civic life*. Nashville: Vanderbilt University Press, pp29–58.

Zanker, R. and Lealand, G. (2009) 'New Zealand as Middle Earth: Local and popular communication in a small nation'. In Miller, T. (ed) *The contemporary Hollywood reader*. Oxford: Routledge, pp155–62.

Index

a priori principles of justice 46–7
action: general theory of 73
action competence 147
action learning 75
adult attention deficit disorder 82, 99, 153
advertising 9
agency 7–8: barriers to 67–9; and family
   income 68; freedom of 7; frustrated
   50–2; importance 64–7; as personal
   responsibility 68; as resistance 71–3, 78;
   see also social agency
alcohol abuse 51–2, 95, 142
Alliance for Future Generations 136
Almond, G. 68
altruism: appeals to 8
animal rights 108
anxiety 34, 55
Arato, A. 73
Arendt, H. 2, 65–6, 116, 135
Arnstein, S. 70
Ashdown forest 131, 132
Asian Tsunami (2004): deaths 50, 83
Augé, M. 86
authoritarian decision making 53–4
autonomy 64, 67; interdependent 66;
   self-governing 79–80

Bandura, A. 46, 69, 147
Barber, B. 5, 9, 139
Barry, J. 72, 73, 103
Bauman, Z. 128
Beaumont, E. 77
Birmingham, K. 97
Black American citizenship 69
blame 44, 54 146; *see also* justice as
   responsibility

Boal, A. 75
Bohman, J. 72, 112, 129
Bourdieu, P. 69
brand awareness 31; branded
   consumption 29
Brooks, R. 128–9
bullying 51–2, 77, 95, 115, 142, 143

CAFOD 145
capabilities: central 50
capabilities philosophy 111, 150
carbon footprint 144; reducing
   104–5
Carbon Handprint UK 144–5
Carson, R. 1, 2, 126, 151, 155
charter schools 155
'chauffeuring' 87
Chawla, L. 58, 69, 110
child development theory 3, 65, 152
'choice architecture' 8
Christchurch earthquakes 28, 70–1, 98,
   153–6; stresses caused by 55
Citizen-Consumers 65
citizen participation: ladder of 70
citizen schools 114, 151
Citizen-Scientists 32
citizenship: as collective action 30,
   36–8; as mutual interdependence
   152; as networked social agency 149;
   as participation 29–30; as personal
   responsibility 12, 30–2, 139; as
   relationship of rights and duties 11;
   rethinking from child's perspective
   3–5; as sponsored participation 38–9;
   see also ecological citizenship; non-
   citizenship